IMMUNITY FOR MURDER

IMMUNITY FOR MURDER

THE VERONICA TAFT STORY

DAVID M. BEERS

COPYRIGHT

Immunity for Murder: The Veronica Taft Story
Written by David M. Beers

Published in United States of America
This edition published 2021

Copyright @ 2021 David M. Beers

All rights reserved. No part of this book may be reproduced, scanned, or distributed in any printed or electronic form without permission of the author. The unauthorized reproduction of a copyrighted work is illegal. Criminal copyright infringement, including infringement without monetary gain, is investigated by the FBI and is punishable by fines and federal imprisonment. Please do not participate in or encourage privacy of copyrighted materials in violation of the author's rights. Purchase only authorized editions.

This is a work of nonfiction, however, some of the names used in this book have been changed to protect those individuals' privacy.

Paperback ISBN: 978-1-7378690-0-9
eBook ISBN: 978-1-7378690-1-6

Cover design, editing, formatting, and layout by Evening Sky Publishing Services

DEDICATION

In memory of:
Lyric Lonell Taft

June 2, 2008 – December 30, 2010

CONTENTS

Prologue — 1

Part I
BACKGROUND

1. Mother in Crisis — 7
2. A Little History — 10

Part II
THE INVESTIGATION

3. Early Investigation — 17
4. Charles Pratt - Interview — 20
5. Veronica Taft – Interview #1 — 37
6. Crime Scene — 64
7. Autopsy — 69
8. Continued Investigation — 73
9. Funeral Home — 82
10. Complaining Witnesses — 84
11. Early Theory — 90
12. CPS — 93
13. Veronica Taft – Interview #2 — 102
14. More CPS — 119
15. Seeking Legal Advice — 131
16. Evidence Exam — 134
17. A New Search Warrant — 138
18. Veronica Taft – Interview #3 — 151
19. Premature Decision — 153
20. Pretend Justice — 157
21. A Third Search Warrant — 161
22. Bloody Diaper – A Second Look — 166
23. Cruel Prosecution — 170

24. Lie Detector	175
25. Jesse Noel	178

Part III
THE ARREST

26. Arrested for Murder	193
27. Grand Jury	199

Part IV
PREPARING VERONICA'S DEFENSE

28. In Defense of Veronica	215
29. Veronica Taft - Jail Interview	225
30. Deanna Bryant	237
31. Lyric's God Mother	246
32. Where is SpongeBob?	254
33. Continued Investigation	258
34. A Lifelong Friend	264
35. Meeting with CPS	268
36. Prep for Trial	270

Part V
THE TRIAL

37. The Drama Begins	275
38. CPS Legal Matter	298
39. Trial Resumes	300
40. Closing Arguments & Deliberations	306
41. Verdict	310
42. Aftermath	312
43. Sentencing	315
44. 25 to Life	316

Part VI
THE APPEAL

45. Appeal	321
46. Appellate Court Decision	328

Part VII
THE AFTERMATH

47. Starting Over — 337
48. Power of Authority — 347
49. A Ruthless Killer — 349
50. Summing Up — 359
51. Return to Fayette Street — 374
52. They Called It Justice — 376

Part VIII
ADDENDUM

53. Notice of Claim — 381
54. Career Changes — 382

Note from the Author — 383
Acknowledgments — 384
About the Author — 386
Also by David M. Beers — 388

PROLOGUE

"Yo, the nigger's not gettin' up. The nigger's not breathin'. He be cold." Those were the words spoken to Veronica Taft by Charles "Chucky" Pratt when returning to her bedroom after checking on her four young children on the morning of December 30, 2010. Having found her only son, 2½-year-old Lyric, unresponsive and unable to wake him. Veronica started flipping out, screaming, "What do mean he's cold and not breathing? Go get him, bring him to me." Chucky ran back to the children's bedroom, picked up Lyric, and quickly brought him to his mother. In desperation, she immediately yelled at him and slapped his back, trying to wake him. But quickly realized he was cold, purple-colored, and not breathing. She immediately started CPR while screaming at Chucky to call 9-1-1. He'd just finished dialing when she suddenly snatched the phone away and placed a hysterical call to 9-1-1 herself at 10:53 a.m. Then, half-dressed, with the phone still in hand, she flew down the stairs and out into the street, screaming hysterically, "Call the police" and yelling, "Does anyone know CPR?" A startled neighbor responded quickly and ran upstairs with her but was stopped by

Chucky, asking who he was. He just shoved Chucky out of the way, ran to Lyric, and started CPR.

By 10:56 a.m., just a couple blocks away, Superior Ambulance was dispatched to Taft's 2nd floor apartment at 4½ Fayette Street in Binghamton, NY, reporting of a child not breathing. Meanwhile, a very hysterical mother stood by, thinking her son may already be dead as she watched over her neighbor doing CPR. All the while, anxiously awaiting the arrival of the ambulance and hoping for a miracle.

Chucky just stood there before Veronica shoved him aside, saying, "Get away from me." Then watched as Chucky suddenly punched the living room wall, once with each fist, leaving a large gaping hole. With crumbling pieces of wallboard and plaster falling to the floor next to the family Christmas tree.

| Taft Apartment

Arriving two minutes later, EMTs ran upstairs and immediately took over the life-saving efforts on Lyric. They were followed shortly after that by the first responding police officers from the Binghamton Police Department (BPD). Besides being cold and not breathing, EMTs also noticed Lyric's abdomen was bloated, causing the jean pants he was wearing to be extremely tight. They quickly removed them to ease the pressure. They also noted multiple abrasions and contusions on Lyric's head, face, and neck. The dire situation was recognized immediately by the lead EMT, who quickly scooped Lyric into his arms and rushed him downstairs to the waiting ambulance while continuing CPR. Later, he reported that Lyric's extremities were cold, but his core was still warm.

Following close behind, Veronica jumped into the ambulance with Lyric, and by 11:06 a.m., they were on their way to the ER at Lourdes Hospital. All the while, continuing CPR, intubation, and other resuscitation efforts until their arrival just four minutes later at 11:10 a.m. Immediately upon arrival, the waiting ER staff rushed in and took over.

Lyric was in good hands as ER doctors and staff worked feverishly in their efforts to revive his cold and lifeless body. However, upon arrival, he was already in full cardiopulmonary arrest, with a complete absence of spontaneous pulse respiration or blood pressure. And by 11:15 a.m., his rectal body temperature had plunged more than twelve degrees, registering a critically low, 86 degrees Fahrenheit. Lyric's clothing was removed and replaced with warm compacts and blankets during the hospital's life-saving efforts. And a warm saline solution was pumped into his stomach. A witnessing patrol officer secured Lyric's clothing, placed them into separate evidence bags, and labeled them.

| Lyric Taft

Veronica anxiously stood by in the waiting area as investigators began questioning her about what had happened. At the same time, along with hospital staff, they attempted to comfort her as she waited nervously, praying and desperately hoping that her son may still be alive.

Meanwhile, doctors and staff continued their heroic efforts despite how hopeless it seemed, using any/all medical means available for nearly an hour. But Lyric's body monitor remained flatlined throughout, and his body temperature continued to drop. There was never any return of spontaneous pulse, respiration, or blood pressure. And the early onset of rigor mortis[1] was starting to appear. Tragically, at 12:06 p.m., doctors were forced to make the call, and it became official – Lyric was dead.

---

1. *Rigor mortis*: Biochemical changes in the body produce stiffening, which usually appears within 2 to 4 hours after death. Beginning in the muscles of the jaw and neck, then proceeds downward in the body to the trunk and extremities. Becoming complete within 6 to 12 hours.

I

BACKGROUND

1

MOTHER IN CRISIS

Undoubtedly, one of the more difficult things a doctor has to do is make a death notification. And that task becomes even more difficult when it involves a sudden and unexpected young child's death. Needless to say, Veronica was devastated upon learning of her son's death. Officers and hospital staff tried their best to console the traumatized and grieving mother who'd gone into a deep state of shock. But to her, their words of comfort fell on deaf ears and seemed meaningless.

Later, medical records described how Veronica had initially been traumatized due to her son's uncertain condition, then traumatized further upon learning of his death and then described as a woman in crisis. Emotionally upset, crying, overwhelmed, searching for meaning, and in need of grief support.

Despite all that, within 30 minutes of learning about the death of her son, Veronica, who was still in shock, visibly shaken, and emotionally distraught, was escorted from the hospital back to the police station. She sat in a small interrogation room waiting to be questioned further. Previously, Charles Pratt had been escorted by the BPD directly from Fayette Street to their station for his interview. By the time Veronica arrived, Pratt had already been there for over an hour.

Meanwhile, back at the hospital, doctors and staff continued their assessment of Lyric by ordering a CT scan of his body. Earlier during their life-saving efforts, they observed and documented many suspicious injuries all over his body. Previously, EMTs and BPD officers had made their observations of Lyric's injuries. As a result, Investigator Matt Zandy from the BPD's forensic ID Unit was sent to the ER with instructions to photograph Lyric's injuries.

According to hospital medical records, although not all-inclusive, the following injuries were noted. None of which revealed any signs of external bleeding:

- Bruising to forehead & occipital region,
- Bruising to front and back of both cheeks, including a large abrasion – possibly a burn on the left ear,
- Abrasions/lacerations on cheeks in front of both ears – suggestive of fingernail marks,
- Large bruising with abrasion on the upper left chest,
- Abdomen – distended and firm,
- Bruising and abrasions on palms of both hands, right heel, and upper back.

Additionally, it was noted in the ER flowchart records at 11:43 a.m. that early signs of rigor mortis were observed in Lyric's lower extremities; then again, at 11:51 a.m., it was noticed in his jaw. Later, the medical narrative noted the following: *"At both ankles, there was plantarflexion[1] what over time appeared to be early rigor."*

. . .

Author's note: As noted, rigor mortis typically starts to appear within 2-4 hours after death, becoming maximal within 6-12 hours. As such, the noted signs of early rigor at the ER should be helpful when trying to estimate the time of death. A later chapter will address this further.

Due to the severity and suspicious nature of Lyric's injuries, authorities were near, if not already, convinced that his injuries were *not* the result of some accidental cause but rather a violent assault at the hands of an adult. They were already thinking homicide, but they also knew there would need to be an autopsy to make it official. Accordingly, Dr. James Terzian, a local forensic medical examiner at Lourdes Hospital, was contacted. He agreed, and they made arrangements to perform the autopsy the next day.

---

1. *Plantarflexion*: Movement of the foot in which the foot or toes flex downward toward the sole.

2

A LITTLE HISTORY

With a population of around 45,000, the City of Binghamton is a small city that serves as the County Seat for Broome County, NY, which has approximately 200,000. Binghamton was named in honor of a wealthy land investor from Philadelphia, PA, by the name of William Bingham. He had envisioned building a new community around the confluence of the Chenango and Susquehanna Rivers, located in south-central NY, just north of the PA border, about 200 miles upstate from New York City. When the County of Broome was created in 1806, it was named after John Broome, the Lt. Governor of NYS at the time.

Veronica Lynn Taft, a.k.a., "Ron" or "Roni," was the oldest of four children, with a younger sister and two brothers. Growing up with a loving mother and father, she enjoyed a pleasant home life with her younger siblings in a modest middle-class home near Whitney Point, NY, and attended Whitney Point schools.

Veronica stood only five feet three inches tall, with hazel eyes and light brown hair. While attending school at a young age, she was often teased, bullied, and ridiculed by students and school officials. By age 12, she was diagnosed with ADD/ADHD[1], classifying her as learning disabled. Although, her disorder never became severe enough to require medication. It did, however, continue to affect her ability to learn in the mainstream. After that, she began attending an Alternative Learning Center (ALC). There she found her niche, applied herself more efficiently, and her ability to learn excelled.

As an ALC student, she was affiliated with the Whitney Point School District. Therefore, she was still able to participate in their extracurricular activities. She joined the varsity cheerleading squad. With her athletic ability, combined with her small stature, she quickly advanced to become the team's "flyer." Upon completion of her education at ALC, Veronica received recognition as a high honor-roll student. Upon graduating, she received her HSE/TASC[2] diploma.

After high school, Veronica spread her wings and moved to Johnson City, NY – a small village west of Binghamton. There, she met and started a relationship with Izdihar "Izzie" Noori. Later, they became parents to two girls they named Haveen and Amira. Their relationship was relatively short-lived after Veronica fell victim to several repeated incidents of domestic violence. Some of which occurred in front of the children and led to CPS[3] involvement.

After severing her relationship with Noori, she later met and began a new relationship with Lonell Barnes, leading to two more children. A boy named Lyric and another girl named Zoey. She now had four small children in as many years. Unfortunately, this relationship was short-lived as well. It started deteriorating when Veronica learned that Barnes was cheating on her. It evolved into more domestic violence incidents, compounded by

Barnes' ongoing mental health issues, including his diagnosis of bipolar disorder and schizophrenia. Again, some of the incidents occurred in front of the children prompting yet another visit and investigation by CPS. As a result, Veronica's children were taken away for a short period.

After getting her kids back, she attempted to sever her relationship with Barnes. She avoided further CPS involvement by moving out of state to live with a friend for a few months, taking her children with her. But by August of 2010, she moved back to Binghamton after learning that Barnes was being treated in a mental health facility and no longer a threat. After that, she moved back with her kids and found a small 2nd-floor apartment on Fayette Street and a job working nights at Binghamton High School. At the time, she was 23-years old.

In late August or early September 2010, a friend introduced Veronica to Charles "Chucky" Pratt, who had recently moved to Binghamton from the Bronx. He found a small apartment a short walk from Fayette Street. There was a mutual attraction, and they started seeing each other regularly. Veronica learned from Chucky about his criminal history of selling drugs and serving time in state prison. But he'd assured her that his drug-dealing days were over. Within a short time, their relationship became intimate. Later, when Chucky met her children, he'd treated them very well, and they all seemed to enjoy having him around. Lyric, especially being the only boy, followed him around constantly.

Recognizing how well he seemed to be in his interactions with the children, Veronica felt comfortable in asking him to babysit while she was away at work. Since she worked the night shift, she knew it wouldn't be a huge task because the kids would just be sleeping. Chucky agreed and began babysitting the children, who now ranged in age from 1½ to almost five. At the time, he didn't have a regular job but would take on a few odd jobs from time to time. And Veronica, who was only making minimum wage, was paying him about $90.00 a week to babysit.

Chucky was a 27-year-old black man, who at the time, was four years older than Veronica. Supposedly, he'd been abused and later abandoned by his birth mother and raised in foster care in Bronx, NY. In 2003, he was convicted on two Class B felony counts of Criminal Sale of a Controlled Substance, one within a school zone. He was sentenced to two-to-six years in state prison and committed to the Bare Hill Correctional Facility, a medium-security prison in the Town of Malone, Franklin County, NY. In 2005, he was released on parole but soon violated with another drug charge. He returned to prison, where he served out his remaining sentence. He was released on January 27, 2010, and shortly after that, moved to Binghamton, NY.

Unbeknownst to Veronica, Chucky's drug-dealing days were not over. As it was, he was still actively involved in buying, selling, and using drugs. It may have helped with spending money, but mainly it was to support his drug habit. Veronica was somewhat naïve, thus unaware that Chucky's only genuine interest in life was sex, drugs, and video games. But not always in that order.

From around mid-November 2010 forward, Chucky began routinely babysitting Veronica's four children on weeknights while she worked. For the next six weeks, everything seemed to be going along smoothly. Then suddenly, everything changed. On December 30, 2010, tragedy struck.

---

1. *ADD/ADHD*: Attention deficit disorder/Attention-deficit hyperactivity disorder.
2. *HSE/TASC*: High School Equivalency / Test Assessing Secondary Completion
3. *CPS*: Child Protective Services

II

THE INVESTIGATION

3

EARLY INVESTIGATION

Shortly after EMTs arrived at the scene and took over the life-saving efforts on Lyric, a terrified, hysterical, and incoherent phone call was made by Veronica to her mother, Hope Taft. She called Hope's private work number at nearby Binghamton General Hospital, where she worked, and asked to speak with Hope. The floor nurse who answered couldn't understand what she was saying but did recognize the name Hope and called her to the phone. When answering, she barely recognized her daughter and knew something was very wrong. All she heard was that Lyric was blue, and she needed her to come over right away. In a panic herself, she ran out of the hospital and quickly drove over to Veronica's apartment, arriving within a matter of minutes. She was told that the ambulance with Lyric and Veronica had just left for the hospital. Veronica, who had been using Chucky's phone, returned it to him before she left, leaving Hope with no way to reach her.

Hope recognized Chucky, who was still standing at the scene and spoke to him briefly, but he claimed not to know what happened and wasn't saying much. She introduced herself to the officers as Veronica's mother and asked what was happening. After hearing some sketchy details about what was going on, she offered to help with the other children. After that, she was escorted upstairs into the apartment to help the children get dressed, then collect clothing and other items they would need. When she returned downstairs, she looked for Chucky again, but he'd just been taken away to the police station. The children had been placed in protective custody and also taken to the station. CPS had already been notified and would be there when they arrived. The officers advised Hope that the other kids were fine and offered to take her to the hospital to be with her daughter. As they left the scene and headed towards the hospital, they abruptly changed directions and went directly to the station.

Meanwhile, back at the scene, believing this situation involved a criminal element, the BPD maintained an active police presence in anticipation of a search warrant that would allow them to search and forensically examine Taft's apartment. As they made an application for a search warrant, a uniformed officer was assigned to safeguard the scene and start a crime scene log. Investigator Matt Zandy from the BPD forensic ID Unit was already on the scene, taking photos around the exterior and conducting a preliminary walk-through of the apartment. Shortly after completing that assignment, he was reassigned, as mentioned, to respond to the ER at Lourdes Hospital and obtain photographs of Lyric's injuries.

Ever since the 9-1-1 call at 10:53 a.m., a lot had happened in a relatively short period. Many things were happening simultaneously at the scene, hospital, and BPD station. During the early stage of any major investigation, things can quickly become very chaotic. At times, everything and everyone involved seems to be rushing in several separate directions simultaneously. The importance of keeping the lines of communication open and transparent between the different entities involved is crucial. Should there be a breakdown or lack of shared communication, the investigation can quickly become compromised, resulting in lost opportunities or steering the investigation in the wrong direction.

Did a lack of communication ever compromise this investigation? Were there lost opportunities? Did the investigation stray off course? A future chapter will answer all those questions. But for now, let's return to the investigators' busy squad room at headquarters to find out what they were learning from their interviews with Charles Pratt and Veronica Taft.

The squad room was buzzing with activity. Several investigators were already engaged and carrying out various assignments. Charles Pratt was brought to the station early, placed into a private interrogation room, and waited to be interviewed. CPS caseworkers were arriving to get briefed on the situation, then take custody and see to the needs of the surviving children. Arrangements were also being made to have the children interviewed. Hope Taft had been brought in at the request of CPS. Arrangements were being made for her to take temporary custody of the children. Later, the officers at the hospital with Veronica brought her to the station and placed her in a separate interrogation room. She awaited her interview. Other off-duty investigators and supervisory personnel were called to report back to duty. All of this had taken place in about an hour-and-a-half. All mandatory notifications had been made. So, by 12:30 p.m. on December 30, 2010, a major investigation of the suspected homicide of 2½-year-old Lyric Taft was up and running full-throttle.

4

CHARLES PRATT - INTERVIEW

Charles Pratt – Interview (Timestamp – approx. 72 mins fast)

Chucky was dressed in gray jeans and wearing a black jacket. He stood five feet ten inches tall, with short black hair, and weighed 170 pounds. He had been waiting in the interrogation room only a few minutes when one of the investigators walked in and asked if he needed a drink or anything. For some odd reason, Chucky still had his cell phone with him when one of the officers said, "The Captain said you can make a phone call if you need to." As soon as the officer left the room, Chucky immediately placed a call to his friend "Max," later identified as Martin Rodriguez.

Author's note: The following is a summary taken from the written transcript of the videotaped interview of Charles Pratt. As bizarre as it may seem at times, the exact language and terminology he used are included for authenticity. Notably, much of what Pratt was heard saying takes place while he's alone, outside the presence of investigating officers.

Only Chucky's side of the conversation could be heard. He started by saying, "Yo. Yeah, man. I'm fucking sitting in this room, son, in the investigation room. Yeah. This is crazy, son. Plus, they doing – they doing their little CSI shit inside the room and shit." He then talks about doing CPR and says, "Son, when – when we was doin' CPR, son, it sounded like something was in his fucking throat son…because he wasn't breathing son. Yeah. I went to sleep. Yo, my nigger yo. I put them down around like 11:00, 11:15. So I went to sleep like 11:30 son, quarter of 12:00 because I was tired." He then described how the baby, Zoey, started crying and woke him up, and he had just put her back to bed when Veronica came home. Then continued saying, "So, I went back in the room with Veronica. We chilling, talking, you know what I mean? We both fell asleep. So, we gets back up. You know what I mean? I gets up because I had to go to the bathroom."

Then, he heard the kids in their room while he was up and knew they were waking up. Then continued saying, "I opened the door, went in the room. I'm like, yo, you know what I mean, the kids is not up yet. So, I'm starting to wake the kids up and shit. The two girls is already up. So, I'm tapping Lyric like, yo, get up.

You want to eat, come on, get up, get up. So, the nigger not moving, son. The nigger's lips is purple, son. The niggers face and body start feeling mad warm, and cold. You feel me? So, I'm like, whoa, what the fuck is going on, son. You know what I mean? So, the only thing I noticed was a bump on his head. Like what the fuck is – you know what I mean? So, I told Veronica, I say yo, Lyric is not getting up. She was like, wake him up. I say he's not getting up, yo. Lyric is not breathing, yo. She like, what you mean, he's cold? I say yo, the nigger is not getting up. The nigger is not breathing, yo. She – I brung Lyric to her, yo. She started flipping, son. After that, son, all hell broke loose. These niggers looking at me weird. I'm the only black nigger in here, son. Son, this is fucking crazy, son. This is crazy, son. No. I'm sitting in this room. I don't know how long I'm going to be in here, son." He listened for a moment, then continued saying, "Veronica…fuck man. She at the hospital, son. They wouldn't even let me be by her side, son. That's what I'm saying. I'm saying yo, I'm – I'm looking at it like you all looking at me like I'm a suspect."

Author's note: In that interrogation room, Pratt was not only a major witness but a potential suspect. Without being searched and allowing him to keep and use his cell phone while unattended, was, at the very least, poor judgment, if not a direct violation of protocol. Shortly, we'll learn what happened once they realized their mistake.

Pratt ends his call with Max and immediately places another call to his stepbrother, Jemel "Melo" Fields, who he'd just spoken to earlier before leaving the scene. Apparently, during that call, he'd already asked Jemel to look up a number for an attorney to call. In other words, he was already in search of an attorney while still at the scene. Then, during this call, after Jemel gives him the attorney's number, he asks him to repeat it and then asks, "Who is this...can I call – can I call him now? Should I call him now or what? I'm going to call you back." He then hung up and dialed the number. There was no answer.

He called Jemel back and told him no one was picking up. He then asks if he knows any other number he can call then continues saying, "Yo, because I don't – I've been sitting here for like 10 minutes now, yo. Son, the nigger was about to push me inside the car, son. I said – I said – I said the nigger was trying to push me inside the car and shit, yo. Yeah, man. One of the nigger's man, I had to stop the nigger, yo. I had to talk to his partner. Listen, man, I don't got a problem getting in the car, man, but I ain't gonna let your partner just keep on pushing me because now I feel I'm being – I'm being a suspect here, yo. Why you can't ask me the questions right here? I asked them, I say, is I'm getting locked up? Is I'm getting arrested? He said no. We're just doing it for investigation because a two-year-old died in the house as we was there, you know what I mean? He may have died when she came in. He may have died when I was watching him when he was asleep. I don't know my nigger. This little nigger be running around doing mad shit, you feel me? So, who knows, you know what I mean? And that shit ain't right."

Earlier, Pratt received a call but didn't recognize the number, so he didn't answer. He was now receiving another call and hung up with Jemel. It was Hope Taft, Veronica's mom. He answered and said, "Hello. Huh? Yes, I did. What's going on? Because they got me in this fucking room, and I'm like – like fucking scared, yo. Where – is Veronica okay? Is she okay? Uh-uh. Oh, they – they didn't put you in a car with her? All right. Have her call me, please, please." Before hanging up, he also learned that Veronica had tried calling him earlier from the hospital. He still had the number in his phone and hit redial. A woman answered, and he asked to speak with Veronica and said, "Yes. I'm sorry. It was a girl named Veronica Taft who just came in and used this line right here. Her son just passed away. I'm her boyfriend. I'm looking for her. Veronica Taft. She was just there using your phone. Oh my god. All right. Yeah. I appreciate it." Chucky spoke briefly to a different person on the phone and repeated his request to talk with Veronica Taft.

Veronica was located and came to the phone. Chucky said, "Baby, I am so fucking scared right here, yo. Like this shit just tops the fucking cake right now. Yo, they got me in this room, staying here for like 15 minutes already, yo. Nobody talked to me. No. They – yo, yo, they looked at me like – like I was the fucking killer, yo, like I was the fucking suspect, yo. And the guy started fucking pushing me, yo. Are you fucking serious? Yo, Veronica, what they saying? Yeah. What's he saying, baby? Is they – nothing at all?" Then he continued, "I know I put them down as soon as you left…because I know this, though. I know Peeky[1], and all of them was in the room. They was watching a movie, and I told Peeky, once the movie go off, turn it off and go to bed, all right?" He then explained that when he was going to bed, the movie was still on and said, "The movie was still – yeah. The movie was still on. So, I went in the room. They was all asleep. Every one of them was asleep. You know what I mean? So, I turned the TV off and – huh? Yeah. I just turned the TV off, and I just walked out. And then I closed the door."

He then started talking about his situation again and said, "They're fucking pushing me, babe. They're fucking pushing me, yo. Yo man. It's my fault, yo. I should have been there, yo." Finally, he turned back to Veronica and her situation and said, "Where you at now? You – you waiting in the ER? And why they can't tell you nothing, yo? Yo, he – he got to be okay. He got to be okay, yo. They taking that long, baby, they taking that long, yo, pray for him. Pray for him. Pray for him. It's taking them that long, baby, you know what I mean? He was still part warm. He was still warm in the heart. Don't worry about it. Baby, I'll be on my way over there as soon as I'm done with them, yo. If they taking too long, yo, I'm about to call me a lawyer and – and tell them what's going on because I am fucking scared, yo. I never went through this shit in my life."

Notably, when Chucky was trying to locate Veronica at the hospital, he told the person he was talking to that "her son just passed away." How would he know that? Earlier, when he spoke with his brother, he said, "he may have died when I was watching him." Now, he tells Veronica, "They looked at me like – like I was the fucking killer." All references to Lyric already being dead. At the time he spoke with Veronica, it was only about 11:35 a.m. As we've already learned, Lyric's death wasn't announced until 12:06 p.m. Yet he tells Veronica, "He got to be okay," and "don't worry about it." Also notable was that when he first spoke with Veronica, he immediately started complaining about his situation, never asking Veronica anything about herself, or more importantly, how Lyric was doing. But let's continue to learn what happened next and what else he had to say.

As soon as he hung up with Veronica, he called Max again and told him, "They left me here, son, and went to talk to her, son." A uniformed officer entered the room then and interrupted his call, demanding he give him his phone. Chucky immediately protested and told Max, "Hold on. Yo, they taking my phone. The sergeant said I could have my phone." As the officer reached for his phone, he said, "Can you let go? Can you let go?" The officer said firmly, "Give me the phone." They argued back and forth, and he repeated, "Give me the phone." Still speaking with Max, Chucky said, "I'm not going to fight them, son. Should I give them my phone or what, yo? Is – I'm being arrested? Is – I'm being incarcerated?" The officer again said, "Give me the phone. I was told by the sergeant to come back here and take the phone." Chucky responded, "Why? I want my lawyer. Give me a lawyer. I'm not giving up none of my personal unless I have a lawyer. You all is treating me like I did something wrong here. I want a lawyer."

For now, Chucky won this battle as the officer, likely trying to avoid a physical confrontation, left the room without the phone. Chucky continued speaking with Max and said, "Son, the nigger walked out and locked the door, son. They locked me in here, son. Son, they – they locked me in here, son. This is not good, son. This is not good, son. This is not good, man. This is not good, yo. Yeah. Yeah. Yeah. No. They went to go see Veronica, son." He then spoke briefly about needing to turn his phone off because his battery was low but then continued saying, "Yo, these niggers is bugging son. They're not getting my phone, son. These niggers is not getting my phone, man. Yo, tell these niggers, yo, the nigger tried to touch me, man. Tell the nigger – he grabbed me and everything. The only thing you heard was get off, get off me, yo. We want to know what's going on with this nigger. No, man. These niggers is bugging, man. They ain't taking my phone, son. They bugging, son. They looking at – now they looking at me like a fucking suspect, son."

In case you were wondering, Chucky was hyperactive, on his feet, nervously pacing back and forth, and practically bouncing off the walls. Most likely, he was very high on drugs as he continued venting with Max, saying, "Son, this is – this is crazy, son. This – the doctors? Oh, oh, oh. They doing – they doing a – I think a scan or something on him right now. She's saying that they ain't saying yet. They ain't nothing yet. And I'm saying, well, baby, is been a minute, yo. He must be alive. He got to be alive." He then spoke briefly about speaking with Veronica at the hospital and with her mom and continued with, "I talked with her, she was like, yo, they doing X-ray on him right now and everything, but they ain't telling me nothing yet." He listened for a moment, then said, "So, are you telling me that he's alive, yo? Is he alive, yo? Please, man, tell me, son, because this is weird, son. I'm the only black man in that fucking shit, son. I'm the only fucking black man in that fucking room, in that house, son."

He talked a bit more about not giving up his phone and how he was being treated, then said, "Son, I don't think they going to give me an attorney son. That's what I'm saying, yo. They ain't saying no charge or nothing. That's what I'm saying, but at the end of the day, they over there arrested me – they over there talking to Veronica, son. They over there talking to Veronica." Just before he was about to shut off his phone with the dying battery, he provided Max with the phone number for Veronica's mom, Hope Taft.

As soon as he finished his call with Max, the door opened, and Investigator Anthony Diles entered the room with a uniformed sergeant. It seemed as though they might have been monitoring the situation inside the room or at least aware of the phone issue. Diles took the lead and started using a more tactful approach with Chucky, trying to reason with him. Diles asked, "Are you okay? Chucky replied, "No, I'm not okay, yo. This guy is grabbing me. He's trying to grab me and take my phone. I want a lawyer. I want a lawyer. If I'm not being – if I'm not being questioned with my lawyer present, you all not getting nothing out of me. You understand what I'm saying?" Diles kept his cool and continued trying to defuse his hostile attitude. But Chucky continued with, "If I'm not being detained here, I want a lawyer. I want to get out. I don't know what the fuck is going on right now. I am scared for my fucking life."

Diles described the difficulty of not having all the details because he had just gotten there, and they were still trying to sort things out. Therefore, until they could do that and get some answers, it was necessary to detain him. Despite his explanation, Chucky still couldn't understand why he was being detained. Explaining further, Diles said, "I literally just got here…I don't know a lot of what's going on either way, okay? We're looking into that. I'm not here to bust your balls or anything like that. I want to get to the bottom of this too. You've already expressed you don't want to talk to us about things, so that does kind of limit me on things. But, again, doesn't necessarily stop anything at this point. At this point, do you have to stay here for a while until we figure out what's going on? Yes." Chucky asked, "On what grounds? What are you looking into?" Diles answered, "If you want to call it, you're being detained, absolutely you're being detained. You've got to stay here for the time being. And I don't have any choice on that."

The dialogue between Diles and Chucky continued back and forth for several minutes before Chucky finally started to mellow – a little. As Diles continued to explain, Chucky finally started to say that he understood. Diles, realizing that his tactful approach was working, hit Chucky with his purpose in coming in and said, "One thing I do have to do, though, I can't have you in here with a cell phone. It's against our rules," then continued to explain why. Surprisingly, Chucky seemed to understand and wasn't nearly as hostile. They continued talking for several more minutes. The hostility had faded, and the conversation turned a bit more friendly. Chucky was offered a drink but asked for a cigarette instead. Diles said, "I'll see what I can do."

Before leaving, Diles asked him if he had anything in his pockets, "knives, guns, anything like that?" He said no but was asked to empty his pockets onto the table. There were several items in his pockets but no weapons. They did hold onto his lighter and told him he would get it back when they were done. With Chucky's lighter and cell phone in hand, Diles and the sergeant left the room. Chucky was heard saying, "They locked me up, man. They locked me up." Then he started banging on the door. Diles came back in and started a new conversation with him. Chucky was concerned about officers speaking with

Veronica and asking why she hadn't been brought to the police station. Diles said, "How do you know she hasn't?" They continued to talk for a couple more minutes, then Diles left the room again.

The door had just barely closed when he blurted out, "This is crazy. This is driving me out of my fucking head, yo, my head, yo. Fuck that, man. I don't understand fucking why I can't be at the hospital. I'm going to jail. This is crazy. This is fucking crazy." He then yelled through the door, "I need to know what's going on, yo." Then yelling louder said, "Investigator! I need to know what's going on. I'm not being charged. Please, let me out. Let me make my statement. This is weird. This is weird. I need to get out of here or give me a lawyer. Hello! Hello! Hello! Can I get some service over here?"

After that, Diles reentered the room and said, "What's up? It's going to be a while." Chucky said, "Hold on, sir. Everybody is getting interviewed. Everything is getting investigated, but I'm the only one sitting here. Nobody's talking to me." Diles replied, "You're not the only one sitting here. I can't talk to you. You requested an attorney, right?" Chucky replied, "No. Well, where's my attorney then? I don't have an attorney." Diles responded again, "I realize. We're done, okay," and walked out of the room. Becoming irate once again, Chucky yelled out, "Holy shit! I need a phone call, sir. You holding me against my will, sir. Holy crap, yo. They bugging, yo. Sir, you all holding me against my will. Hello! Hello!"

Sergeant Tom Eggleston entered the room, making his first appearance, and said firmly, "Charles. Have a seat." Chucky continued to insist he was being held against his will, becoming even more irate. Initially, Eggleston tried to reason with him just to get him to listen. Chucky's ranting and raving worsened before Eggleston finally said forcefully, "If you don't – if you don't knock it off, I'm going to put that shackle on you." Chucky wasn't fazed a bit and continued asking why he was being arrested and insisting he hadn't done anything.

Eggleston, raising his voice, repeatedly said, "Listen to me. Listen to me." While Eggleston was trying to explain the serious nature of the situation, Chucky said, "I understand, but everybody is being – everybody is being questioned but me." Eggleston said, "That's not true. We're talking to everybody." Chucky fired back, "That's what the other guy said. Why you all lyin' to me?" Eggleston replied, "Don't yell at me." Chucky asked again, "Why you all lyin' to me?" Eggleston, raising his voice, "Don't yell at me." Chucky said, "Why – I'm scared. I am fucking scared for my life, yo." Eggleston said, "As you should be. Because we need to talk about a very serious matter here in a very short time."

Eggleston tried to get him to relax and calm down, by assuring him that someone would be in soon to talk to him. Chucky complained about how long he'd been waiting and that someone had already interviewed Veronica at the hospital. Then demanded to know why no one was talking to him. Eggleston said, "You've got to give us a break here. We're trying to get – go along as best we can. I just walked in here. I didn't speak to anybody yet." They briefly continued to banter back and forth, then Chucky said, "All right. Is I'm being charged? Eggleston replied, "Do you want to talk to us?" Chucky said, "Yes, please. Right now!" Eggleston left the room after telling Chucky he was going for his notepad. As the door closed, Chucky said, "Everybody else is being spoke to. Yo, this is crazy. I'm looking like a fucking suspect here, yo. I'm looking like a suspect, yo."

Diles and Eggleston reentered the room. Eggleston formerly introduced himself as Diles asked, "What do you want to talk about?" Chucky answered, "I'd like to know what's going on right now. I will tell you everything that started from when I came in the house around 10:15, 10:30 by the time – at night by the time my girlfriend had to go to work." He continued to lay out his story, describing his version of events, including his interactions with the children, both before and after Veronica went to work and while he was there babysitting. He described putting everybody to bed between 11:00 and 11:30 p.m. but clarified that only the two older girls were. Claiming they were watching a movie when he put them to bed, he instructed them to turn it off before going to sleep. He then added, "I'm closing this door because if I close the door, they won't come out. You understand what I'm saying? Because when they come out, they start touching stuff."

He then fast-forwarded to the following day after Veronica returned from work around 7:15 a.m. The baby, he said, Zoey, had woken up crying, so he'd fixed her a bottle and put her back in bed. The other kids were still sleeping. He'd gone back and laid down with Veronica, where they talked for a while and then fell asleep. Later, he woke up to go to the bathroom. By then, he added, "...everybody started getting up – getting up. The only one who was not getting up was Lyric, and I'm about to make breakfast. So, I'm like, Lyric, get up, get up, get up. Lyric won't get up. Now, he's half cold, half warm. It be cold in that room, so I'm not gettin' no assumptions of anything, you understand what I'm saying? So, when I picked him up, I was like, oh my god, what the fuck is going on? I went to her. I told her straight before I even do anything. I said, yo, listen, Lyric is not gettin up. She like, what you mean he's not gettin' up? He's not gettin' up. Wake him up. I say he feel cold. What, the room is cold. I said no. He feel cold. You know what I mean? So, she told me to bring him, so I brung him." Eggleston said, "Mm-mm." Chucky continued, "Next thing you know, she starts flippin'. I don't know nothin'. I don't know nothin'. I just – I just – you're not even writing down what I'm saying right now." Eggleston said, "I'm listening because I want to listen to you." "Okay," he said.

He then backed up and told Eggleston where he was and who he was with before going over to Veronica's apartment. When asked, he said Veronica worked nights as a janitor at the High School while he babysat her four children. He then changed the topic and said, "Now, I'm – I'm asking the questions here. Nobody – everybody is giving me the runaround. All right, attorney, yes. The reason why I asked for it cause I be gettin' scared. Nobody's asking me questions, nobody nothin'. The only thing I hear is get in the car, get in the car, pushin' me." Eggleston responded, "Well – what we have is we have a real serious problem with Lyric. You understand?" Chucky answered, "Mm-mm." Eggleston continued, "…right? You understand that he's not – he – he's not doing well." Chucky replied, "What you mean? I'm not understanding." Eggleston said, "He's very – he's hurt real bad, and we're trying to figure out how that happened and why that happened."

The conversation then changed to his knowledge of the children, their ages, sleeping arrangements, and description of their bedroom. When questioned about how the kids played and got along, he said they would often roughhouse with each other. Then he added, "Yeah. They play a lot. They play a lot. They do hit each other too, at the same time." Turning to Lyric, Eggleston asked, "And he was already asleep when you got there." Chucky replied, "Yeah. When I got there, he was already asleep." Eggleston then said, "Your girlfriend and Lyric are at the hospital. The doctors are working on him." Chucky asked, "Is he alright? Is he stable?" Eggleston responded, "I don't know that, and I'm – it doesn't look good from what we're being told by the hospital right now. So, you understand our concern, obviously?" Chucky said, "Yeah, I understand."

After Chucky and Diles speak briefly, Eggleston said, "You understand, okay, when something like this happens, obviously, we're looking at who's in the house." Chucky said, "And I was the one who was in the house." Eggleston responded, "Right." Chucky then expressed his concerns and asked if he was going to be locked up. Eggleston replied, "No. But here's what we have to do. You're not under arrest. I want you to understand that. But we do need to speak with you about this, and we have the right to keep you here until we determine exactly what happened, but it doesn't mean that you're under arrest, okay?"

Eggleston told him that his girlfriend's mother was there with the kids. And hopefully, the investigators at the hospital with Veronica would be bringing her back soon. In the meantime, they had a lot to do and many other people to talk to, and it would take some time. Eggleston then said, "Hopefully, you're not going to be here all day, but you've got to bear with us, okay, just a little bit. In the meantime, I have to go make a couple phone calls to try to find out a little bit more, okay?" Eggleston then asked if he could get him some water or something. Chucky said, "I want a cigarette. I am like – my nerves is really shot right now." Eggleston said he'd work on it.

Eggleston asked Chucky for some of his pedigree information and jotted it down. He then asked about some of Veronica's past relationships, including the fathers of her children. Later, he asked if Veronica disciplined her children and how she did it. Chucky explained that she would spank them now and then, but "She don't OD," he said. Eggleston's questioning turned back to Lyric, and he asked, "But he was already in bed?" Chucky responded, "He was already in bed." Eggleston said, "And asleep or allegedly asleep? Chucky replied, "Allegedly."

Before leaving the room, Eggleston told Chucky he would work on getting him that cigarette and then left. A few minutes later, Eggleston returned to the room with a cigarette in hand, but before offering it to him, he asked a few more questions about who was where in the bedroom. He then walked over close to Chucky and offered him his cigarette. Chucky reached for it with his left hand. As Eggleston was lighting it, he noticed an injury and pointed to Chucky's knuckles. He asked, "What happened to your hand?" Chucky replied, "I punched the wall." Eggleston asked, "Oh, at home?" Chucky replied, "Yeah. I was…" Diles, who had been at the scene earlier, was standing behind Eggleston, interrupted and said, "Is that what the hole is?" Chucky said, "Yeah. I was very frustrated." Eggleston replied, "Okay. I just noticed that so." Chucky replied, "Yeah. Both of them," as he held up his right hand also. Diles again asked, "Was that – that was this morning?" After noticing the injured knuckles of his right hand, Eggleston said, "Oh, is that – oh, that too, huh?" Chucky responded, saying, "Yeah. Both of – it was the wall." Eggleston replied, "Jeez."

| Discovery of Pratt's bloody knuckles

While Chucky was still being interviewed, the BPD had already learned about the severe injuries to Lyric's head, face, and neck, including a burn mark near his left ear and a pattern of three gouge marks on both sides of Lyric's neck in front of his ears. That, according to the ER doctors, appeared to have been made by fingernails. Furthermore, they also had the corresponding photographs that were taken at the hospital. Surprisingly, no photographs were ever taken of Chucky's fingernails or bleeding knuckles. Nor were any scrapings taken from under his fingernails. From experience, I found it very strange how they could simply overlook such elementary yet important tasks. A valuable opportunity lost.

As the interview continued, Chucky added a little more to his story when questioned further about the kids in the bedroom. He said, "I put the girls in their room as soon as their mother left because she gave – matter of fact, she went in the room and gave the girls kisses and Lyric and all them kisses before she went to work. So, she was in the room with them."

For the most part, the interview was over, but investigators continued to come and go over the next several minutes. On one occasion, shortly after they left the room, Chucky was alone and heard saying, "He got to be okay, yo. He got to be okay. It was on my watch. It was on my watch." Later, when one of the investigators stepped in to check on him, he was told that Veronica had just returned from the hospital and was in the other room. He'd asked to see her but was told that couldn't happen right now because she was still being interviewed. Shortly after the investigator left, Chucky yelled out, "Veronica!" He waited for a moment but heard no response. Then, he yelled again, "This is not right. I'm the only one here, yo. I know that. I know I'm the only one here. Only one here, yo. I'm about to go crazy, yo. They ain't give me my phone calls." Again, yelling through the door, "Investigator!" Then he continued saying, "All day long. Hauling me down like I'm a fucking suspect, yo. I'm a fucking suspect, yo. Get the fuck out of here, yo. I ain't do it, man. I ain't do it. You all got to let me go, man. You got no cause to arrest me, press any charges. Let me go, fucking shit, yo."

Eggleston walked back in for the last time and told him he was about to let him go. When asked, Chucky assured him that he was not going anywhere and said, "You have my phone number." Eggleston said, "Okay. Now, understand this. Right now, you can't go to 4½ Fayette Street because we – well, let me

– let me – just…" Before he could finish, he was suddenly interrupted by another investigator walking into the room. A moment later, Eggleston looked at Chucky and said, "Have a seat." He sat down in his chair across the table and said, "I just want to let you know that I have some bad news, okay? The hospital did all they could for Lyric, but he didn't make it, okay? So, what I'm saying to you, Charles, is you can go back to your house, but you can't go over to 4½ Fayette Street, okay?" Chucky asked, "Why?" "Because we need to be there because we've got – we've got to look to see what might have caused these injuries. So, technically – for lack of a better term, it's a crime scene, okay?" Chucky understood and agreed to stay away from the scene.

Even though Chucky had been detained for nearly four hours, the actual length of his questioning only lasted about 20 minutes. After Eggleston verified his contact information, Chucky was told he was free to go and escorted out of the room. However, while walking into the squad room, Chucky continued talking and providing additional information. We'll learn shortly what more he had to say.

As the story unfolds, we hear a lot more about Charles Pratt. But for now, let's jump over to the waiting room outside the ER at the hospital, where Veronica Taft is nervously waiting for word on Lyric. At the same time, Investigators Joe Cornell and Jeff Wagner were anxiously trying to learn more about what happened and used the opportunity to ask her a few questions.

---

1. *Peeky*: Nickname for Haveen - Veronica's oldest daughter.

5

VERONICA TAFT – INTERVIEW #1

Author's note: A more formal interview with Veronica would occur once they got back to BPD headquarters. But the following is a brief summary of what they learned at the hospital.

During questioning at the hospital, Veronica explained how she worked last night at the Binghamton High School, doing custodial work – working from 11:00 p.m. until 7:00 a.m. that morning. She stated that after returning home, she would typically check on the kids before going to bed. But this morning, she didn't check on them and went straight to bed.

Veronica was also asked about Charles Pratt. She explained that he was her boyfriend responsible for the children while she was at work. She explained how they all called him Chucky. Adding further, she did not believe Chucky would have done anything to harm Lyric or any of her children. When asked, she also denied ever suffering any physical abuse from Chucky and that he did not discipline the children. Adding that if she'd ever seen him doing so, he would have problems.

Later, when asked about the children's sleeping arrangements, she explained that all four children slept in one room – the youngest in a crib, and the other three pretty much chose wherever they wanted to sleep on the two bunk beds in the room. Initially, she thought Lyric may have been on the top bunk that night but later said she wasn't positive. She might be getting her days mixed up since she started working the night shift.

Veronica was then told that they had reason to believe that Lyric had been assaulted sometime during the night and that Chucky may very well be responsible for the injuries he sustained.

Shortly after that, Veronica was notified that Lyric had been pronounced dead and was asked to accompany investigators back to BPD headquarters for further questioning. She agreed.

While at the hospital, Veronica was in a state of shock, stunned and emotionally distraught after just learning of the death of her young son Lyric. Regardless, only minutes later, in shock, she was escorted out of the hospital and rushed back to BPD headquarters for further questioning and placed alone in a small interrogation room. At the time, she was dressed in light blue jeans and a gray hooded sweatshirt. It was now about 12:47 p.m.

VERONICA TAFT – INTERVIEW #1 | 39

| Veronica Taft – Interview

Author's note: Like the Pratt interview, the following is a summary taken from the actual written transcript of the videotaped interview of Veronica Taft. Again, for authenticity, the exact language and terminology are used. Similarly, Veronica can also be heard talking to herself outside the presence of investigating officers.

Veronica was escorted into the interrogation room by Investigator Jeff Wagner, who said, "Just have a seat right there, and we'll be right in with you, okay?" He then left the room. Sitting alone at the small table, Veronica began unconsciously, rocking back and forth. Her hands were clenched in prayer as she started talking out loud. She was heard saying, "What happened to my baby? Oh, God! God, please, take care of my baby. Please, take care of my baby. Please take care of my baby. God, please, I love my baby. I love him. Just tell him I love him, and I did everything I could. He wouldn't wake up. Please, God, please, just take care of my baby. That's all. Take care of my baby because I didn't. I didn't check on him. I didn't check on him. Just take care of my baby, God, please. Please, God. I'm so fucking stupid. My beautiful baby boy. He's beautiful. I love him. I can't look at him, though. I can't see him that way. I can't see him that way. I can't. I can't look at my baby. He's dead. I can't even look at him. I can't see him that way. Oh, what happened to my baby? God, please, take care of my baby. He was such a good boy. He was such a good boy. He don't deserve this. No child deserves this. What happened to my baby? Oh, God, I just want to know, God, what happened to my baby? God, what happened to my baby? Oh, God, what happened? God, take care of my baby. That's all. God, just take care of my baby. I love him. I love him more than anything in the world. I'll see you when I get there when my times up. See you when I get there. I love you, my baby boy."

But she didn't stop there and continued saying, "I shouldn't have went to work last night. I don't know why I didn't just stay home, took the night off. Oh, God, I shouldn't have went to work, shouldn't have went to work. Should have checked on him this morning. Should have. Should have checked on him this morning, but I didn't. I should have checked on my baby boy, my baby boy, my little baby boy. Why didn't I check on him? I'm fucking stupid. Why didn't I check on him? I'm fucking stupid. I'm so stupid, so stupid. My baby, let's hope – such a good baby. Let's hope – I hope he didn't suffer or anything. I hope he knows I love him, my baby boy. I loved him so much. I love him. I love him. I love him. God, just take care of my baby, that's all. I love him. Take care of my baby. What do I tell my other babies? I'm not going to say their father killed him. How do I tell them that? How do I tell them that? Chucky couldn't have done that to him. No way. He loved them kids. He's never – he's never touched them. He couldn't have. If he did, I'm going to hurt him. He's going to suffer if he did something to my baby, but I don't think he did. There's no way."

Wagner reentered the room and asked if she needed anything. "I have to pee real bad," she said. So, they took her to the restroom. She added, "I might be a minute. I'm like, really cramped up. I'm just making myself upset." Wagner said, "I understand." A few minutes later, she returned to the room, accompanied by Investigator Cornell. They spoke very briefly before Cornell left the room, leaving Veronica alone again.

Once again, she started talking out loud, repeating much of what she said earlier. However, there were some interesting new things she was saying as well. She started talking about Chucky, saying there was no way he would do anything. Then she said, "He's too good to them kids. He didn't act no different. I don't know how this could have happened." Thinking she might be responsible and not yet knowing what happened, she added, "I'm fucking stupid letting him on the top bunk. He probably fell off. They said he got a bruise on his forehead. He probably fell off the top bunk. I'm a fucking idiot, yo. I shouldn't have let him up on the bed. He should be in his own bed in his own room. He just wants to sleep with his sisters because he loves them." Again, she starts repeating much of what she said earlier – continuing to beat herself up for not checking on him and still wondering what to tell her other babies. Then she started second-guessing herself whether she could have done something more. In other words, she was blaming herself and demonstrating all the classic signs of survivor's guilt.

Later, she said, "I don't know what happened. I need to know what happened. I need to know what happened." Suddenly, her thoughts turned back to Chucky when she said, "I hope to God that – that Chucky wouldn't do anything to him. I don't think he would, because he's – he's so good to them, and he didn't – he disciplined them. There's no way. He bumped his head, or I don't know. I don't know. I don't know. He (Chucky) didn't act no different. The truth will come out if he did because I'll fucking hurt him. If he fucking hurt my baby, he better suffer."

. . .

Author's note: Veronica was clearly suffering from cognitive dissonance. In other words, her mind was in a major tug-of-war. On the one hand, wanting to believe Chucky couldn't have done this while at the same time considering he may have.

Continuing, she said, "But I don't think he did. There's no way. Why would he? No matter what, nothing should happen to a baby. But, I mean, he's such a good boy. There's no way. I don't know. I don't know. I guess you never know – just no way. I don't know. No way he did it. He's all calm and everything. He brought my baby to me. He was my baby. My baby was gone. I tried to wake him up. He wouldn't wake up, though. My other babies, thank God they're little because…"

Wagner and Cornell reentered the room and started by writing down Veronica's pedigree information. Cornell then explained the nature of their investigation and read her Miranda rights. She understood and agreed to speak with them; she read and signed the Miranda form. It was now 1:13 p.m., just a little over one hour since Lyric was pronounced dead.

Wagner and Cornell had already conducted a preliminary interview of Veronica at the hospital and were with her when she was notified of Lyric's death. So, Cornell started by saying, "Okay. We're going to probably be going over a lot of things we've already spoken to you about." Veronica replied, "Right." Having already been through a previous line of questioning, she asked, "Can I not do this again after this?" Cornell said, "Well, we're going to try not to go through it as many times as – okay, so yes – okay."

After some basic background questions about the children, sleeping arrangements, past relationships with other men, and her work history, they started asking many background questions about Chucky. Later, the questions turned to his relationship with the children. Veronica explained that the kids liked him a lot. She also believed that he liked them. She had only known Chucky for 2-3 months, but there had never been any problems between him and the children. When asked about disciplining the children, she explained that both she and Chucky would discipline the children when necessary. Admitting there were times when she would 'pop' their hands, but never their bodies. Then she added that Chucky never hit the children because she wouldn't allow it. If anything, he might sit them in a corner for some time-out.

Veronica was also questioned, explaining how she'd been working full-time on the night shift, doing maintenance work at the high school. She worked weekdays from 11:00 p.m. until 7:00 a.m., including last night, and Chucky would babysit the four children while she was at work. Their continued questioning was very detailed and covered the entire gamut of all pertinent areas needed for their investigation.

Despite Veronica's distraught and fragile condition due to the recent loss of her young son, she held up remarkably well, answering all of their questions spontaneously, without hesitation or anger. However, there were many times when she was seen hanging her head, rocking back and forth unconsciously, and could often be heard whimpering or crying.

Notably, not everyone who experiences emotional trauma from a tragic loss has the desire, willingness, or even the ability to answer questions, let alone undergo lengthy police interrogation effectively. Veronica was very much in a state of shock, suffering from confusion and a disoriented state of mind. Given the proximity of her tragedy and the timing of her interview, her memory of specific details might have very likely been distorted, fragmented, or lost entirely. Therefore, while not intentional, there might have been some inconsistencies.

Continuing, the line of questioning turned to what was happening and what she did before she left for work. She thought it was around 9:00 p.m. when she put Lyric in his room and turned on his movie. When asked, she couldn't remember if she had closed the door but then said, "I didn't put it up." She did recall hearing the TV on. Having been to the scene earlier, Wagner had noticed that the bedroom door was broken and off its hinges. So he asked, "Now, that door is broken, though, right? You have to set it there?" "Yeah. You've got to set it," she said. Then added that her oldest knew how to move it to get in and out of the room. Wagner asked if Chucky was there with his brother Melo before she went to work. She nodded.

The questioning then turned to her phone. She didn't have a cell phone, but she would call home from her work phone. She remembered calling Chucky that night and said, "I called him exactly like 11:20 because I always call after I get to work….and then I called him again…between 12:30 and 1:30; I want to say." Adding further that she called the 2nd time to talk with Chucky about coming home to get a movie to take back and watch at work. But they got too busy and couldn't do that. Wagner asked, "Was he awake when you called him? Charles?" Veronica replied, "Oh yeah. He was awake." She added that Chucky had her work number and could call any time. During further questioning about where each child slept, she said it varied because they would take turns on the top and bottom bunk. But last night, she wasn't sure who was sleeping where. She admitted that her days were very similar, and she could be getting her days mixed up between last night and the night before. She may have gone in and kissed them goodbye before going to work. But she'd gotten up in a hurry last night and couldn't remember if she had gone back in their room or not.

Turning to Charles, Wagner asked, "You said Charles is from New York City? Did you tell me that?" Veronica replied, "I didn't tell you that, but yeah, he's from New York City. The Bronx, I think." The interview then shifted back to what happened at her apartment earlier this morning, starting from when Chucky first found Lyric unresponsive. The answers to her questions were very similar to Chucky's version. After describing how she first tried to wake him up and noticing that his lips were purple, she started CPR immediately. Wagner said, "Well, you did the right thing." Veronica replied, "Yeah. But I did it on the bed. I should have done it on the floor. It was supposed to be a hard surface. Then I put him on the floor and tried on the floor." Wagner again said, "Okay. You know what, you did it pretty quick, though, and it didn't make – you did the right thing. You did the right thing, okay?" Veronica said, "I should have checked on him." "Well, you did the right thing," he said.

Cornell left the room as Wagner continued the interview and started asking about the kids sleeping and bathroom habits, such as getting up during the night. According to Veronica, her oldest, Haveen, was the only one who would get up to go to the bathroom during the night. Lyric was still in diapers. He then asked when his last diaper change was. She had to think for a moment but then said she thought it was sometime after they ate dinner but wasn't sure of the time. She seemed to think it was just before she laid down before going to work. Wagner asked, "Did you have to wake him to change his diaper? Veronica replied, "No. No. No. He was awake." Wagner asked, "Where did you change his diaper?" "In my room on the floor," she said. Wagner again asked, "Then you went and put him back in bed?" Veronica responded, "Yeah. Before that, he wasn't in bed. He was in there watching a movie. He wasn't asleep. I changed him. I had to come out and change him." Wagner asked a few more questions about the diaper change and then asked, "You put him to go back to bed? She said, "No. I told him to go back to bed." Wagner again asked, "You told him to go back to bed? Was that the last you seen him?" "Yeah."

She was questioned further about the children's bedroom,

specifically the bunk bed, and how her kids would access the top bunk. She explained that there was a ladder, and other than Zoey, the baby, who slept in a crib, all the others could easily climb up and down the ladder. Wagner then asked if she had noticed any bruising on Lyric when she was changing his diaper earlier. She said, "No, nothing at all." When asked about any bruising, scarring, or injuries, she said, "Maybe some little things here and there, but nothing serious." The only thing she could think of was some small dots or marks on his shoulder, where he'd been scratching himself. Wagner asked, "How about his ears?" Somewhat puzzled, she replied, "His ears?" Wagner said, "Yeah. Did you ever have a problem with his ears?" Veronica replied, "They're waxy. That's it." Wagner asked, "No marks on them, no nothing, no abrasions?" "No," she said.

Continuing, he asked, "I'm going to ask you this. What do you think happened?" She replied, "I really don't know." Wagner asked again, "You really don't know?" She said, "I questioned myself about it all day. I don't know. I think, I mean, like maybe he fell, but then like, oh, God forbid Chucky did something, but he wouldn't – I don't think he would because he was – he's so good to them. And he didn't act different this morning. No, no phone calls like you said, like stuff like that, nothing panicky, nothing, nothing out of the ordinary that would, you know, raise a flag. I don't know. I have no clue." Wagner added, "He suffered injuries that – that led to his death. We're trying to figure out how." Veronica replied, "Okay. Honestly, I want to – almost am sure that Charles wouldn't do nothing to him, but I wasn't there. I don't know. I've been asking myself like is it possible or anything, but there's – I don't know."

The interview then shifts to the fathers of her children, and she explained how one was physically abusive, and the other one had cheated on her. She was also asked about boyfriends since then. She'd had two – a young man named Jesse and then

Chucky. Wagner acted surprised when she told him that her relationship with Chucky had become intimate. It was his understanding that she was only using him to babysit. She explained, "No. He's my boyfriend." Wagner asked, "Do you just want to not believe that he might have done something because…." She quickly interrupted, saying, "Hell, no. No. If he did it, he's going to pay. Fuck that. No. He's going to pay."

During continued questioning, she told them about another man named Raymond, who babysits when she and Chucky aren't around during the day. They noted his name and then turned back to Chucky and asked, "Has he ever hit you?" Veronica replied, "No. He'd be done. I went through enough of that." Wagner continued, "Does he have a criminal history that you know of?" She answered, "The only history he has that I know of is that he – when he lived in the city, for drugs, for dealing drugs." Wagner said, "Okay. And how long did he go away for that? Did he tell you?" Veronica replied, "A while because he got caught twice." Wagner asked, "Is he still dealing drugs?" At first, she said, "No. No. No." But then said, "Let me find out." Wagner asked, "Is he using? Are you using?" She answered, "No. No. I don't even smoke cigarettes." She then told them that Chucky smoked both cigarettes and weed, and she thought he chose to be at his friend Max's house more because they smoked pot, and she doesn't allow it.

Investigators decided to take a break, but they asked Veronica if she needed a drink or something to eat before leaving the room. She asked, "What's going on with my kids?" Wagner said, "Well, the last I know, they're out with your mom." Cornell said, "Yeah. We'll check on that," and they left the room. Veronica was alone once again. As soon as they shut the door, she started talking aloud again, repeating much of what she said earlier. But this time, she added some interesting new thoughts and spontaneous remarks as follows:

"He better not have touched him. I don't think he did. I'm not in denial. It's just that, my poor baby boy. I can't believe my son died. I never thought this would happen to me. There's no way that – that there's no way Chucky did anything to Lyric. I'm not in denial. They're not.... He's such a good boy. He's so good. I don't know. My baby died. What the hell? I never thought this would happen to me. What happened to my baby? My baby fell? My baby died. I want my baby back. When I see my other babies, I can't upset them. Why? Why would this happen to my baby?"

Continuing, she added, "If it was done, then – then whoever did it, if God forbid Chucky did something to him, he will be held accountable, but there's just no way. Like, of course, there's a way, but there's no way he did it. I'm not in denial. He's just so good to them, and the kids are just so good. They like play and have fun and get hurt here and there, you know, because that's what kids do, fall. I hope that their playing and falling didn't lead to death, but I'd rather that than to know that my boyfriend did it. What kind of mom would I be? How could this happen?" Despite what she said about not being in denial, she clearly was. In other words, she was still wrestling with her cognitive dissonance.

Veronica continued talking out loud steadily for several more minutes while waiting for Cornell and Wagner to return. Some of her remaining thoughts and comments have been abbreviated to include the more pertinent things she said as follows:

"What happened to my baby? My baby got hurt. I mean. Even if he fell and it was an accident, and Chucky knew, he didn't act like he knew anything, nothing. We'll find out, though. God is watching. Whoever did it will be punished, whatever happened. I never thought this would happen. This is bullshit. He's always so beautiful. I named him Lyric, and he was so beautiful when he was born. He was like a beautiful song. I hope

Chucky didn't do that to him. I hope he didn't because what reason? I know kids are a pain in the butt sometimes, but mine are really good. It's not denial, just – it's not I don't want to believe that he would do that. I don't know, but if he did that, he's going to pay. God is going to get him Judgment Day. Whenever his time is up, God will get him. I'm confident of that. I hope to God that. God, you took him, and you hold him under your – under your arms and just love my baby boy. I love you, Lyric. I love you so much." She continues talking for a couple more minutes and then says, "I hope someone comes in here soon. It's not fair. It's not fair. It's not fair." She then stood up, knocked on the door, and asked, "Is anyone at the door?"

Cornell and Wagner reentered the room. They'd likely been listening. Cornell says, "Yes?" She replied, "Yeah. I don't want to wait here anymore." Cornell said, "Well. We're going to come back in a minute. You don't have to wait." Continuing, he said, "I just want to ask you. I think you said something to me earlier. You said you gave the kids a kiss before you went to work?" She replied, "The older one." Cornell asked, "The older one? Okay. Where was she?" Veronica responded, "Heading towards her room. I wasn't even in the room. I didn't even look at him." Cornell said, "Okay. Okay." She then added, "I remember looking in the room before – not before I went to work but before I laid down, and he was watching a movie. And it was *Mean Girls*. I said, are you watching *Mean Girls*? He said I'm watching *Mean Girls*. And I said, okay."

Wagner then shifted gears and started asking more questions about Chucky. Veronica explained that she had been in a relationship with him since September. Wagner then asked, "Did he tell you he was arrested for assault back in July here in Binghamton?" Then questioned her further as to why she hadn't mentioned that earlier. She explained that it was her understanding the charge was getting dropped because the guy told his lawyer to drop the charges because he knew he was in the wrong.

Wagner shifted gears again and asked, "Did you have Child Protective at your house recently?" Veronica openly admitted that she did and said, "A bunch of stuff." But when Wagner pushed for more specific details, she said, "Everything under the sun." Wagner then asked, "Well, could you tell me that, what?" Veronica replied, "I'm doing drugs. I'm dealing drugs. I'm molesting my children. I'm doing everything with them. But the worker that came out, she said, we could tell this is malicious stuff, blah, blah. And I actually got a thing in the mail about two weeks ago saying it's closed, blah, blah, blah." He then questioned her further about her experience with CPS, and she openly explained everything she could recall, including the names of those who had filed malicious complaints against her.

Questioning then turned to her past relationship with the fathers of her children. She explained her history with them, how their relationships ended, and that neither father has any relationship with their children. Wagner then confronted her about getting herself involved in abusive relationships. She admitted that the first relationship was physically abusive, but "the other one was more emotional and stuff like that," she said. Wagner said, "So it kind of sounds like you find yourself in bad relationship after bad relationship." Veronica replied, "Well, I see where you're going with this." Wagner said, "No, I'm not. Not you. I'm talking Charles. I'm not saying it's your fault. Don't get me wrong, and don't take this the wrong way. Some women find themselves with the wrong guy continually. It's nothing to do with the woman, but it happens. And I think I'm sitting across the table from one right now."

Veronica defended Chucky, claiming he was not abusive at all. Wagner said, "I can tell you this. When we wanted to talk to him, he wasn't at all happy with us, and he was – he seemed like he was ready to fight if he had to. So, you know what, I've been at this job a long time, and people aren't normally like that. So, that guy has a temper." Cornell jumped in and said, "He wants nothing to do with us, and he's sort of the one that was responsible for the child when you were gone. And like Jeff said, I thought we were going to end up fighting with him. And you're saying that he doesn't have a temper?" She said, "No, he really don't. He's…" Wagner interrupted, "He does. I can tell you this, Veronica, I've been doing this job a long time, and I've never had anybody in a situation like this as uncooperative as he was. That just isn't normal." She responded, "Right. I'm not in denial or anything like that. It's just that I feel like I would have noticed something. Wagner responded, "Well, it's either that or, you know what, sometimes boyfriend and girlfriend want to protect the other one." Veronica snapped back, "Hell, no. I didn't protect him." Wagner said, "Well, the thing is you don't know what happened." Veronica replied, "I don't. I don't." Wagner said, "You don't have a crystal ball, and neither do we. So, the good part of you wants to believe Charles didn't do anything, but I think deep down you might have a suspicion that he did something to Lyric." Veronica replied, "Well, something happened to my son, obviously. I wasn't there. So, it's either he did, or it was an accident. It's one or the other." Wagner said, "We don't think this was an accident." She said, "It sucks too, though, because he was so great, not abusive and all that shit. And if he did this, I don't know where the fuck that came from."

As the interview continued, they rehashed some of the same information for clarification and then wanted to learn what she knew about the hole punched in the wall at her apartment. Cornell started by saying, "Now, look, I don't know if you told me, Jeff, when – when Charles brought Lyric to you this morning, there was mention about some – some hole he had punched in a wall?" Wagner followed up and asked, "And there was a hole in some wall of the apartment?" Veronica confirmed there was a hole punched in the wall, as she had watched Chucky do it. To verify, Wagner asked, "You're sure he punched a hole in the wall?" Veronica says, "Yeah. Right there. He did it – right then and there before the EMTs walked in. I think he did it at the same time my neighbor was there from across the road. His name is Chris, I believe."

Briefly entertaining the possible 'falling out of bed' scenario, Wagner asked Veronica if she had heard anything from the kid's room before Lyric was discovered. She said, "I heard her (Haveen) playing and stuff. I heard her in the room." Wagner asked, "If she felt something was wrong, would she have come in and told you – right then if Lyric was lying on the floor?" She answered, "Yeah, absolutely. She's a very smart girl." Wagner said, "Okay. Okay. So, I guess what I'm getting at is you can see where I'm going with this?" Veronica said, "Yeah, I can see." Wagner added, "He didn't fall. Lyric didn't fall and land in bed and have all these injuries happen to him. If he would have fallen, the worst-case scenario if he fell and those injuries happened in a fall, he would have been on the floor." She agreed but said, "I don't know where he was." Wagner continued with, "So, at some point during the night, Lyric was out of that bedroom, and he was put back in bed. Do you see what I'm saying?" She agreed. Wagner added, "pretty clear-cut, especially with what you told me about Haveen." Wagner then left the room, and Cornell stayed behind with Veronica. She said, "I'm not trying to cover for the guy. I swear to God." Cornell then explained their position and purpose finding out what really happened, whether this was an accident or something else. And they were still waiting to hear more from the doctors who were continuing their examination – admitting that they didn't have all the answers yet.

Only a few minutes went by before Wagner reentered the

room, and the interview continued. It's now about 2:26 p.m. He picked up the questioning and asked, "Hey, I just want to run a couple of things by you. You leave for work last night. Your kids are in bed in the bedroom?" She replied, "Heading towards two of them, yeah." Wagner asked, "Okay. Who did you walk out with?" She said, "Myself. Oh, my neighbor downstairs came by last night, the girl downstairs. She stopped by last night like ten minutes before I walked out, and I was on my bed just, you know, getting my clothes on." Continuing, he asked, "Your kids weren't in bed when you left?" She answered, "Two of them were in the room, and two of them were heading towards that way. I told you they were probably playing a game and finishing up their movie, the other two."

With his following statement, it was apparent they had learned something more from Chucky while they were out of the room. Wagner said, "Well, Charles is telling us none of them were in bed when you left, and he fed them after you left, French fries and Tater-tots and things like that." Veronica says, "Oh, yeah, that is – he did feed them directly. You are 100 percent correct. I'm not changing the story. That's right – a late dinner. I didn't eat nothing before I left. He fed them a late dinner – because he's the one that's there." Later, she added, "He did feed them last night. I'm totally wrong." Following up, Wagner asked, "How do you know he fed them?" "Because the fries and stuff were in my oven before I laid down. He did feed them."

Author's note: Whatever Pratt said about the kids not being in bed and having fed them after Veronica left for work occurred off-camera after leaving the interrogation room.

. . .

Wagner challenged her about putting the kids to bed before she went to work. She attempted to clarify by saying they were in the room, but they were just watching a movie. Wagner said, "The problem, Veronica, we have is you told our captain that you put Lyric to bed on the bottom bunk before you went to work." She said, "He was in there watching a movie." Wagner again said, "You told us you put him in the top bunk. Then you told us in here that you took him in to change before you laid down." Veronica responded, "I did change him before I laid down – that's accurate." Wagner again asked, "And then – he walked away, and that was the last you seen him?" Veronica replied, "Yes. But he was in the room watching a movie. That's what he went back to do, on the bottom bunk watching a movie."

Veronica was having some trouble articulating what she was trying to say. Either that or Wagner was confused or misunderstood what she was trying to tell him and was trying to make it look as though there was a discrepancy in her story. Perhaps, it was a little of both. They clearly were not on the same page. Regardless, Veronica appeared sincere in what she was saying but was a little confused in her current state of mind.

Earlier, I mentioned how difficult it could be for someone who has experienced a traumatic event to recall specific details accurately. From what we just witnessed during the interview, that certainly seemed to be the case with Veronica. It reminded me of another case a few years earlier that I recall – a very tragic and traumatic event involving a husband and wife – the wife died, but her husband survived. During questioning immediately after, the surviving husband, who was still in shock, gave conflicting accounts of what happened. Later, they were used against him. So, I was already of the opinion that experiencing a major traumatic event can have an adverse effect on memory. At least in the short-term, if not longer. In my attempt to confirm my opinion, I decided to turn to the medical experts.

It didn't take long to find what I was looking for. There was a wealth of information on the topic – much more than I expected. Each accredited site I checked provided similar information, all of which supported my early opinion. One, in particular, jumped out at me because it addressed the specific issue rather well. I found it in an organization called CASA PALMERA.

Located in Del Mar, California, CASA PALMERA is a nationally recognized treatment center for adults, offering a wide variety of specialized treatment options including, trauma recovery. There I discovered a key article that addressed the specific issue of memory loss due to trauma, titled, *Emotional or Psychological Trauma and Memory Loss*, which read in part as follows:

"Emotional or psychological trauma can also affect your memory. Memory loss is a natural survival skill and defense mechanism humans develop to protect themselves from psychological damage. Violence, sexual abuse, and other emotionally traumatic events can lead to dissociative amnesia, which helps a person cope by allowing them to temporarily forget details of the event. With this type of memory loss, which is also called psychogenic amnesia or functional amnesia, a person will often suppress memories of a traumatic event until they are ready to handle them, which may never occur. Emotional or psychological trauma can also lead to post-traumatic stress disorder, which can manifest itself in different ways including flashbacks of the event and intrusive, unwanted thoughts about the trauma."

From my perspective, that described exactly what was happening to Veronica. But let's continue with the interview.

The questioning continued for a few more minutes as they covered some miscellaneous topics about the new puppy they had, her work schedule, and the time she arrived home that morning, including why she had to walk rather than get a ride like usual. Veronica answered all their questions, and they were apparently satisfied with her answers. Nothing was challenged. Wagner then asked, "Now, do you feel you're in trouble here?" She said, "No." Wagner said, "Okay. Good. Because the only thing that could get you in trouble is if you weren't telling us the truth." "Right," she said. Wagner followed up with, "Then that could land you in a world of trouble. We don't want to see that happen." She said, "Right. Okay." Wagner stated, "He's crying over there. He – he's a wreck right now. He's starting to talk and tell us some things." Veronica said, "Okay. Good. Good."

Continuing, Wagner said, "So, is there anything he's going to tell us that we're going to have to come in and talk to you about – that you know of?" Veronica answered, "No. Absolutely not. I'm not worried about it. I'll take a lie detector. Do you guys do that here? I'm willing to do that." Wagner replied, "Well, we'll keep that in the back of our mind. Do you think we should give you one?" She replied, "Well, if it will clear your guy's head because I don't want you guys to think I don't know anything about my – my son. I don't want to do that." Wagner said, "I don't know – I'll be honest, I don't have a crystal ball right now. I don't know if you know, or you don't know." She said, "Yeah. I don't." Wagner then added, "I do know I'm a little concerned that your story has changed a few different times." Veronica explained that her workdays are all pretty much the same, and she may have gotten her days mixed up.

Wagner continued with, "I mean, don't take this the wrong way, Veronica, but your son died today. I would remember. I would remember if I've had tragedy in my life when the last time I seen my loved one was." Veronica agreed and said, "Right. Right. You're right."

. . .

Author's note: For the most part, I would tend to agree with Wagner. However, as noted above, after just experiencing the death of a small child, then trying to remember specific details about what happened? Maybe – maybe not.

Later, Cornell changed the subject and asked, "When you spoke to Charles between 12:30 and 1:30, what did he say he was doing?" She answered, "He said, "I just got done cleaning. I did the dishes. I cleaned the kitchen." That's all he said." During further questioning, she remembered the kids having been fed earlier in the day.

Continuing, Wagner shifted gears again and asked, "Does Charles ever have to change Lyric during the night? I mean, you don't want your baby to sleep with a diaper full of pee – or poop, did you? She replied, "No. No. I remember changing him in my room and sending him back to his room." Wagner clarified his question, asking, "No. I'm not – I'm talking during the middle of the night. Who changes him?" She answered, "Chucky would have to, obviously."

At this point, Wagner and Cornell looked at each other. Neither had any more questions at this time. They spoke with Veronica for a few more minutes. She was told her apartment was now considered a crime scene, and she wouldn't be allowed to go back there. She said, "I don't want to go back to my house." She wanted to see her kids and was told they were now with her mother and no longer in the building. They had been taken to the Child Advocacy Center (CAC) to be interviewed. Veronica understood and said, "Yeah. Whatever clears me out of here faster. You guys with your lie detector – I just wanna go home." Cornell and Wagner left the room, telling her they'd be back with her shortly.

Like before, alone in the room, she started talking out loud and started out saying, "My baby. You better not have done that to my baby because he's going to be sorry if he did. He better not fucking did anything to my baby, or I'll fucking kill him myself. Well, I can't say that. Fucking something will happen to him." Fast-forwarding a little, she continued saying, "My baby is dead. Oh, God, why is this happening to me? Damn. I did fuck up on the story. That is true. They did eat late last night, and I'm a fucking idiot for that, and now I look all guilty because I didn't pay attention like an idiot. I should have. I should have like because, you know, they're going to look at me like a – I'll take a lie detector. Then they could see that I'm not covering for him, and I won't cover for him."

Continuing, she laid out the entire scenario in detail from the best of her recollection but often second-guessing herself about her memory's accuracy. Remarkably, it's very consistent with what she just told Wagner and Cornell, with very few exceptions. As she was reviewing the details out loud, she remembered a few new things that just came to mind. Later she continued saying, "They think I'm covering for the guy? Fuck that. Somebody accosted my son. I'm not covering for him. I'll take a lie detector if they want me to. I have to calm down because I know my heart is racing fast, and it will make me guilty no matter what. I know how that works. Take a lie detector, so they know that I don't – I don't know what happened. I wasn't aware of it, totally innocent of this."

Once again, she repeatedly professed her love for Lyric and then started going back over the same details again, desperately trying to remember what she saw and what happened – often kicking herself for not being able to remember everything. Later still, she added, "Man, how can I fuck up and say that about last night? They really must think I would know something because I get my nights mixed up because I'm so confused the nights I'm working. I can't remember what the hell

I worked the night before, let alone what I did before I went to work."

In one of her final solo dissertations, shortly before the investigators returned to the room, she was heard saying, "I'm sorry, Lyric. I'm sorry. I'm sorry something happened to you, and I wasn't there to protect you. My poor son. It's cold in here. Lyric. I'm so sorry. I'm sorry, honey. I'm sorry you get – you were killed, or you got hurt and passed away. I'm so sorry. Dammit, dammit, dammit." In her final words just before they entered, she added, "Cover for him. Cover for somebody that killed my kid? Are you fucking crazy? I don't know if he did it. It seems like he did just because that's what you're telling me. That's what they're saying. That he was put to death, basically. But I need to know. I need them to tell me. I wouldn't want to cover for somebody that hurt my baby. This is bullshit."

Sergeant Eggleston and Investigator Wagner entered the room. The time now was about 3:00 p.m. Eggleston had just completed his interview with Chucky and sent him home. He introduced himself to Veronica and took the lead with a new set of questions. He was already convinced that Lyric's injuries resulted from a vicious assault and not from some type of accident. However, his questioning was designed to try and eliminate any accidental theory. He started by asking if Lyric was accident prone or had a history of falling a lot. Later, he asked a series of specific questions about the children's bedroom, focusing on the upper and lower bunk bed, including height, width, and spacing. At times, Veronica used the table and chairs in the room as props to help explain her answers.

Eggleston wasn't entirely done questioning her when she interrupted and asked, "Did he (Chucky) say anything?" Eggleston replied, "Well, I'll get into that in a minute," and then resumed his questioning. More questions about the kids, the bed, sleeping habits, and sleeping arrangements. Finally, Eggleston shifted gears and started asking many of the same questions already asked and answered earlier. It wasn't as if he didn't trust that Cornell and Wagner hadn't asked all the right questions. But from a supervisory perspective, he was likely on alert for any discrepancies in her answers.

Eggleston's line of questioning shifted to her experiences with CPS. She'd had several. She explained how she'd lost her children for a short period of time due to an abusive relationship she had with their father. Later, she had a relationship with another man who became the father of her two youngest children, explaining further that he kept getting in trouble and going to jail. Fearing that CPS might retake her children, she and the children moved to the state of Maine, where they lived with a friend and had just recently moved back to the Binghamton area. She further explained some of her other experiences with CPS, including several malicious complaints by different individuals with which she'd had a falling out. Some of the complaints she said included "everything under the sun." Everything from taking drugs, selling drugs, prostitution, and beating or molesting her children. CPS investigated every time someone called. One of the CPS caseworkers had told her on more than one occasion, "I could tell these are malicious things because it was everything under the sun."

Eggleston then questioned her as to whether or not she knew if Charles was dealing drugs. She knew he had dealt drugs in the past but didn't think he was currently doing so. At least not of which she was aware. But she did add, "My thing is with him, though, I told him if he deals drugs or – that's – that's his thing. I don't want to know about it. I don't want it at my house. I don't want to see it."

Eggleston then took her back to the time shortly after she left for work and asked, "And Charles had said that you mentioned that the kids had to eat? Is that correct?" "Yes," she said. Then explained that if the kids were still up and Charles was going to eat, "You've got to feed the kids too." Eggleston asks, "Now, Charles was up all night, I take it?" She says, "I have no clue. I didn't talk to him." Eggleston again said, "The neighbor says that there was music going on all night long." She said, "Okay. Then yeah." Eggleston continued, "Because he's telling us he went to sleep. I mean, is that like him, you know?" There was no answer before he continued with, "Now, his initial words to the officer that responded there was that he locked the four kids in their bedroom." She replied, "It doesn't lock." Eggleston, "I know the door is off the hinges. And he also said that he got them all to bed after he fed them. Initially, that he fed them all after you left for work." She nodded in agreement.

Later, Eggleston asked, "Let me ask you this. What would be a reason for somebody to hurt your son?" Sobbing softly, she said, "I don't know. That's what's bothering me. That's why I don't get like – I'm going back and forth in my head like, man, if he did that, what could have drove him to do it?"

Continuing, Eggleston asked, "Haveen, has she ever told you – has she ever told you about Charles spanking her with a spoon?" "No," she said. The next question was, "Have you ever seen Charles spank her with – spank any of your children with a spoon?" She answered no but then told him that the girl she told him about earlier, who had called CPS on her, had spanked the children with a spoon.

Moving on, Eggleston said, "We don't have enough information right now to know the extent of your son's injuries. What we're being told is that he has some internal injuries, as well as a possible fractured skull, okay?" Veronica started crying again and said, "Right," and continued whimpering. Eggleston continued with, "It's our experience that those types of injuries don't occur from a fall." More visibly shaking and still crying, she said, "Then he's going to pay for what he did then." Eggleston then hit her with two key questions starting with, "And I'm going to ask you right now, did you hurt your son?" Responding immediately, she said, "Absolutely not. Absolutely not." He followed up with, "Do you know who hurt your son?" She replied, "Well, Chucky was the only one there. It had to be him." He asked again, "Do you know who hurt your son?" Crying even harder now, she said, "No. It has to be him. If he didn't – my son didn't get hurt himself. He had to have done it."

Eggleston once again went back over the events that occurred after she got home from work up until the time Lyric was found unresponsive and 9-1-1 was called. During this review of questioning, he asked, "Did he (Charles) have any injuries to his hands?" She said, "I didn't look. I didn't look." Eggleston asked, "But he was punching the walls?" She answered, "He punched the wall when I was trying CPR…when he wasn't responding, and he punched the wall – a few times."

Previously, Veronica had told him that she had attempted to wake him by slapping him on the back before doing CPR. She'd said, "Like pat him like, you know, like when someone chokes, and you pat them." Inquiring further about this, Eggleston asked, "Did you, besides the CPR, did you like slap his cheeks at all like to get a response, anything like that? Anything around his face? Do you recall that at all?" She replied, "No. I don't think I hit him in his face."

Later, Eggleston asked once again, "Do you know what happened to your son?" "No. I wish I did." Eggleston said, "You know, we're not saying anybody did anything wrong, but what we're saying is that if those injuries are, in fact, if those are accurate, we're not going to know that until the doctor gets done. And just so you know, at least for right now, we let Charles go home." Replying, with a look of disbelief on her face, she said, "Are you serious?" Eggleston replied, "Yeah. We had to. Okay? It doesn't mean anything." She said, "Okay. I'll make sure I keep tabs on where he's at, though." Eggleston said, "He wants us to tell you to get ahold of him. However, here's what I'm going to suggest to you. I'd listen to what he has – hear what he's telling you, and then you can let us know, too." Veronica said she was going to bring a recorder and talk to him. Eggleston said, "You can do whatever you want. I can't tell you what to do." "Fuck that," she said, "If he did something to my son, he needs to pay for it."

Eggleston explained a few more things as to what was going to happen as their investigation moved forward. But the interview was over. Veronica walked out of the room with her interviewers, who had called a friend to come to pick her up. But while she was waiting, she was placed back in the interview room and left alone again while waiting for her ride. As soon as the door closed, her head dropped into her lap. She started crying again and was heard saying, "My baby died. I don't want to go through this. My baby is gone. For what reason would he have to put him to bed like hurt him? The doctors are going to figure out what happened to my baby. If Chucky did it, I'm going to get him caught. I'm going to make him confess to what he did, and he's going to be fucking locked up for life for that shit, killing my baby if he did it. He's going to be locked up for life if he did that to my baby. My baby. My baby boy. My head hurts. How did this happen?" She continued talking out loud for a few more minutes, blaming herself for not being there, and then talking about the clothing needs for her children. Then, she started to repeat many of the same things she'd said before. Finally, the door opened, and Cornell stepped in and said, "Your friend is here." Veronica made her exit, but her experience in the interrogation room was far from over.

CRIME SCENE

If you recall, before Charles Pratt's interview was over, Investigator Anthony Diles left the room, and Sergeant Eggleston continued. Diles had been reassigned to start drafting a search warrant application for Taft's apartment. At the time, Diles had over sixteen years of experience, ten years with other agencies, and the last six with the BPD. That said, his application was very thorough, generously broad, and all-encompassing. To justify his search request, he provided a case summary of what was known at the time, then started describing and listing the various types of evidence that he believed may be present based on his experience. In other words, he asked for the court's authority to search just about anything and everything that might aid their investigation in trying to determine not only what happened but who may be responsible for the death of Lyric Taft. Once completed, a Binghamton City Court Judge was contacted and was available to review the application.

Knowing that his fellow officers were still waiting at the scene for the warrant, Diles ran the application up to the judge's chambers and met with the judge who reviewed his application.

Shortly after that, the application was approved, and the search warrant was granted. Supervisors and other team members were notified.

With the search warrant in hand, investigators made additional preparations. Once that was done, at about 5:53 p.m., they made entry into Taft's apartment to execute the warrant and process the scene. A uniformed patrol officer had been posted at the scene to maintain its integrity. Arriving with the warrant, Investigator Matt Zandy of the forensic ID Unit took the lead, along with his assistant, Patrol Officer Jessica Griffin. Investigators Joe Cornell and Jeff Wager were also present.

Earlier, when Zandy first went to the scene that morning, he described the exterior of Taft's apartment building and its orientation on Fayette Street. He'd also done an early walk-through of the interior where he described the various rooms and their orientation within the apartment.

Now, with the search warrant, Zandy reported first making entry into the living room area. He noticed a large hole on the west wall of the living room, adjacent to the south side of a bedroom door. He noted pieces of drywall and plaster on the floor underneath and took photographs and measurements. The hole measured $8\frac{1}{4}$ inches wide, $16\frac{1}{2}$ inches in height, and was centered $55\frac{1}{2}$ inches off the floor. Strangely, however, none of the broken wallboard or plaster pieces were ever examined or collected as evidence.

| Hole in Living Room Wall

Zandy noted reddish-brown colored staining on the front of a gas-fired space heater in the southeast corner of the living room. Sterile swabs of the stains were taken and collected by Griffin. Later, under closer examination, it was determined that the staining was not blood. As previously noted, Zandy was already aware that Lyric's injuries were all internal with no indication of external bleeding.

Having learned that Lyric had been found unresponsive in the children's bedroom, Zandy turned his attention there. He photographed and described the room, its contents, and their orientation within the room. Having also learned that Lyric was found on the bottom bunk, he focused further attention there. He described the bottom bunk as having a futon-type mattress with a black cover, which appeared dirty, with various stains and food particles. He also noticed and described what appeared to be a brown, possibly dried vomit stain on the front edge of the mattress. After taking additional photographs, he took measurements of the bedroom and bunk bed. He documented these on a small hand-drawn diagram. Later, the mattress cover was removed and collected as evidence.

| Kid's Bedroom

Surprisingly, other than some additional photographs and what was just described, nothing further was done. There were no narrative descriptions, measurements, or diagrams of the living room, kitchen, bathroom, game room, or even Veronica's bedroom. It was now only 6:57 p.m. So, they had just completed their entire examination, assessment, and processing of a suspected homicide crime scene in one hour and four minutes. The whole official report filed by the BPD ID Unit consisted of just one short, half-page narrative and less than a half-page of notes.

I would consider Matt Zandy one of the nicest guys you'd ever want to meet. However, professionally, I was concerned. I found it rather remarkable how everything that needed to be done could have been done so quickly. In my experience as a crime scene investigator with the New York state police, I'd processed numerous crime scenes, including several homicides. The process is slow and methodical, like using a fine-tooth comb, thus very lengthy and time-consuming. Even more so in a suspected homicide, with little or no physical evidence.

After reviewing the ID Unit report, it was apparent that the crime scene processing had been abbreviated. Other than photographs, several things were either left undone or incomplete. As mentioned, other than the children's bedroom, there were no descriptions or measurements taken of any other rooms in the apartment or their contents. Other than the space heater in the living room, they didn't even mention the family Christmas tree standing in the corner near the hole in the wall.

There were garbage cans, large unopened plastic bags, baskets of dirty laundry, and miscellaneous articles of clothing scattered about the apartment. All of which were photographed but never examined. For a suspected homicide, this crime scene was given up much too soon. And while working under the authority of a search warrant, there's only one opportunity to do what needs to be done. By giving up the crime scene prematurely, the probative value of any evidence found after that would be compromised. And any future return to the crime scene because you *forgot* to do something could have negative consequences down the road. As we'll learn shortly, that's precisely what happened as the investigation unfolded.

7

AUTOPSY

At about 9:30 a.m. on December 31, 2010, Dr. James Terzian commenced the autopsy examination of Lyric Taft's body. Present during the autopsy, in addition to his morgue assistant, were two members of the BPD forensic ID Unit identified as Investigator Matt Zandy and Patrol Officer Jessica Griffin. Also present were Broome County District Attorney Gerald Mollen and his Chief Investigator, Tom Tynan, and briefly, BPD Investigator Anthony Diles.

Throughout the entire examination, Investigator Zandy took photographs as other witnessing members engaged in informal discussions with Dr. Terzian about his findings. Dr. Terzian began with an external examination by describing Lyric's body as a mixed-race male toddler who appeared well-developed and well-nourished, measuring 35.5 inches in length and weighing 32 pounds, 10 ounces. Further, there were no signs of *livor mortis*[1], which was consistent with exsanguination. From there, he went on to describe his external injuries. The following, although not all-inclusive, is a summary of his findings:

- Contusions of the forehead
- Irregular & linear contusions to occipital region
- Abrasion above the left eye
- Patterned contusion with various abrasions on the chest
- Abdomen – protuberant, tense & darkened
- Angular abrasions on both sides of the upper back
- Other contusions and irregular abrasions elsewhere on the back
- Abrasion on the outer edge of left ear
- Series of irregular & rounded abrasions below the left ear
- Three curved abrasions, anterior & inferior to right ear – resembling fingernail marks

From there, he continued with his internal exam. Again, while not all-inclusive, this is a summary of his findings:

"Found within the abdominal cavity was at least 700 cc's (2 pints) of dark, unclotted, red blood. (Approximately 50% of his entire blood volume), with a lacerated liver identified as the main source of hemorrhage. Furthermore, the liver had become detached from the spine."

Author's note: Later, Dr. Terzian offered a comparative description of the lacerated liver to the likeness of "splitting open of a ripe tomato."

Digestive system:

"*Regurgitated food matter in the esophagus. Stomach contents containing approximately 50 grams of dark, mucoid, unidentifiable food matter. (collected & frozen for further study)."*

Central nervous system:
"Under the reflected scalp revealed at least one-half dozen areas of dark red-purple flat hemorrhage distributed over both sides of the frontal & parietal areas. The brain appeared somewhat swollen symmetrically."

Respiratory system:
"Lungs – areas of alveolar edema – fresh intra-alveolar hemorrhage – aspirated vegetable matter."

In his clinical summary, Dr. Terzian noted that he had been in dialogue with Investigator Matt Zandy from the BPD, investigating the death that involved suspected child abuse. He further noted that he had reviewed the emergency room record, which included Lyric's rectal temperature as 86.0 degrees Fahrenheit. He also identified the report of Dr. James Stoughton as the ER physician who had noticed bruising on the head, arms, and legs of Lyric and filled out a "Report of Suspected Child Abuse or Maltreatment" form.

Author's note: The narrative graphic descriptions of Lyric's injuries revealed the vicious nature of his brutal assault but paled by comparison to the visual images depicted in the photographs.

. . .

In Dr. Terzian's final summary, he wrote, *"This 2½-year-old male toddler died of exsanguination, secondary to multiple blunt force injuries to the abdomen and head. The findings are consistent with death within less than one hour of sustaining the abdominal injuries. The manner of death was homicide."*

---

1. *Livor mortis:* A pooling of the blood in the body due to gravity and the lack of blood circulation as a result of the cessation of cardiac activity.

8

CONTINUED INVESTIGATION

Both Veronica and Chucky had told investigators about Jemel "Melo" Fields having been at the apartment before Veronica left for work. BPD had also learned that Chucky had called Jemel while he was waiting in the interview room. As the only other adult present that night, they needed to speak with him. Investigator Anthony Diles was assigned to and interviewed Fields by telephone. It was still December 30, 2010.

Fields said that he had met up with Chucky around 10:00 a.m. that morning at Veronica's apartment. He recalled seeing Veronica and all of her children, including Lyric. They all appeared fine. After breakfast, they went over to his friend Max's apartment, where they played video games all day until returning to Veronica's apartment later that night between 10:00 and 10:30 p.m. Fields said that when he arrived with Chucky, Taft and her children were the only ones there. Taft was either in her bedroom or in the kid's bedroom with her youngest daughter. He recalled seeing the two oldest girls in the game room in the back of the apartment. All three girls appeared to be fine. He had not seen Lyric but believed he was in his bedroom. Later, he said a skinny

Hispanic female from the 1st floor knocked on the door, came inside, and talked to Taft in her bedroom for a few minutes. Taft then left for work around 10:45 p.m., and the skinny girl went with her.

After she left, Chucky made dinner consisting of Mac & Cheese, French fries, and Tater-tots, and all four kids had eaten. He thought he'd seen Lyric come out of the bedroom to eat but wasn't sure. He fixed a plate for himself but ate in the game room in the back. He thought the kids were eating at their table in the kitchen. He remembered that Chucky had fixed four plates for the kids but had not seen if they had all eaten because Chucky had cleared the plates before he came out of the game room. Later, he said Chucky put the kids to bed after eating and wedged their bedroom door into place.

Fields had limited contact with Taft and her children but had never seen her or Chucky strike the kids or use any physical punishment. He added that they were usually well-behaved. That night, the kids were not acting up or causing any trouble before he left. He knew that Chucky spent a lot of time at Taft's apartment and babysat her children during the night when she worked.

Fields remembered calling Chucky's cell phone twice this morning and left a voicemail when he didn't answer. A short time later, around 10:30 or so, he saw that Chucky had called him twice. But he missed his calls, so he called him back again. This time he answered his call and said that Taft's son had died, he was not breathing, and his face was blue. Fields believed he had this conversation with Chucky while still at Taft's apartment before the EMTs arrived.

Four days later, on January 3, 2011, Investigator Diles and the Assistant District Attorney (ADA) from the Broome County DA's office traveled to Norwich, NY, for a more detailed interview of Jemel Fields, who was currently living there with his girlfriend.

Fields explained that he and Chucky were half-brothers, having the same mother. His permanent residence was in Ohio, but he'd been staying in upstate NY since mid-December. He'd been to Taft's apartment on five or six occasions, adding that the Taft children appeared to behave normally for their age. Moreover, that Lyric appeared to be relatively quiet and well-behaved. The only disciplining he'd observed was when Veronica would yell at the kids but then added that they responded to that and did as they were told.

Diles and the ADA then revisited what he'd told Diles earlier, reiterating the same story. This time, with a few additions. Taking him back to the morning of December 29th, Fields had met up with Chucky at Taft's apartment that morning and had breakfast. He recalled seeing all of the children that morning, including Lyric, wearing a SpongeBob outfit and appearing fine. Later, they showed him a series of photographs depicting the bruises and abrasions on Lyric's head. He didn't recall seeing any marks on him that morning. Like he'd told Diles earlier, after breakfast, they went back over to Max's house and played video games the rest of the day. Then, about 10:00 p.m., they left Max's house and headed to Taft's apartment. He explained further that he had to stop at Chucky's apartment to pick up a cell phone charger, so he was a few minutes behind him arriving at Taft's place. When he arrived, he recalled a Spanish woman from downstairs walking up the stairs with him. She'd asked him to tell Veronica she wanted to talk to her. When he entered Taft's apartment, he relayed the message to Veronica, who was lying down in bed. The Spanish woman came in behind him and stayed with Veronica until she left for work. He recalled seeing the two oldest girls watching a movie, and the one-year-old was in and out of the room. But did not recall seeing Lyric.

Like before, he said Chucky made dinner of Mac & Cheese, fries, and Tater-tots and fixed four plates for the children. He'd also fixed one for himself and went into the game room to eat while the kids ate at a small table in the living room. Later, when he came out with his empty plate, he noticed the kids had finished eating and saw their empty dishes. He assumed they had all eaten. Then sometime around 12:20 or 12:30 a.m., he went back to Chucky's place to sleep. By that time, the children were all in their room and may have been sleeping. Before leaving, he noticed that Chucky was in his sleep clothes, cleaning up the house and taking care of the dog.

Fields also remembered calling Chucky around 10:00 a.m. the following day and leaving a voicemail message. Then, around 11:00 a.m., he noticed two missed calls from Chucky and called him back. That's when Chucky told him that "her son died." Chucky sounded upset, and he could hear Veronica screaming in the background. Chucky said to him that he didn't know how he died. He hung up from talking with Chucky but called him back a few minutes later and learned he was being taken to the police station for questioning. Several minutes later, Chucky called him back from the police station and told him he was in a room, and no one was talking to him.

Near the end of his interview, Diles informed Fields and later wrote in his report that, "*The results of the investigation and the autopsy clearly put the time of death in the early morning hours of December 30, 2010.*" Adding also that an adult definitely caused the injuries. Then he pointed out that there were only three possibilities: Taft, Pratt, or Fields. When Fields was asked directly whether he had done it, he answered, "No. I did not." Then agreed that Taft and Pratt were the only other possibilities.

Author's note: Later, the information Diles just shared with Fields regarding the time of death becomes more significant.

As mentioned, Veronica had reportedly left for work at Binghamton High School on December 29th at about 10:45 p.m. Also reported was that she had worked there with two coworkers from 11:00 p.m. until 7:00 a.m. the following morning. In as much, right after the autopsy on December 31st, Investigators Wagner and Cornell were assigned to try and verify that she did, in fact, work as reported.

The on-duty custodian, identified as Michael Thorne, verified the employment of Veronica by showing, then provided them with a copy of her timesheet, which indicated that she had worked all night. Later, they were able to locate and interview Michael Decker, Jr., and learned that he was the one who picked up and drove Veronica to work that night. He also assured investigators that she had worked with him all night and never left. And it was his signature on her timesheet. Later, Decker read and signed a supporting deposition prepared by Cornell, with the information he provided.

In addition to interviewing Veronica's coworkers and verifying her timesheet, the Investigators also obtained and reviewed video footage from some of the city's street cams. Through these, Veronica was seen leaving her apartment with Decker at about 10:56 p.m. and later seen leaving work and walking home just after 7:00 a.m.

Later still, a review of the phone records confirmed Veronica's calls from work to Chucky's cell phone, just like she said. In addition, phone records revealed that she'd also made two other calls – one to her mother and another to her friend Chelsie.

Chucky's friend, Martin "Max" Rodriguez, is another name we've already heard. The two spent a great deal of time together, smoking weed and playing video games for hours on end. Chucky had also called him from the interrogation room on the morning of December 30th. Max was located and interviewed in his small basement apartment on Henry Street.

During the interview, he acknowledged being friends with Chucky and knowing his brother, Melo, or Jemel Fields. The two of them would often come over to his apartment, where they would play the video game, *Call of Duty*. On the night in question, it was no different. As usual, the three of them were there, playing video games before Chucky had to babysit. He wasn't positive but believed he had left his apartment by 9:45 p.m. He knew Chucky would babysit overnight for his girlfriend. He'd seen him with the kids before and seemed very responsible. Since the incident, he had only seen him two or three times. On one of those occasions, he was with Veronica. He described Chucky as acting very distant since the death and thought he was quite concerned and upset over what happened to the baby.

While canvassing the neighborhood, investigators located and interviewed Wanda Torres. She lived on the bottom floor at 4½ Fayette Street. She had just moved in about a month earlier. She was home on the night of December 29th into the 30th. She recalled hearing loud music playing from upstairs for most of the night. She knew who Veronica and her boyfriend were, but she didn't speak to them very often. She claimed there were times when she could hear Veronica upstairs yelling at her kids. She had also heard from a neighbor that she was a prostitute.

During the interview with Wanda Torres, another woman identified as Lynette Pica was also present and interviewed. She had been visiting Wanda on the night in question and so was also there. She recalled when she arrived that day. She wandered upstairs to ask for a cigarette. She thought it was about 8:00 p.m., and when she got up there, she saw about four black males smoking marijuana. She knew one of them was Veronica's boyfriend, who would spend the night watching the kids. She was only up there for a few minutes and didn't notice the kids. Before leaving, she added, Veronica often appeared to be "fucked up" or high and was heard yelling at her kids.

Three days later, Lynette Pica was reinterviewed. When asked, she admitted that it could have been later than 8:00 p.m. when she went upstairs that night. She hadn't paid much attention to the time. She was then asked if she could remember seeing anyone else going up the stairs at the same time as her? She recalled Jemel was also going up the stairs. Even though three days earlier, she'd only mentioned recognizing Veronica's boyfriend. This time she said she went into the apartment, talked to Veronica, and saw all the kids who appeared to be fine. She advised further that she had somehow scared the baby, Zoey, then recalled Lyric telling her to leave her alone. She hadn't noticed any problems with Lyric, such as bumps or bruises.

Pica opened up more, mentioning further that Veronica put the kids to bed while she was up there. Then they sat on the bed and talked about possibly getting together on New Year's Day. When Veronica left for work, she went downstairs with her. Chucky and Jemel were still upstairs with the kids. Shortly after going downstairs, the music upstairs was turned up.

Another neighbor at 4 Fayette Street was also interviewed. Contrary to what Wanda Torres claimed regarding loud music, this neighbor had been up all night, playing video games, hearing no loud music or unusual noise.

Earlier, Veronica identified her daytime babysitter as Raymond Ramos, who she claimed was babysitting her kids and fed them earlier on December 29th. Ramos was located and interviewed by BPD at his Liberty Street apartment on January 4th. Ramos acknowledged babysitting for Veronica as recently as

December 29th. He'd been watching the kids over the past few months on about fifteen different occasions and believed they were all well cared for. On the day in question, Ramos was at Veronica's apartment between 1:00 and 5:00 p.m. watching the kids that day. While he was there, the kids were playing and acting fine. He recalled feeding them twice: once around 1:00 p.m. and then again around 5:00 p.m. with peanut butter & jelly sandwiches.

Also, while there, he played a video game on the TV in the back room. Lyric, he said, was in and out of the room often. He didn't notice any bruises or scratches on him while he was there. Later, he added that the oldest daughter, Haveen, changed the other kid's diapers while he was there. He knew that Chucky would often be there and knew him to watch the kids overnight. He didn't see Veronica with the kids very often because when he came over, she would leave. She did pay him a few dollars to watch the kids. It was his opinion that Chucky only appeared interested in Veronica's youngest child, Zoey, when he was around.

Previously, we learned about one of Veronica's neighbors, who had come to her aid that morning to help with CPR. He was later identified as Christopher Winans, who lived directly across the street at 3 Fayette Street. On January 6, 2011, upon request, Winans reported to BPD Headquarters for an interview. Winans advised that his wife had yelled to him and asked if he knew CPR on the day in question. His wife told him that the girl across the street was screaming about a problem with her kid. He went outside, and the girl he knew as Veronica was hysterical. She was yelling that her child was not breathing. He then followed her across the street and ran up to her apartment on the 2nd floor. Just outside her apartment, he was stopped by a black male, who asked him who he was. From the doorway, he could see a child on the bed with Veronica. So, he just pushed the black male aside and went in to help the child. As he started CPR, Veronica left the room briefly and, when she returned, told him he had to do CPR on a hard surface. She then put her child on the floor, and he continued doing CPR for a couple more minutes until the medics arrived and took over.

Winans had noticed bruises on the left side of the child's face. Then told investigators that to him, they looked like knuckle marks. He'd also noticed that the black guy showed no emotion, adding that he was just talking on his phone and did not seem concerned about what was going on. He had also heard the guy telling whoever he was talking to that his kid was dead.

As a follow-up to what they had learned from Chris Winans, they interviewed his wife, Linda Winans. According to Linda, she had been sitting on the front porch having a cigarette on the day in question. Suddenly, a white female that lived across the street came outside her apartment yelling, "Call the police." She was on a cell phone and didn't know CPR. Linda knew she had four kids and became concerned. She knew her husband knew CPR and yelled upstairs to tell him the lady needed someone who knew CPR. He came downstairs and went across the street to her apartment.

Linda followed her husband and entered the Taft apartment, where she saw her husband doing CPR on a young child in a bedroom. While she was there, she observed a black male trying to hug the female who lived there. She heard the female tell the black male, "Get away from me," while she talked on the phone. She also recalled hearing her say, "Mom" and later, "Get over here, (Unknown name) is dead." She added that the female was crying the entire time she saw her. The black male, she said, "Appeared to be calm."

9

FUNERAL HOME

Before speaking with Chris Winans, as a result of the autopsy and the photographs taken, the BPD already had a good working knowledge of what Lyric's injuries consisted of and how they looked. For example, they already knew about Lyric's neck injuries that appeared to have been caused by fingernails. However, during their interview with Chris Winans, they learned something new. Winans, who had been up close and personal doing CPR, observed what he thought looked like knuckle marks on the left side of Lyric's face.

With the newest revelation from Winans, the BPD went back to take a closer look at the photos. Under closer review, they agreed with Winans that knuckles from a closed fist punch to the face might have caused the injuries on the left side of Lyric's face. But the only photos they had were not very definitive. At the time, Lyric had already been dead for nine days, and they had already taken his body to a funeral home. When they called the funeral home, they got lucky and learned that his body was still there because funeral arrangements were still pending. Shortly after that, an application was made for another search warrant, seeking to reexamine, rephotograph, and further document Lyric's injuries, including additional measurements.

Investigator Matt Zandy and Sergeant Michelle Stebbins responded to the funeral home when the new search warrant was granted. They were given access to Lyric's body to take additional photos and measurements. Although the more recent photos showed more clarity, they still couldn't confirm whether the marks were or were not, knuckle marks made from a punch. Regardless of the means, some powerful force had been used to cause the numerous severe injuries that were present.

A few days later, a funeral was held for Lyric. Anyone who has ever gone through the emotional and painful experience of attending the funeral of a small child knows how difficult that is. I've had my own experience. It's tough. Imagine how much more painful it is for the child's mother, staring at a tiny little casket or urn, holding the remains of her baby as the reality of his death finally sinks in.

Several of Veronica's friends and family were in attendance for the sad occasion. Included were some of Veronica's so-called friends. However, they were not on the best terms, and their relationships with her had become estranged. More about that shortly. Despite any personal issues with Veronica, they still loved her children. They set aside their differences, albeit temporarily, to pay tribute to Lyric at his funeral. But like I said, it was only temporary. Chucky was a no-show at the funeral.

10

COMPLAINING WITNESSES

Lyric's tragic death occurred during the holiday week between Christmas and New Year. Hence, word of his death spread quickly throughout the regional community with little detail via the local media. Within hours, calls started filtering in from those who knew Veronica Taft. Each was expressing their concerns regarding the circumstances surrounding Lyric's death. Then, they claimed to have information alleging some troubling experiences they had with Veronica.

Interestingly, the CPS caseworkers working closely with the BPD readily recognized the names of those who called, having dealt with them earlier. All involved complaints filed against Veronica that were investigated previously.

Typically, due to the often sensitive nature of their work, including privacy issues, CPS records are confidential. Access to those records would require a court order or judicial subpoena. However, this was a major homicide investigation involving a savage and brutal killing of a defenseless 2½-year-old toddler. Therefore, CPS voluntarily turned over to the BPD any/all records they had on Veronica Taft in a cooperative effort. The majority of which, due to their bizarre, vindictive, and malicious nature, were ruled unfounded.

Moreover, the records revealed some of the long-standing, estranged, and bad-blood relationships. They included a lot of trash talk and back-stabbing. At times, Veronica tried avoiding them to prevent further CPS involvement, but their bizarre allegations of crying wolf continued.

Author's note: During my early assessment of this 'crying wolf' sisterhood of so-called witnesses, I'd been using some rather harsh adjectives to describe them. Here, however, I'll refer to them as a coterie of loathsome "cry-ladies." With one common interest – making Veronica Taft's life miserable.

Far from all-inclusive, but merely to offer a glimpse at some of the allegations made, the following list was extracted directly from CPS, SCR[1], and BPD records:

- Buys, sells, and abuses drugs around her children,
- A host to drug dealers,
- Repeated acts of physical abuse to all of her children – especially Lyric,
- Picks up children by the hair and throws them across the room,
- Lyric was left unattended and drank poison from underneath the sink,
- A street-walker who prostitutes herself and pimps, other young girls,
- Cooks crack in her bathtub,
- Walks around naked in front of the children,
- Lyric's face filled with splinters,

- Kids always had marks and bruising – every time they were there,
- House always a disaster (food on floor, dirty laundry, maggots in the sink),
- Kids & clothing always filthy,
- Water was black after bathing kids,
- Put lotion on Lyric's penis and taught him how to masturbate,
- Lyric had different scratches and/or bruises during every visit,
- Punched her daughter in the crotch and said, "that's how sex feels."

Talk about overkill. And this wasn't even the complete list. Had only a handful been true, Veronica would have been labeled the meanest, nastiest and most, badass mother in town. Admittedly, she may never be featured in *Parent's* magazine or receive any mother of the year award. But she had been doing rather well despite the many parental challenges she faced as a young single mom with four small children on a poverty-level income. Unlike some single parents on public assistance, Veronica supplemented hers by working full-time at minimum wage. Previously, as a cafeteria worker in two Binghamton schools and more recently doing night-shift maintenance work at the high school. As a result, she provided a more suitable and comfortable place to live and raise her children. With four growing children under the age of five, all with hungry mouths to feed, she kept food on the table and clean clothes on their backs. Yet, there were still those, especially the loathsome cry-ladies, who had an ax to grind. They were quick to criticize and condemn her as an abusive and unfit mother with their non-stop, false, and malicious allegations.

Later, after learning what happened to Lyric, these same

yahoos viewed his death as the perfect opportunity to renew, as well as bolster, their egregious allegations. Which, by design, was driven by their vengeful agenda. Or perhaps, a bit of jealousy. After all, they had seen how Veronica was doing well on her own and no longer had any use or need for them. Once, they had been friends. But over the years, their own lives had been shattered by their issues. Regardless of their actual motive, they'd cried wolf so often that by the time Lyric died, they believed their lies to be true. It's been said that "some liars are so expert they deceive themselves." Or that "the most dangerous liars are those who actually believe they are telling the truth." Indeed. So, by the time authorities interviewed them, their fine-tuned lies seemed even more convincing.

As for the BPD, when they were looking to support their case against Veronica further, this was just what they wanted to hear. As for the cry-ladies? They were more than willing to step up their vengeful agenda to try and 'help the cause.' The BPD readily embraced anything and everything they had to say, even after learning of their tainted backgrounds and history. They ignored or showed no interest in their undeniable lack of credibility.

Each of these cry-ladies had major, and I mean significant, credibility issues. Simply put – they had none. They had no positive traits whatsoever. And it wasn't just their fabricated lies against Veronica. Their own lives were shattered, which led to their own set of issues with CPS and law enforcement. Their criminal convictions included, but were not limited to, "obtaining public assistance by fraud, obstructing governmental administration, identity theft, breaking & entering, forgery, larceny," and more. One had lost her children after being taken away by CPS. Still, another had been cited by CPS for lack of supervision after wandering off, leaving Veronica's four children unattended while she was babysitting.

The same credibility issue can be examined further where caseworkers responded and later documented the results of their investigations into the numerous allegations made time after time against Veronica Taft. According to the official CPS records, a few of the more notable examples of the written comments made by the investigating caseworkers regarding their findings include:

- 3/22/07 – SCR report: Unfounded – no credible evidence to substantiate maltreatment of the child. Mother (Veronica) took a drug test at the request of CW – negative results,
- 9/15/07 – DSS report: Unannounced home visit. Everything fine – "appears to be some vindictiveness going on" between mother and teen daughter, towards Veronica,
- 9/26/07 – SCR report: Unfounded – no evidence to indicate maltreatment,
- 9/06/10 – SCR report: Unfounded – no credible evidence to substantiate a failure to provide adequate supervision and provisions for children. Mother went for drug test – was clean. The children have never presented with any marks on multiple home visits by multiple CW's,
- 9/13/10 – SCR report: Unfounded – no credible evidence to substantiate the allegations. The children do not have marks, and the child allegedly sexually abused is too young to articulate having his penis stroked for purposes of sexual gratification. The person reporting this info is not deemed to be credible. Veronica has gone for random drug screen and has never appeared under the influence on any of the multiple unannounced home visits.

So, there you have it. These are all their words, not mine. But interestingly and more importantly, out of all those cry-ladies who'd made prior allegations against Veronica, none of them had any direct knowledge or information about what happened to Lyric on the night he was killed. Yet, they were more than anxious to share all the sordid rumors they'd heard, which had quickly spread amongst themselves. Authorities were all ears.

We've probably not heard the last from the loathsome cry-ladies. Despite their lack of credibility, they were telling authorities precisely what they wanted to hear. All of which was needed if they were to build a case and move forward against Veronica. They could use these lies to establish an alleged pattern or history of abusive behavior. They certainly didn't have any direct evidence. So, the only way forward was to put on their reality blinders, turn a blind eye, and accept these incredulous allegations. Unfortunately, they chose to do so. As for Veronica, she was now clearly in their crosshairs as the number one suspect.

---

1. *SCR*: Statewide Central Register of Child Abuse and Maltreatment – a/k/a, "The Hotline."

11

EARLY THEORY

Initially, all the evidence was lining up against Charles Pratt, and all eyes were on him as the suspected killer. This theory was supported by several things: the time of death, Veronica's alibi, his bizarre behavior, early demands for an attorney, and the comment he made during a phone call to his brother when he said, "This little nigger be running around doing mad shit."

So, what "little nigger" was he referring to? I think we all know the answer to that. Lyric. Additionally, due to Pratt's irrational and uncooperative behavior, including his bad temper, investigators had already been telling Veronica and CPS that it looked as though Chucky had killed Lyric sometime after she went to work. In as much, the case against Pratt was starting to look like a slam dunk. His arrest was appearing imminent.

Shockingly, that early theory was short-lived – very short-lived. Something had prompted a radical change in their thought process. It caused an abrupt shifting of gears, which turned the focus of their investigation on Veronica instead. And the case against Pratt? Not even a blip on the radar. Without any explanation, his suspicion just suddenly disappeared.

Admittedly, I was stunned. I couldn't understand and asked myself, "What prompted this abrupt change in the investigation?" And equally important was the question, "How was Chucky eliminated as a suspect?" Not having the answers to those questions was very troubling. So far, I hadn't seen anything to show how Chucky could possibly have been eliminated. So, I asked myself what was really going on here? Had any tangible evidence been found that either implicated Veronica or cleared Chucky? If so, where was it? Let's see it. Lay it on the table.

From my perspective, other than the loathsome cry-ladies, there was no such evidence. But at the same time, I was thinking to myself, "Oh please! Don't tell me they're seriously considering that coterie as any means of 'proof' against Veronica." That was nuts. Besides, they estimated the time of death between 3:00-4:00 a.m., and Veronica's work alibi was iron-clad, which was verified four ways.

Therefore, to prove Veronica was the killer, they had three options:

1. Prove she was at home about an hour before the estimated time of death,
2. Prove she killed Lyric *after* she arrived home from work at 7:15 a.m. and before making the 9-1-1 call, or
3. Prove she killed Lyric *before* she went to work.

Notably, option one was ruled out rather quickly by Veronica's alibi. Option two had also been ruled out with Dr. Terzian's opinion that Lyric had not been killed after 7:00 a.m. Therefore, option three was all that remained. But there was a significant problem with this option as well. They had to be asking themselves, "How do we get around the time of death?" Good question because the problem was obvious. For Veronica to have done this, they would have to find a way to push back the time of death to a time *before* she went to work, which would mean six hours or more. In other words, in the 9:00 p.m. timeframe. If that's the case, evidence would be needed to explain why Lyric's rectal temperature wouldn't have been much lower. Furthermore, proof would be required to explain why his body wouldn't have been in a more advanced stage of rigor mortis. More on this later.

If you recall, the witness, Lynette Pica, told them about seeing Veronica that night before she went to work. And that she saw all the kids who appeared fine, including Lyric, who had actually spoken to her just before Veronica left for work.

Therefore, option three had already been ruled out as well, with everything still pointing to Chucky. But if they continued to pursue this, and it indeed appeared as though they were, I was anxious to learn how they would do it. In the meantime, I kept asking myself, "Why Veronica Taft and not Charles Pratt?"

For now, I encourage you to be asking yourself that same question because this was far from over. As the story unfolds, what you're about to learn regarding other decisions made and things done or not done, will only raise more questions and cause greater concern. Bear with me as we move forward to discover what was happening and being found during the ongoing investigation.

12

CPS

As mentioned previously, due to the suspicious nature of Lyric's injuries that resulted in his death, the BPD suspected homicide from the get-go. Because Veronica was considered a possible suspect with three surviving children, CPS had been called. After that, both BPD and CPS launched their independent investigations into Lyric's death. While BPD focused on the criminal element, CPS focused more on the welfare of the surviving children. But because their mutual interests in the facts were the same, it only made sense to join forces by working together and sharing information.

Accordingly, CPS quickly set up shop at BPD headquarters, where assigned caseworkers began exchanging information and working together. CPS supervisors quickly pulled all available records on Veronica Taft and held a briefing with their caseworkers.

Records indicated that Veronica's children had been taken away from her before, after she was assaulted by the father of her two youngest children, in their presence. However, she had separated herself from him since that time, and her children were returned to her about a year earlier, in December of 2009. Shortly after, to further distance herself from her abuser, Veronica moved out of NY and took her children to live in Maine. She later returned to NY in August of 2010.

The report further mentioned numerous incidents of severe domestic violence against Veronica at the hands of Izdihar Noori, the father of Haveen and Amira. Additionally, Lonell Barnes, the father of Lyric and Zoey, had also been involved in domestic violence with Veronica. He was currently on probation and being treated for mental health issues and taking medication for schizophrenia. As a result, the family services case involving Veronica had been closed.

Caseworkers then started reaching out to the hospital, EMTs, and the BPD for more information. Besides a few exceptions and some minor discrepancies, most of what we've already learned was noted in their report. Notably, during their interview with the lead EMT, he described Lyric's extremities as, "cool but his core was warm." He'd also noticed that the Taft apartment was "not overly clean but was not overly messy." Later, he also remembered a female on her knees behind him, sobbing hysterically.

The CPS report noted receiving a call from BPD Captain John Shea, who requested they respond to BPD headquarters ASAP. Then added that a two-year-old had been taken to the hospital, and it would likely be a fatality, and at that time, a suspected homicide. Shea further advised some surviving children needed to be interviewed at the CAC. After that, lead caseworker Traci Reynolds responded to the BPD. Meanwhile, Captain Shea called back to report that the child had just been pronounced dead at the hospital and it was a homicide.

Shortly after she arrived at BPD, Reynolds was briefed by Captain Shea with what was known so far, including the names of Veronica Taft and Charles Pratt and a timeline of events.

Shea advised that the ER doctor had backed off on his original homicide assessment and was now saying the injuries could have been from a fall. He had already reported numerous injuries, including a possible fractured skull, lacerated liver, and a stomach full of blood. Reynolds also learned that Veronica was at the hospital with her father and that Hope Taft, the maternal grandmother, was at the BPD to help with the surviving children.

Reynolds further reported that as soon as an investigator was available, they would be taking the two oldest children to the CAC to be interviewed. While she was waiting, Reynolds spoke with Hope Taft and observed the children's interactions with her. She reported that all three children appeared to have good hygiene and were appropriately dressed. All seemed to be free of any suspicious marks and bruises, and none appeared to be in any medical distress. Reynolds's interview with Hope continued.

In summary, Hope said she only knew Pratt a little bit and that his apartment was not far from Veronica's. She also knew he'd been babysitting for Veronica while she worked nights at the school. Hope said she would take the children to her house tonight and agreed to have only supervised contact with her daughter and the children. Continuing, when asked, she said she never had any concerns regarding the children while in Veronica's care. And that she had never observed any unusual marks or bruises on any of the children. When asked, she denied that Veronica used any drugs and stated that she had never been a drug user.

When Reynolds explained the need to interview the two oldest children at the CAC due to their young age, Hope expressed reluctance. But after Reynolds explained the necessity of assessing the safety of the children due to the serious allegations involving the death of a child, Hope agreed. She also agreed not to allow any contact between Charles Pratt and the children.

Shortly after that, Hope accompanied Reynolds and BPD Investigator Corey Minor to the CAC to interview the two oldest children, Haveen and Amira. Despite their tender age, Hope was excluded from the interview.

According to the CPS report, Haveen appeared a little shy but engaged in conversation with Reynolds and Minor. Amira, however, would not speak with them. After that, absent Amira, Haveen was interviewed on this occasion and again later as well. Unfortunately, each time she was interviewed, the story was never the same. At times, she completely contradicted what she said earlier. Other times, she refused to talk at all, which was likely due to any number of things, including her tender young age, fear in her mother's absence, and confusion by the sudden death of her little brother. But most likely, it was her fear of being interviewed by adult authority figures she'd never seen before. Then over time, her confusion was compounded further by various things she'd either heard or was being told by others. That's hard enough for an adult, let alone a tiny five-year-old child.

After the CAC interview, Reynolds continued her interview with Hope. She confirmed that Veronica had lived in Maine for a couple of months with a friend because she was having issues with the children's fathers. Later, the questioning turned to Lyric. According to Hope, Lyric was a very active child who would be "bouncing off the walls" at times. She stated further that she saw a little of his dad in him. Then she explained that his dad was bipolar and schizophrenic. She felt Lyric had similar signs of this.

When asked about what she could remember about this morning, she'd received a call from Veronica around 10:30 stating that Lyric was blue. She knew something was wrong because Veronica usually wouldn't call before noon. She knew Veronica had gotten home from work, was tired and not feeling well, and went straight to bed. Later, when asked, she explained how Veronica would use timeout as a form of discipline.

When they had finished at CAC, they all returned to the BPD. After which, Hope and the children left to go home. Before leaving, Reynolds said she'd be checking in with her at the house later that night.

While still in the squad room, Reynolds noted that Broome County DA Gerald Mollen and BPD Captain John Shea were both there. She heard Shea announce that Charles Pratt was currently being interviewed but was not being very cooperative. Then later, Sergeant Tom Eggleston entered and advised that Pratt had asked for an attorney and was being released.

Reynolds was also anxious to interview Veronica, but she was still in interrogation. So, she decided to wait, knowing that she could conduct her interview once she was done.

After more than four hours of questioning, Veronica had just been told, "Your ride is here," and she was free to leave with her friend who'd just arrived to pick her up. But as soon as she walked out of the interrogation room, Reynolds was right there waiting. Before she could leave, she would have to be interviewed all over again. For a grieving mother who was emotionally traumatized by her baby's sudden death, there was no concern or compassion for her whatsoever. I was amazed she held up as well as she did.

There's no need to explain what we've already learned from Veronica because her interview with Reynolds was consistent with what she'd already told the BPD. However, there were some additional items Reynolds covered that the BPD did not. In as much, I'll summarize.

When questioned about her children, Veronica explained that all of her children were healthy and never had any previous injuries. Stating further, that they all ate well and had good appetites. She said that all of the children were fine when she left for work. When asked, she denied seeing any unusual marks or bruises on the children before going to work that evening and said all the children were acting fine.

When questioned about any drug or alcohol arrests, she adamantly denied any allegations of drug use, claiming that she had only tried pot as a teenager. However, she knew that Pratt had been arrested in the past for dealing crack. She mentioned that she was arrested for assault in the past but was acquitted of all charges, and the arresting officer was fired. When asked, she denied knowing whether Pratt was using drugs and stated that he worked construction and got paid under the table.

When asked about any mental health issues, she advised that she had been diagnosed with ADD/ADHD in the 7th grade but denied ever taking any medication for it. Then she denied having any other mental health issues.

Turning to Charles Pratt, she was asked about their relationship. Shortly after Charles had moved up from the Bronx in April, they'd been together for a few months. She added that they'd met through a friend. She denied that Charles had ever been violent towards her or the children.

Veronica also spoke briefly about her broken and abusive relationships with the fathers of her children, Izdihar Noori, and Lonell Barnes. She advised that she hadn't seen Noori in many months, and Barnes was currently in jail.

Turning to her finances, she claimed she was making under 200 dollars a week and received assistance from DSS to pay her bills. She also received help with food stamps, WIC and had Medicaid for the children.

Reynolds then explained the safety plan that was made due to the allegations. Veronica agreed to have her mother keep the children, where her visitation would be supervised. Later, Reynolds was interrupted when Veronica said, "I want to know the results of the autopsy." Then added, "He wasn't sick. Something happened to him."

As the interview ended, Reynolds explained, and Veronica agreed that the children would not have any contact with Charles Pratt. She then introduced her friend and said she would be spending the night with her. She also included a phone number where she could be reached. Reynolds also reported that before leaving the BPD, she'd been advised that a search warrant was in the works for the Taft apartment.

Then, reporting further that later that night, she and Senior Caseworker Linda Voigt traveled to the Taft residence in Lisle, NY, to meet with Hope and Tom Taft, reexamine the children, and assess the suitability of their home. The Taft residence was found to be above minimal standards, which was nicely decorated and furnished. Also, exceptionally neat, clean, and warm, with adequate sleeping arrangements for the children.

Pictures were taken of each of the children, and they were each examined for any unusual marks of bruises. There were none. Reynolds also noted that while they were there, the children would not speak to caseworkers.

Reynolds's final entry on 12/30/10 read as follows:

"24-hour risk assessment: Lyric was pronounced dead on today's date; his death is suspicious as it appears that Lyric had sustained external and internal injuries. The three surviving children were free of any suspicious marks or bruises, and a safety plan has been made with the maternal grandmother. Investigation is continuing."

On Friday, December 31st, Reynolds checked in with Lourdes Hospital pathology to learn that an autopsy was scheduled to begin at 9:30 a.m. and would likely take a couple of hours. Later, she called Captain Shea and discovered that the autopsy was still ongoing, but they'd learned there was no skull fracture. Later still, she called Dr. Terzian to learn that Lyric's death had been ruled a homicide, and the cause of death was due to blunt force trauma to the head and a ruptured liver.

Reynolds also checked in with Hope Taft to check on the children and remind her of the agreement not to allow Veronica unsupervised visitation. Hope confirmed the agreement and said Veronica had not yet been to the house. She also confirmed that Charles Pratt would not be allowed around the children.

On Saturday, January 1st, Reynolds placed a call to Sergeant Tom Eggleston at the BPD, who reported that the investigation was continuing that day. He added that Lyric had been beaten. He had bruises all over his face, head, and ears, as well as swelling and bleeding of the brain. He also had a lacerated liver. Eggleston reported further that Lyric's body temperature at the time was 86 degrees and that usually, a body loses two degrees per hour after death, but with a child, it could be a little quicker. He further stated that it looked as if Lyric died sometime within the 3:00-4:00 a.m. time frame. He still had food in his stomach at the time of death, and his abdomen was filled with blood. Reynolds was also advised that the mother (Veronica) was verified to be at work at that time. Continuing, he added that Lyric's death could have been quick, and he may not have cried due to the brain injury. Both the head injury and lacerated liver would have been fatal. Furthermore, they were working on a more concrete timeline between injuries and death, although Dr. Terzian felt his death was relatively quick. According to Terzian, Lyric did not have any old injuries.

After speaking with Eggleston on the phone, Reynolds responded to the BPD. Upon arrival, she learned and reported Veronica had just been picked up and brought in for another interview. She also learned that she'd been found in Pratt's apartment when they went to get her. Reynolds was unaware that Veronica had offered to try and learn more from Chucky about what happened during her first interview. In as much, Eggleston encouraged her to report back to him anything she might discover.

Reynolds stuck around as Veronica was being interviewed for her second time. It's unclear whether she observed the interview on the closed-circuit monitor or learned what took place from investigators. Regardless, she reported Veronica gave her statement and, shortly after that, requested an attorney. She also reported that Veronica had been shown pictures of Lyric's injuries but insisted she didn't know what happened to him.

While this was happening, Reynolds placed a call to her supervisor to update her on the case and request that a foster home be located in case a safety plan could not be made. Reynolds then described in her report how Veronica became uncooperative and was yelling and screaming. She continued to do so as she called and talked to her parents, who were coming to get her. Reynolds expressed her concern that Veronica might go to her mom's house and disrupt the safety plan. Her supervisor advised she would start that process.

Before learning what CPS did next, we will pause to review what happened during the second interview with Veronica. But we'll return shortly to reveal what more was happening with CPS.

13

VERONICA TAFT – INTERVIEW #2

Roughly 48-hours after her first interview, investigators decided to bring Veronica back in for a second voluntary interview. In the interim, Veronica stayed with friends and family and had not returned to her apartment. But during her first interview, she'd told Sergeant Eggleston that she was going to try and connect with Charles to see if she could learn anything more and report back. After failing to find Veronica at her apartment, they checked for her at Pratt's place. Sure enough, she was there. When they told her they would like to speak with her further, she agreed. But Chucky, who was right there, was heard whispering in her ear, trying to convince her she didn't have to go. Investigators also asked Chucky for a second interview, but he refused.

Veronica's second interview did not end well. Initially, it was just a repeat of her interview two days earlier where she answered all their questions and retold the same story. Then, during the second phase of her interview, she was asked to provide a written statement. She agreed, but that meant being requestioned and retelling the same story for what was now the third time. Her cooperation continued as they prepared her written statement, which she later read and signed. Ordinarily, the interview would have ended there. With Veronica believing she was done and about to walk out the door. Instead, investigators reentered the room to resume the third phase of questioning. Veronica's interview was far from over.

| Veronica's Second Interview

Author's note: Veronica's second interview was also videotaped. The following summarizes that interview, which again will include some of the exact language and terminology used. Including, once again, some of what was said outside the presence of interviewing officers.

Veronica was led back into the interrogation room around 10:25 a.m., only about 48-hours since her first interview. She was dressed in a heavy winter coat and wearing a knit hat. Although she appeared a bit nervous, she seemed somewhat more relaxed.

During her first interview, she'd been questioned by Investigators Wagner and Cornell. They had since been replaced, and for her second interview, she was about to be reinterviewed by Investigators Corey Minor and Anthony Diles.

For the most part, the first phase of her second interview was a somewhat routine follow-up to her first interview. Even before asking their first question, Veronica said, "I don't want to see any pictures."

Minor started right out, saying, "I'll be honest with you. Somebody killed your son. Let me put it this way, Veronica, whoever did this and I've already got a pretty good idea who did this, and whoever did this was full of hate and rage for what they did to your son." Continuing, he added, "I don't think this would have happened if you were in the house." "Hell no," she said. Minor added, "I think you would have protected him, but unfortunately, you were at work trying to do what was best for your family."

Knowing she was at work when Lyric was killed, Veronica asked, "What was the time of death that the autopsy said?" The autopsy had just been completed the day before, so Minor already knew the answer was between 3:00 and 4:00 a.m. But rather than tell her that, he just said, "That's what we're working on."

From there, Diles started to describe, in graphic detail, the extent and severity of Lyric's injuries. After asking if he suffered, she was told of his head injuries, how his brain had swollen, and how he may have survived about an hour after being injured. Veronica broke down into tears.

Minor continued with, "There are only three people who could have done this: Charles, Jemel, or you before you left for work. Did you have anything to do with this?" "No. No way. No way," she said. Then added, "Once you establish the time of death, you will know that." Minor asked, "What makes you say that?" She said, "Because it had to happen when I was gone. I saw him before I left, and he was fine. Then he ate, and that was after I left."

The interview then shifted to Charles, who they commonly refer to as "Chucky" during the interview. Minor mentioned having found her with Chucky that morning, then reminded her that Chucky was trying to convince her and encouraging her not to go in for another interview. Minor then said, "You were lying next to the person who killed your son." He also reminded her that Chucky had been asked to come in for another interview but refused. She explained how she'd wanted Chucky to come with her, but he wouldn't.

Minor continued with, "Somebody beat your son – beat the shit out of him." Then he went on to describe Lyric's injuries again and asked, "How was Charles acting?" She replied, "He was freaking out. He punched the wall."

Referring to one of Veronica's children who was interviewed, Minor said, "She's heard Charles disciplining them with a spoon." Later, turning back to Veronica, he added, "By your own words, there was only one person in that house – Chucky."

Partway through the interview, both Minor and Diles took a break and left the room. Veronica was left alone with the camera still running. Much like her first interview, she started whimpering, crying out loud, and talking to herself. Quietly, yet unconsciously, rocking back and forth in her chair, she was heard saying, "My poor baby. I hope he didn't suffer." She continued to cry. Later, she was heard repeating many of the same things she said while alone during the first interview.

Several minutes went by before Minor and Diles reentered the room. Even though Veronica had asked not to see any photos, Minor pulled out no less than a half-dozen full-blown color photos of Lyric, graphically depicting his injuries, and spread them out on the table in front of her. She took one look, gasped, and said, "Oh my God. Oh my God," quickly breaking into tears. Diles then pointed to one of the pictures and said, "The whole back of his head was full of blood." Veronica whimpered and cried. She turned nearly hysterical as she cried out, "Why? Why?" Minor jumped in and said, "And the kids are telling us that they've heard him discipline Lyric." Diles kept the ball rolling and said, "His abdomen was full of blood. Fifty percent of his blood was in his belly." After taking a moment to compose herself a little, she said, "What do you want me to do?" Minor again said, "I'll be honest with you. He was dead when you got home from work. The only thing that could have saved him is if you were home."

While pointing to the pictures, Minor asked, "Why did he tell you not to come in today?" Then answered himself, saying, "Because he did this to your son." Diles followed up, saying, "Now we gotta decide which side of the fence you're on." This was followed by Minor asking, "So what do you want to do? Protect your son or protect the guy who did this?" Considering that line of questioning, it was apparent they believed she knew what happened and was covering for Chucky.

Veronica continued crying but, after seeing the pictures, agreed that Lyric's injuries were not from a fall. Minor followed up further, saying, "He was trying to control the situation. He's controlling you because he didn't want you to come down here." Diles added, "He was whispering to you not to come." Veronica explained that she had spoken with her mom, who encouraged her to come in and talk with them.

Still visibly upset, she continued to study the pictures laid out before her as her interviewers pointed out and described Lyric's respective injuries. Continuing, Minor asked, "What's been going on in your life since he came in? Because something tells me, this isn't the first time this kid has taken an ass-kicking." Acting somewhat surprised, Veronica replied, "Really? I've never seen him scared around him." Diles followed up, asking, "Have you ever noticed anything before this?" Veronica replied, "No. That's why I'm so dumbfounded. I'm shocked. Not one of my kids has a single mark on them."

. . .

Author's note: Notably, Minor's comment about Lyric having been beaten before was already disputed during the autopsy the day before, where Dr. Terzian reported finding no evidence of any old injuries.

Previously, both Chucky and Veronica told the BPD about a new puppy they had, that according to Chucky, had peed on the bed that night. Knowing this, Minor said, "I've got a very good idea of what happened. That dog pissed on the bed and set Chucky off, and he took it out on him." Seriously? So, in Minor's opinion, the puppy peeing on the bed was the motive to kill Lyric? That didn't make any sense at all. Veronica just shook her head and said, "No."

Diles changed the subject and asked, "Are you going to go back to him later?" Veronica said, "I need to speak with him because I need to hear it from him."

Diles and Minor left the room for a few minutes, taking the photographs with them. When they returned, Minor asked, "Has Chucky said anything to you about this?" She explained having tried to talk to him, but he wouldn't talk about it. Continuing, Minor said, "You know we have to talk to your girls again. Do you have a problem with that?" She replied, "Yeah. I don't want them going through that shit again."

Shortly, we'll learn that they didn't like that response. But Veronica, knowing her girls had already been interviewed, was simply trying to shield them from any further psychological harm. Besides, Haveen was only five, and Amira, just three-and-a-half.

Following up, Minor asked, "How do you know your girls haven't been beaten too?" She answered, "They don't have a mark on them, and they would tell me, especially my oldest." Minor added, "For some reason, you're torn here." "I'm not torn," she countered. Then she quickly added, "I'm ready to go." Minor replied, "Just sit tight," and then left the room.

About two minutes later, Diles reentered the room with Sergeant Tom Eggleston, who pulled up his chair face to face with Veronica and began speaking firmly. It was apparent he'd been monitoring the interview from the squad room and heard her response to interviewing her children. He started by saying, "We need your cooperation on this. You need to be open for us to do an unobstructed investigation." Raising his voice, he added, "And if that means talking to your kids, that's what we're going to do. The most important thing is to find out what and who killed your son. Killed your son. Do you understand what I'm saying to you?"

Veronica replied, "Yep." He continued with, "You have to convince me that you know nothing about that, okay?" He then followed up with a threat saying, "Where this goes from here depends a lot on you. And whether or not you see your children for a long period of time depends on your cooperation." Veronica said, "Okay. Okay." He then added, "CPS is here now, and they're working with us, and they're going to go with us up to Whitney Point as soon as we're done here." Veronica interrupted, saying, "I'm going up there." Eggleston snapped back, saying, "Only if you're going to cooperate. But if you're going to go up there and not allow us to talk to those kids, you're not gonna go. We're gonna talk to them because they were the only ones that were in the house when this happened. Unless you did this before you went to work." Veronica replied, "No." Eggleston asked, "Do you understand?" Veronica replied, "Yes." Eggleston said, "The only thing on your mind should be justice for your son, not some loyalty to Chucky or anybody else. But for your son who was defenseless and innocent." Eggleston then stood, but before he left the room, she said, "I'm definitely not on Charles' side."

Diles then set up his laptop computer on the table to take her statement.

Over the next hour, Veronica laid out her story once again as Diles typed it into what would soon become her formal written statement. Once completed, Diles left the room to have the statement printed out. Then returned and asked her to read it over. He then left the room again, leaving her alone to read her statement. After reading her statement and while waiting for Diles to return, Veronica once again started talking to herself and was heard saying, "There's no way. I can't believe Charles could have done this." But then she added, "He killed my poor baby. He's going to pay for it. They'll put him away for a long time. Lyric, I'm so sorry. Mommy's so sorry. If he did this, lock him up. What do you need me for?"

Diles reentered the room and had her sign her statement. Then, he left again. Understandably, Veronica assumed she was done and would soon be on her way. Little did she know, her situation was about to become a lot worse.

Shortly after signing her statement, Veronica expected to leave when Diles and Minor returned to the room. From the nature of the questioning that followed and their demeanor, it was apparent their focus had suddenly shifted to Veronica as a suspect. This was later supported by Diles' own words during a court proceeding when he said, "It happened that the tides turned."

Continuing, Minor sat down across from Veronica and took the lead. Surprisingly, before asking his first question, he said, "We're making some headway." Unbeknownst to Veronica, she was about to learn that the tides had turned as Minor began by reading her Miranda rights.

Remember, Veronica had already been interviewed for over two hours, where she voluntarily answered all their questions and repeated the same story – twice, which later included her formal written statement. Why Miranda now? But more importantly, why no Miranda before her two-hour interrogation and written statement? Ordinarily, that's not how it's done. In fairness, however, at least initially, their only viable suspect was Charles Pratt. After all, Veronica was cleared by her iron-clad alibi and the estimated time of death between 3:00 and 4:00 a.m. Therefore, there was no need to Mirandize her because she was only a cooperating witness.

In contrast, however, even before Miranda, whether they would admit it or not, Veronica was still a suspect in the minds of investigators. This fact was supported by the fact that she'd been shown the enlarged graphic photographs of her dead son, even though she'd told them earlier she didn't want to see them. In my view, they were trying to use the photos as a means to trigger an emotional reaction, which they hoped would lead to either her confession or her admitting knowledge of what Chucky had done. Otherwise, had they truly believed she was a surviving victim rather than a suspect, they would have spared her the painful viewing of her son's gruesome photographs. If nothing more than protecting the interview's integrity, Miranda should have been given before it started.

Veronica was surprised by the sudden reading of Miranda and asked, "Should I have my lawyer here?" Minor replied, "You're actually helping us find out what happened to your son." She replied, "It's not helping. I wasn't there. How many times have I said the same thing over and over again? How is that going to help? The only way you guys are going to get him is if I can get him to confess to me." Ignoring just about everything she just said, Minor told her she could have a lawyer, but if she did that, "he would only tell you not to talk with us." As a result, Veronica agreed to continue cooperating by reading and signing the Miranda form and then agreeing to continue speaking with them further.

Minor started the next phase of her interview by saying, "We've been talking to some other people." Then started to lay out the accusations being made by, you guessed it, the loathsome cry-ladies. Veronica said she knew all about the allegations of her being a drug dealer, abusing her kids, and so on. She also explained her dealings with CPS and offered to have her hair tested for drugs. She further explained the ongoing issues she was having with those making the complaints. Minor continued, "They're telling us that you've been yelling, and it gets louder at times." Then he started pressing her on, yelling at or hitting her kids. All the while, zeroing in on the deadly 'black spoon.' Veronica admitted to having and using black spoons in her kitchen but denied ever hitting her kids with one. She did admit to 'popping' the kids on the hand or butt with her hand at times. But again, never with a black spoon. Later, she said she might have struck the black spoon on the edge of a table as a warning. Then emphasized that if she did 'pop' them with her hand, it would never be hard enough to leave a mark.

Diles tried to soften her up by admitting and describing how he was physically disciplined as a child. Veronica wasn't impressed and didn't budge from her denial of using the black spoon.

Minor then addressed the heart of their new theory by saying, "We have some allegations that you smoke crack, and you're a street-walker." With a snarky look on her face, Veronica replied, "That's nothing new – I've heard that before. They told that to CPS." When asked about any drug use, she admitted having tried marijuana a handful of times but other than that, never any hard drugs and very little alcohol.

Diles jumped in again, suggesting, "Temperatures can flare. Patience wears out." Veronica raised her voice and fired right back, saying, "I didn't kill my son." By now, she was fully aware the tides had turned, and they were looking at her as a suspect.

Shifting their questioning back to the last time she saw Lyric, she explained once again that he was in his bedroom watching a movie with his sisters. When asked what movie, she said, "*Mean Girls* or maybe *Mrs. Doubtfire*. They liked watching both of those." She then added, "I thought I heard Lyric say goodbye, mommy, but I can't be sure."

Continuing, Minor said, "He was in that room when you left. We can't account where Lyric was from the time you left for work until it happened. The girls are saying he was in the room the whole time." Veronica replied, "Yes, but that may have been after he ate. He had to have left because he ate." Minor said, "Yes, but that was stuff left from when you fed him." She replied, "No. Cause, you can tell how long it's been there, can't you?" Then, referring to the interview of her girls, she asked, "Did you ever ask them if they ate dinner together? Because I asked her if they ate dinner together, and she said yes." Minor dodged that question saying, "She's not going to talk to people, but I mean she does say some things, but I'm not going to tell you exactly what she said right now." More importantly, he didn't want to admit to some of what Haveen had told them during her interview about the times when Chucky would hit them with a black spoon.

Veronica attempted to defend herself further, saying, "Chucky said he fed them all after I left." Minor asked, "Did he eat then, or was that from before?" She explained how they might have eaten earlier, around 5:00 p.m., but wasn't sure. Then she added, "They ate after I left. But you guys know that." Minor said, "Because Chucky was telling you that?" Remembering what she'd been told earlier, she said, "Yeah, and you guys said you found potatoes in his stomach, so obviously, he did get up and ate." Minor was backed into a corner because he had told her that earlier. In response, however, he back-pedaled away from that, saying, "I said it was consistent with potatoes. That doesn't necessarily mean it was potatoes."

Given my experience, knowing how frequently the words "consistent with" are used to support a criminal theory, I found Minor's explanation somewhat amusing. But more importantly, I was curious to know why he had made his comment in the first place. If you recall, the autopsy report documented that the substance found in Lyric's stomach was an "unidentifiable" food matter. Since the autopsy was just the day before, the obvious question was, how did it suddenly go from "unidentifiable" to "consistent with" potatoes? Had there been a subsequent attempt to identify the food? Or was this simply some of Minor's speculation before Veronica became their new suspect? In other words, back when they were still looking at Chucky. Regardless, other than Minor himself, there was no official report or finding that the substance was consistent with potatoes or anything else. But if it wasn't potatoes, what else could it be? According to Ray Ramos, he'd fed all the kids peanut butter and jelly sandwiches at 5:00 p.m., which, according to the new theory, would have been four to five hours before his mother killed him.

Bottom line: this was not a guessing game. A woman's life was at stake. Trying to identify Lyric's last meal was crucial and should have been a high priority. Unfortunately, the initial visual exam had failed. Therefore, it would logically require advanced testing by a more scientific means, with the technological know-how just a phone call away. And didn't we learn earlier that the stomach contents had been sent out for that purpose? If so, where are the results?

Author's note: Notably, in further regard to the stomach contents, the same medical examiner who performed the autopsy would later punch a huge hole in the new theory. More on this later.

. . .

Having been prompted by the stomach contents issue, Veronica started speaking about her interest in forensic science by reading and watching television shows like *CSI*. Minor asked, "Do you make it a regular habit of reading about what stomach contents are going to be after death?" She answered, "No, but it's awesome." Minor again asked, "Does it interest you to know that people can't get away with things?" Veronica replied, "Yeah, it's awesome. They shouldn't be able to get away with anything."

Diles tried downplaying it further, saying, "Believe me, that CSI-world is 90 percent fiction. That's why it's entertainment cause it's bull shit."

Okay. I'll be the first to agree. Some CSI-related material on television or cinema can be a bit far-fetched or exaggerated at times. All in the interest of entertainment. But 90 percent fiction? Now that's an exaggeration. Besides, if it were 90 percent fiction and all bull shit, no one would be watching. That being said, I questioned why Minor and Diles were so concerned about Veronica's interest and knowledge of forensic science. Especially when she'd been asking them about establishing the time of death and length of time food remains in the stomach. Those were legitimate concerns and important questions that needed to be answered – knowing that one or both could prove her innocence. But more importantly, it could also point to the real killer. In as much, I think they grossly underestimated her level of understanding.

Changing the subject, Minor continued looking at the photographs of Lyric spread out in front of him. Then pointed to her hands and asked, "Do you have long fingernails?" She immediately responded by holding up and showing her hands, saying, "No, I bite them bad."

Hmm! What do you suppose prompted that question? Because they had already learned earlier, from the photographs and autopsy report, that the fingernails of Lyric's killer penetrated and abraded his skin behind both ears. A killer with long fingernails.

Minor continued with, "We've got this narrowed down to three people." Veronica quickly snapped back, saying, "Well, it wasn't me. I was at work. If you guys find out what time he died, you'll see that I wasn't there." She was basically telling them how to do their job by pointing out yet again the need to establish the time of death. But unbeknownst to Veronica, they had already done that. For whatever reason, they weren't sharing that with her.

Continuing, Minor turned up the heat, saying, "What I'm getting at? That kid was dead when you left." Veronica snapped back quickly again, saying, "No way. I put him in his room before I left." She added further that he was awake and watching a movie with his sisters. Minor continued with, "I'm going to be honest with ya. Something in this stinks. Stinks real bad. Stinks real bad." Veronica said, "Obviously, someone killed my son." Minor said, "Yeah, but the question is, who did it, and did you know about it?" Answering firmly once again, she said, "No. No way. I didn't do it, and I don't know about it." Minor again said, "I mean, somebody did this to him." Veronica said, "I wouldn't have done that to my baby – never." Minor said, "Well, something happened." "Obviously," she said. Then added, "You need to get him to confess to it. He needs to be put away."

Things were about to turn ugly when Minor asked, "Why are you so concerned about the time of death?" Whoa! Whoa! Hold on just a minute. Here we go again. Before she answered, let's stop here for a second and ask, why wouldn't she be concerned about the time of death? Of course, she was concerned. Her concern was evident and justified. Knowing that she had a rock-solid alibi, the time of death would help eliminate her as a suspect. She had a right to know and was anxious to find out. She'd already mentioned it several times. And even though they knew the answer, she was never told. On the flip side, had the time of death been established *before* she left for work, they would have been throwing that in her face repeatedly. Either that or she would already have been arrested.

It turned even uglier after Veronica answered by saying, "Because you guys are accusing me now saying I was the last to see him, and that's bull crap." Minor jumped in quickly, saying, "No one's accusing you." Now she's furious. She raised her voice and fired back with both barrels, saying, "Bull crap. Because I'm still the one sittin here, aren't I? Why isn't he in here getting interrogated? Why am I? This is bull shit. I would never do that to my kid." Minor replied, "Is it bull shit because I need to ask you some questions?" Still fired up, she snapped back, saying, "Yeah, it is bull shit that you're asking me when I wasn't there." Whether he realized it or not, Minor had met his match and was about to lose her. But in his effort to keep her talking, he tried imposing a little guilt, saying, "So, you don't want to cooperate so we can find out what happened?" Still fired up, she answered firmly, "No. I want to cooperate and find out. It's just that you guys are not going to sit here and tell me that I'm one of the three people cause that's bull shit." Minor snapped back, saying, "You are one of the three people." Now, in total frustration, with a disgusted look on her face, she suddenly just stood up and said, "I'm leaving," and walked out the door.

Appearing rather surprised, both Diles and Minor quickly followed her into the squad room, trying to coax her back in, saying, politely, "Why don't you come back in so we can talk." She was having no part of it as she started crying and said, "Why? No. No." Her crying turned hysterical as she was heard asking to call her mom. But a moment later, they did walk her back into the interrogation room as Minor said, "We're going to get you a phone call." At which point, she was left alone in the room again, frightened, visibly shaken, and crying hysterically as she paced back and forth in the small room. Then she started banging on the door, yelling and demanding her phone call. She can be heard crying and sobbing, saying repeatedly, "I want my phone call. I want my phone call." At times, some of what she said was muffled out by her hysteria. But one of her final comments was loud and clear when she said, "This is bull shit. I can't believe this shit."

A few minutes went by before Minor finally reentered the room and said, "We're going to get you out of here, but here's the deal." She was still bawling as he followed up with this warning, "You're free to go, but just know this. If we find out you had something to do with this, you're going to have to answer for it." Calming slightly, she replied firmly, "I didn't do this." In his final statement, Minor attempted to infer some guilt saying, "If you can go to bed at night and look yourself in the mirror – knowing what happened...." Interrupting, Veronica jumped in quickly, saying, "I don't know what happened." Then Minor continued, "...and it could have been prevented, you're a better person than I am, and you'll have to answer to that in your own way. So, you're free to leave."

The bizarre irony of what Veronica just went through would present itself just two days later. When, as previously mentioned, Jemel Fields was reinterviewed by Investigator Diles on January 3rd. Remember what Diles told him? Word for word from his report, he wrote, *"the results of the investigation and the autopsy clearly put the time of death in the early morning hours."* Yet, he continued to point out to Jemel that Veronica was still one of the suspects.

Whether he realized it or not, Diles contradicted himself because they'd already confirmed Veronica's alibi of her being at work during those early morning hours. How could she still be a suspect? Furthermore, if you recall, just two days earlier, the BPD had also shared that same time of death estimate with CPS. And as we just learned, they turned around and shared that same information with an interested witness, Jemel Fields. Wasn't he one of the original suspects? Why tell him and not Veronica? Then, another two days went by, where they once again reported the exact time estimate to CPS. Therefore, it seemed apparent that they were already convinced and comfortable with the estimated time of death. Otherwise, they wouldn't be sharing it with anyone.

14

MORE CPS

Lead CPS caseworker Traci Reynolds, who was present during Veronica's second interview, had grown concerned after learning of Veronica's response to re-interviewing her children. Fearing she might do something to disrupt the safety plan, a decision was made to conduct an unannounced home visit at the residence of Hope and Tom Taft in Lisle, NY. Shortly after that, a detail was quickly organized, consisting of Reynolds, three investigators, a BPD patrol officer, and some additional New York state police assistance.

Upon arrival at the Taft residence, they knocked on the door. Hope answered and allowed everyone into her home. At the time, Hope was there alone with the three children. Minor started by informing her that the case was now a homicide. She became quiet and appeared visibly shaken but didn't ask any questions regarding his death. When explicitly asked, she denied having heard anything about his death. When asked about Veronica, she explained that her husband Tom had gone to get her. Reynolds reported how Hope maintained her composure but only gave short yes/no answers to all questions. She answered no when asked whether the girls had ever mentioned Lyric or anything about what happened? But she did say that Haveen was having a hard time being away from her mother.

Reynolds and Minor attempted to interview Haveen and Amira, but neither would speak to them. Not even while sitting on Hope's lap with her trying to get them to talk about non-threatening topics.

Reynolds reported again that the home was above minimal standards, including cleanliness, warmth, adequate food, and proper sleeping arrangements for the children. Furthermore, all three girls appeared clean, shy, and free of any suspicious marks and bruises. At Reynolds' request, Hope agreed to have each of the children seen by a doctor on Monday. She agreed further to appear in family court to seek emergency custody. Before leaving, Reynolds was advised that Veronica was currently staying with her grandmother and provided her contact information.

On Sunday, January 2nd, Reynolds called and spoke to Veronica. They reviewed the safety plan, where she had agreed to no contact with the children. Veronica said that she wanted her children at her mom's house. Reynolds then explained that she would be going to court tomorrow. Veronica asked, "Go to court for fucking what?" Reynolds informed her that she would just have to be available to go to court tomorrow. After explaining further that it was for an Order of Protection, Veronica hung up on her.

Later, Reynolds, her supervisor, and a deputy from the Broome County Sheriff's Department conducted another unannounced home visit at the Taft residence. Her reported findings mirrored those reported previously. But while she was there, Hope was advised that the safety plan could become long-term, and she would need to be prepared for that. She understood and agreed that if needed, she would raise the children. She said that she was willing to go to court tomorrow to seek emergency custody of the children, including an order of protection against Veronica that would prevent her from having anything other than supervised contact with her children.

On Monday, January 3rd, an assigned caseworker responded to the Broome County Correctional Facility and conducted a face-to-face interview with inmate Lonell K. Barnes, the father of Lyric and Zoey Taft, Veronica's two youngest children. His interview was quite lengthy, and for the most part, he had nothing good to say about Veronica. However, shortly into his interview, he stated, "I know for a fact that Veronica's new boyfriend did this." When asked how he knew this, he said he had learned from Veronica about her new job working nights while her boyfriend watched the children. Later, he'd also learned that Lyric had been killed while she was at work.

Barnes then admitted his abusive history with Veronica, which included numerous incidents of domestic violence. He also admitted to being arrested at least seven times for missing court, disturbing the peace, resisting arrest, menacing, assault, and other charges he couldn't remember. But then he admitted that several of the charges were for domestic violence with Veronica. When asked, he denied having any substance abuse or mental health history.

Similarly, another caseworker contacted and interviewed Izdihar Noori, the father of Veronica's two oldest children, Haveen and Amira, in one of the interview rooms at DSS. During his interview, he, too, acknowledged his history of domestic violence with Veronica and claimed to have completed anger management and domestic violence counseling. He hadn't seen Haveen or Amira for about three years. Even though he was allowed supervised visitation, he refused. He added that he didn't know much about what was going on in Veronica's life either. However, he did say that when he was with Veronica, she was a good mom. Before ending the interview, Noori provided a few others who may have more information about Veronica.

Later, Reynolds interviewed Lyric and Zoey's paternal grandmother over the phone. The grandmother had last seen Lyric and Zoey on the Thursday before Christmas and had taken some pictures. She claimed that the children were fine, stating that they were both running around and appeared happy and healthy. She remembered bathing the children and hadn't noticed any unusual marks or bruises on either of them. In addition, she admitted to hearing rumors of drug activity and the children being left home alone. Also, that Veronica would lock the children in their rooms. She admitted having no personal knowledge of any of this but offered to try and get the names of those who may have witnessed it.

On Tuesday, January 4th, after reviewing the case with her supervisors, Reynolds placed a call to Hope Taft. She was making doctor appointments for the girls today and said they were all doing fine. She also added that Veronica was meeting with her attorney now. Reynolds then placed a call to Veronica and left a message asking her to contact her.

After all the parties were notified, arrangements were made, and a court proceeding was held in Broome County Family Court. After that, an Order of Protection was issued against Veronica and Charles, preventing them from contacting the children. Although, Veronica could have supervised visits through the Department. Hope was given supervision over the children at her residence.

Later, Reynolds received a phone call from Sergeant Eggleston. He'd called to fill her in on the results of their interview with Jemel Fields, Chucky's brother. He also confirmed that Veronica was at work the entire evening on December 29th. Furthermore, a witness had just given them a statement that Veronica mistreated Lyric by locking him in his room, and she was mistreating the other children also. The witness further claimed that Veronica was buying drugs outside her apartment while her children were inside alone.

Sometime later, Reynolds met with Eggleston to review the police photographs of Veronica's apartment. After reviewing the photos, she described the home as being *"minimally furnished with minimal clutter, and the home did not appear to be dirty."* She reported further that *"All the children slept in one room. There was a single bed on top, a double on the bottom, and the baby slept in the same room in a pack-n-play."*

On Wednesday, January 5th, Reynolds placed a call and spoke to Sergeant Eggleston again and learned that the BPD would be meeting with Dr. Terzian the next day to discuss the case further as far as a timeline. He advised further that they were still estimating Lyric died sometime around 3:00-4:00 a.m. and would have died within an hour after being injured.

Another four days had passed since Veronica's grueling interrogation, where they had all but accused her of killing her son. Yet, they were still estimating the early morning time of death. And even though she brought it up several times, they never told her.

Surprisingly, even though a whole week had passed, CPS had not reported any interview or contact with Charles Pratt, even though they were present at the BPD on December 30th when he was first interviewed. Finally, on Thursday, January 6th, Reynolds called his cell number to arrange an interview. It went straight to voicemail, and she left a message. Then tried the next day again with the same result.

On Friday, January 7th, after failing to reach Chucky, Reynolds placed a call and spoke to Veronica, asking if she could come and see her. After explaining why Veronica said she wasn't doing anything without her attorney or mother. Reynolds also asked if she could have Chucky call her. When Veronica asked what for, Reynolds explained that she needed to speak with him regarding the reports. Veronica wasn't certain where he was and said he was "floating around."

Later, when discussing visitation, Veronica informed Reynolds that she refused to visit her children at DSS, saying, "It's disgusting." Stating further that she wanted to see the children at her mom's house. In response, Reynolds claimed that the court order indicated visitation must take place at DSS. Veronica repeated her refusal to do that. Then explained how she wanted visitation at her mom's with her daughter because it was her birthday. Reynolds wouldn't budge, insisting that it had to be at DSS. Veronica still said no.

Notably, Reynolds was not truthful about the court order when telling Veronica that her supervised visits must occur at DSS. The court order said, *"Mother may have supervised visits with the children as agreed and arranged by the Department."*

From my perspective, Reynolds was just playing hardball with Veronica. But in doing so, she was shirking her primary responsibility: the best interest and welfare of the children. Reynolds knew that Hope Taft's home provided a safe, warm and comfortable family environment for the children because they'd been going there almost daily to check on them. What better place for Veronica to visit her children? More importantly, a much more comfortable environment for the children to reunite with their mother. Nothing like the "disgusting" visitation rooms at DSS described by Veronica. She knew it to be "disgusting" from having been there before. Veronica's request for visitation at her mom's house was a much better option all-around, even more so when she'd asked to have it there to celebrate Haveen's birthday.

Earlier: Amira, Zoey & Lyric with mom

Reynolds had the authority to allow the visit at Hope's house and could have done so easily. But for her, this wasn't about the children. Instead, she chose to flex her CPS muscles to let Veronica know who was in charge, even if it meant making things awkward, confusing, and uncomfortable for the young children and an inconvenience for Hope. Just to point out, Veronica had not yet been accused of anything. Regardless, Reynolds remained steadfast, never budging from her hardened decision, insisting that visitation must take place at DSS. Even though the court order never said that.

From that point on, permission was never granted for visitation at Hope's residence. Having been misled under Reynolds' control, if Veronica desired contact with her children, she was forced to comply with Reynolds' decision and go to DSS. Afterward, when faced with no other alternative, she reluctantly did so.

Later, when speaking with Veronica, she explained what visitation was like with her children at DSS. She hated going there, but it was the only way to see her kids, which was limited to one hour. She'd driven down from Syracuse for a scheduled visit on one occasion, arriving five minutes late. Even though her kids were right there waiting, they canceled visitation, and she never got to see them.

On another occasion, she was rushed out early because they had "somewhere else" to be. "Those things were bad enough," Veronica said, but even worse was, "sitting there trying to visit with my kids, surrounded by two or more caseworkers watching over me like a hawk. Staring at me with their beady evil eyes, watching my every move and listening to everything I was saying to my kids. It was awful."

I asked, "So, that's what you meant earlier when you said, 'It's disgusting?'"

"Ain't that the truth. For sure," Veronica replied. Later she added, "Oh, and another thing. Every time I tried talking to my kids, they'd get right in my face and interrupt, telling me I shouldn't be saying this or that, or I was saying something inappropriate." As a final comment, she added, "You know, I understood why they were trying to make things difficult for me, and that was bad enough, but what really pissed me off was how they were treating me in front of my kids and what impact it was having on them. It was all about me. They didn't give a damn about my kids."

Reynolds held another meeting with Sergeant Eggleston to review the case. She learned that they had talked with Dr. Terzian, who felt certain Lyric's death was before 7:00 a.m. He also said that the liver injury was fatal as it had become detached from his spine. Furthermore, Lyric had a head injury which caused swelling of the brain. Either injury would have been fatal, but he died before the brain injury killed him. Eggleston further advised that Lyric had contents in his stomach that were recovered, and those contents had been sent away to try and determine what he had last eaten. Dr. Stopiker, [sic] Chief

Medical Examiner from the Onondaga County Medical Examiner's Office, consulted in the matter.

Author's note: Strangely, other than what was reported by Reynolds, there was no reference to the stomach contents being sent away or any consult with another medical examiner in any BPD reports or Dr. Terzian's autopsy report. More about this later.

On Monday, January 10th, two caseworkers made another unannounced home visit at Hope Taft's residence. Their subsequent report was identical to all previous home visits.

On Tuesday, January 11th, Reynolds placed a call to Veronica and asked if she would attempt to locate Charles. She said she would try and have him contact her. Later, Reynolds received and reviewed a copy of the autopsy report and then reviewed the case with two of her supervisors. They all agreed that the case was indicated and open for ongoing services. After that, Reynolds' report read, *"Dated 12/30/10, is indicated against Charles Pratt for Inadequate Guardianship, Excessive Corporal Punishment, Internal Injuries, Lacerations Bruises and Welts, Lack of Medical Care and Fatality regarding Lyric Taft."* She reported further, *"Charles Pratt was the caretaker of Lyric Taft and his siblings on a regular, consistent basis while their mother, Veronica Taft, worked. Charles met the children's minimal needs while the children were in his care. He supervised them, fed them, and disciplined the children. Charles Pratt is Veronica's paramour."*

Reynolds then laid out the scenario of events leading to when Lyric was found unresponsive and later pronounced dead at the hospital. After describing the nature of Lyric's injuries and that his death had been ruled a homicide, she ended her report with, *"Lyric was in the care of Charles Pratt. According to Dr. Terzian, medical examiner, Lyric died between 3:00 and 4:00 a.m."* She then added,

"Charles Pratt is not cooperative with the investigation and requested an attorney."

Continuing, Reynolds had also indicated Veronica Taft for *"Inadequate Guardianship and Fatality,"* citing her history with CPS of having *"poor parenting skills and allowing inappropriate individuals to care for her children."* She also reported that Veronica was not cooperative with the agency and that a Neglect and Abuse Petition was being filed in Family Court. She included that there had already been an Order of Protection issued against Veronica Taft and Charles Pratt, which prevented them from having any contact with the children.

On Wednesday, January 12th, as promised, Hope had each of the other three children examined by a doctor at the DePaul Clinic. No concerns were noted.

After several attempts, on Monday, January 17th, Reynolds finally received a call back from Charles Pratt. He inquired as to what she wanted. She explained that he was the subject of their report. He said, "What are you talking about?" She had to explain again and then asked him to come in to discuss the allegations with him. After agreeing to come in on Thursday at 10:00 a.m., he said, "This is life or death if you know what I mean?" Then added, "I'm not getting the death penalty for no accident. People are talking shit, and my attorney's guns are loaded." As soon as he hung up, Reynolds immediately called to alert the police of what he'd just said.

On Thursday, January 20th, Reynolds received a phone call from Charles Pratt, telling her he could not keep his 10:00 a.m. appointment and instead would come in at 1:00 p.m. Later, however, he called back again and told her he would not speak with her because his attorney advised him not to. But apparently, he changed his mind and showed up at CPS asking to talk to Reynolds' supervisor. CPS supervisor, Brenda Kellerman, was notified that Pratt was in the building. Soon after that, Kellerman teamed up with another supervisor, and together, they met with Pratt.

According to their report, Chucky started by saying he was unhappy with the investigation but then added that he just wanted it to be finished. Adding further, he said, "I don't like to be disrespected." He then explained how he'd been abandoned by his mother and placed into foster care at ten years old. Then he added how he wanted to go back to NYC and that Binghamton had "hurt" him (while holding his hand over his heart). He said further that he wasn't going to move now because it would "look bad." From there, he claimed that he'd always wanted to be a daycare provider, which was why he was taking care of Veronica's children. They explained to him that there was a procedure they must follow in any investigation, and that was what they were doing.

That's it? Strangely, other than what I just described, there was absolutely nothing reported about the subject matter. There was no interview. They didn't question him about anything. Knowing how difficult it had been to get him in for an interview and not knowing if they ever would, they just blew the perfect opportunity to do that. Why did they even bother having him come in?

In comparison, Veronica had been interviewed extensively and repeatedly, asked to tell her story numerous times. And it had already been established that whatever happened to Lyric happened on Pratt's watch while Veronica was at work. Yet, he was asked nothing about what happened. Nor anything about his relationship with Veronica and the children.

Equally important, not a thing about his criminal and personal history, including any relationships with other women and their children, was asked. As a professional investigative agency, they indeed hadn't demonstrated any of that professionalism here. Something wasn't right. Why wouldn't there be equal interest in both their stories?

We'll learn more about this later. In the meantime, we're going to back up a few days to find out what happened after Veronica stormed out of her second interview in tears.

15

SEEKING LEGAL ADVICE

Even though Veronica had been released without being accused of anything, she recognized the insinuated accusations from the nature of their questions. Knowing she was innocent, she was dumbfounded and overwhelmingly confused. But most of all, she was terrified and trying to understand how all this could be happening. Adding to her confusion, as bizarre as it seemed, she couldn't fathom how the initial focus on Chucky had changed so quickly and how the crosshairs were now focused on her. Her thoughts of fear and confusion were turning to anger and frustration. Then she realized that she couldn't do it alone if she had to go through this again. She would need an attorney.

Shortly after walking out of the BPD, Veronica's search for an attorney was on. Unfortunately, it was a Saturday, so she'd have to wait for a weekday. Knowing she could never afford an attorney herself, she turned to the Broome County Public Defender. Ordinarily, the Public Defender doesn't get involved until an arrest has been made. Fortunately for Veronica, they took the time to listen to what she had to say. After learning there was an active homicide investigation and that she was a suspect, they felt her story was compelling enough to make an exception. After that, she sat down with one of their investigators and laid out her story once again.

After describing everything that happened, she talked about her experience and interviews with the BPD, including when she'd been told she was a crackhead and prostitute and that she had offered to let them test her hair for drugs. Then she explained how she'd further agreed to take a polygraph test to show she was telling the truth. She explained what she'd been told about the autopsy, where partially digested Tater-tots were found in Lyric's stomach.

It was noted that during Veronica's intake interview, she was crying off and on and commented several times about how much she missed her children. Further, that she was confident she'd done nothing wrong and, as far as she knew, would not be charged with this murder.

Then, the very next day, on Wednesday, January 5th, the Broome County DA's office drafted and sent an email to the Broome County Court Clerk. Briefly, it identified Veronica Taft and how she had sought the services of the Public Defender's Office. Then it stated that the Public Defender's Office had a conflict in representing her. Furthermore, it indicated that they were requesting a conference with the judge to see if new counsel could be assigned so that their office could interview her, adding further that no charges have been filed at this time.

Shortly thereafter, the court granted the DA's request and turned to the assigned counsel list to try and find a qualified attorney to represent Veronica. Later, Attorney David Butler from the family law firm of Butler & Butler Law Offices in Vestal, NY, was contacted and agreed to represent her. Dave Butler had years of experience as a highly qualified criminal defense attorney, who, along with brother Matt, followed in the footsteps of their father, Earl Butler. All of whom had long-standing reputations as honorable and respected members within the legal community.

16

EVIDENCE EXAM

As previously mentioned, when Lyric was still being treated in the ER at Lourdes hospital, they had removed his street clothes and the diaper he was wearing, which were then secured into evidence by Patrol Officer John Taylor. Later, they were transported back to **BPD** Headquarters, cataloged, including examination instructions, and placed in the evidence locker. Initially, the first examination instructions for each of the three items, including one diaper, one red shirt, and one black sweatshirt, were to process each item and then check for fingerprints. Unfortunately, the blue jeans Lyric wore that were removed by EMTs at the scene were never recovered.

Typically, the first step in the process would be photographing the clothing, followed by a careful and thorough naked-eye examination. The purpose is to look for anything of evidentiary value, then continue to look for any form of trace evidence such as hairs, blood, other body fluids, foreign fibers, particles, or stains. The next step would require using a Variable Light Source Instrument, known as a "Crime Scope," which uses adjustable and variable light sources to look closer. It tries to identify any latent (hidden) trace evidence that may not be visible to the naked eye, i.e., blood or blood residue on dark material. After that, anything found, whether identifiable or unidentifiable, would be documented and marked for possible further examination by the crime lab. Then, the final step would be to check for fingerprints.

A little over a week had passed when Sergeant Michelle Stebbins, as supervisor of the ID Unit, transferred each of these three items from the evidence locker to the ID Unit lab for processing. She started with item #1 – the diaper. After removing it from the paper bag, she described it as a white disposable diaper with green, blue, and purple graphics. There were two adhesive fastening tabs on the back and two non-adhesive tabs on the front. The interior consisted of absorbent material, and there was elastic around the leg areas. The interior appeared to contain urine, along with a smell that was consistent with urine. The weight of the diaper was heavier in the front than the back and was darker in color.

Turning to the exterior, she described several areas that appeared to be consistent with bloodstains, which included red staining on all four fastening tabs. She then placed red sticky arrows that pointed to each specific area and took a series of photographs. She further noted a long dark hair adhered to the left rear adhesive tab. However, the hair was neither photographed nor collected, and there was no fingerprint exam, not even the smooth fastening tabs.

Author's note: Interestingly, one of the more apparent bloodstains seen on one of the fastening tabs was crescent-shaped and appeared remarkably consistent with that of an adult thumbprint.

. . .

Similarly, she turned to and examined item #2 – the black hooded sweatshirt, describing it as an Old Navy brand, size 2T. It was a black cotton hooded sweatshirt with red & white graphics, "Old Navy" on the front, and a zipper up the front. The sleeves were partially composed of thermal-type material. The item appeared to be well-worn. There was a defect in the back, near the base of the hood, and a vomit-like stain on the right sleeve. She also noted several long wavy hairs, possibly brown, adhered to the garment.

Also examined was item #3. It was described as a red, long-sleeve turtleneck cotton shirt. The brand was "Wonderkids," and the size was 4T. This also appeared to be well worn and had a defect near the neck seam. It was also cut up the middle, which was consistent with removal by EMTs.

Oddly, the black mattress cover recovered from the scene, with the apparent vomit stain, was never examined or tested, which could have been another means of identifying Lyric's last meal.

The discovery of the bloodstains on the diaper's exterior had immediately perked Stebbins interest, and rightfully so. After all, both Dr. Terzian and the ER doctors found and reported that Lyric had no external bleeding. It was all internal. Furthermore, there was no evidence of any bloodletting at the crime scene. And during Veronica's early interview, she told investigators about changing Lyric's diaper just before she went to work. But she presented no signs of being injured. By contrast, that same morning, during Pratt's interview, he was observed with bleeding knuckles on both hands. Knowing these things would have sent up a red flag for Stebbins. As such, she'd logically be asking herself, "Why is there blood on the *outside* of Lyric's diaper? Is it Chucky's? Could he be our killer?" Those were good questions that needed to be answered. Considering the time-consuming efforts just described, she'd recognized the value of documenting the evidence in preparation for submission to the crime lab for further testing, specifically, for serology and DNA.

Remarkably, there was nothing to suggest that the blood was from Lyric or Veronica from what was already known. Chucky was the only one left. But he claimed to have been injured while punching the wall after becoming frustrated with Lyric's situation. They already confirmed the hole in the wall. Therefore, his claim should be considered corroborated, right? Well, not quite. Because here's the problem. If the blood on Lyric's diaper came from Chucky, that would mean he was already injured and bleeding *before* he punched the wall. As such, the evidence would tend to prove his injuries occurred earlier, likely during his savage attack on Lyric while Veronica was at work. If that did happen, he would have a two-fold reason for punching the wall: one, to cover up the area where he'd bashed Lyric's head into the wall, and two, to have an explanation for his bleeding knuckles and to make sure someone witnessed him punching the wall. We'll be learning more about this later but for now, let's fast-forward a few days to find out if anything new was happening during the ongoing investigation.

17

A NEW SEARCH WARRANT

Previously, during the late afternoon of December 30th, the same day Lyric was killed, the BPD obtained and executed a search warrant for Taft's second-floor apartment on Fayette Street. They searched for the items listed on the warrant that could be considered evidence. Other than the photographs and items previously mentioned, nothing more was discovered or secured as evidence. Additionally, Taft's apartment was processed as a crime scene, with a primary focus on the children's bedroom. Later, the search and crime scene processing results were documented in a short narrative report, along with a few notes.

Now, on January 14th, over two weeks had passed. The investigation had been moving forward non-stop. The reason was unclear, but something prompted them to apply for another search warrant for Taft's apartment. Initially, I was clueless as to what they might be looking for now. They had already searched and given up the crime scene back on December 30th. What did they expect to find now? And even if they did find something, what value would it be? Two weeks? Without knowing what may have changed, or who may have been there doing whatever? That's never a good thing. Since then, anything could have happened, including anything that may have been altered, added, removed, or even destroyed. Therefore, the probative value of any newly discovered evidence would fall under heavy scrutiny.

Regardless, they made an application, and a new search warrant was granted. The new application prepared by Investigator Cornell, other than one short paragraph, mirrored the original application prepared by Investigator Diles word for word. The only new paragraph mentioned the December 31st autopsy by Dr. Terzian, where he identified severe trauma to the back of Lyric's head and other parts of his body and noticeable bruises and abrasions on his neck, face, and upper chest. But this was nothing new. Investigators were already aware of Lyric's body trauma, having personally observed and photographed his injuries on December 30th.

Strangely, the new paragraph made no mention of anything new they wanted to search for that hadn't already been listed in their original application. Therefore, I struggled to understand what it was the BPD was trying to do. Then I briefly wondered whether it might have anything to do with their bizarre effort to try and push back the time of death.

Also noted was another paragraph in Diles' original application that Cornell omitted, which addressed the importance of the very reasons I just described above as follows:

"Affiant (Diles) is of the opinion that items described to be seized, 'could be destroyed or removed from locations sought to be searched resulting in the loss of valuable evidence if not seized forthwith.'"

Therefore, they clearly understood the value of maintaining a continuous police presence at the crime scene until they were satisfied that everything that needed to be done had been done. Until then, the crime scene should never be given up. This wasn't their first rodeo. The BPD would have known that. But now they're returning to whatever's left of the crime scene. So, what were the investigators really looking for? Would anything be different this time?

Later, on January 14th, Cornell's application was approved by the court, and a new search warrant was issued. After waiting until January 19th, now *three* weeks later, the warrant was finally executed by ID Unit Supervisor Sergeant Michelle Stebbins, Assistant Investigator Matt Zandy, and Investigators Cornell and Wagner.

My curiosity was killing me. Even before I read Stebbins' narrative report, I turned to her scant few attached notes, where I learned that the time taken to complete this second search was precisely the same as the first search. A whole one hour and four minutes. Thinking to myself, "Here we go again. This ought to be good." I then turned to her narrative report, consisting of one single page.

The second paragraph quickly revealed what I suspected but didn't want to believe. It was now clear that the BPD was looking for something to help push back the time of death. I was now sure they were genuinely targeting Veronica Taft and not Charles Pratt. But it was still a mystery as to why.

As entry was made into the apartment's living room, Stebbins wrote that it seemed to be "extremely warm." Then, as previously noted during the first search warrant, she described the same heater in the living room corner with an open flame visible within the outer covering. From there, they went immediately into the kitchen, where they reported a temperature reading of 74 degrees Fahrenheit.

I now realized what they were trying to do. It certainly seemed like a futile attempt. However, if they could show how "extremely warm" it was, then they could argue that the average cooling rate of the body, known as *algor mortis*,[1] may have been slowed down. It could allow them to argue further that the time of death was earlier than estimated.

"Extremely warm?" I know it's not just me because we all know that a temperature of 74 degrees falls well within the normal comfort range. Therefore, unless Stebbins was an Indigenous person from the extreme North, her report was clearly an exaggeration. And from my view, that was no mistake but rather a deliberate attempt to support their new theory that Veronica had done this before she went to work. As troubling as it was, her apparent mission to 'help the cause' didn't stop there because the more significant concern wasn't so much what she'd done but rather what she failed to do.

As mentioned, the reported temperature in the kitchen was 74 degrees. Yet, there were no photographs nor any indication of how that was obtained. Later, however, we did learn it was taken from a thermostat in the kitchen. But why just the kitchen? Under their new theory, Lyric would have been dead or dying on the bottom bunk in the children's bedroom from around 9:00 p.m. until sometime after 10:30 a.m. the following day. Therefore, if recording the temperature was that important, the children's room should have been the target location, not the kitchen.

Despite other evidence known at the time, it appeared as though they had made a deliberate decision *not* to record the temperature in the kids' room. First of all, it was wintertime, and according to NOAA[2] local area weather records, the outside temperature during the entire time in question was below freezing. Secondly, the only heat source in the apartment was a single-unit space-heater, centrally located in the corner of the living room. Logically, the rooms furthest away, including the kids' bedroom in the rearmost part of the apartment, would be much cooler than the kitchen, which was directly adjacent to the heat source. Thirdly, blankets, sheets, and towels were hung over the windows in every room to keep out the cold drafts. Finally, during Chucky's detention, he made references to Veronica, saying that it was cold in there and then said himself, "It be cold in that room."

The truth is, they knew it was much colder in the children's bedroom. So, why not record it? Because having an official record of the bedroom temperature would defeat their whole purpose in going there. Which, in turn, would destroy the new theory they were so hell-bent on trying to prove. They weren't about to let that happen. Besides, Veronica had already been in their crosshairs for the past three weeks. And any passing thought about doing the right thing was now quickly rejected. Presumably, from their perspective, it was too late to do the right thing. Though, in my opinion, I'd say it's never too late.

I was deeply troubled by their brazen disregard and denial of the truth. Instead, the investigators decided to solve their problem by denying it existed. But we all know, denying the truth doesn't change the facts. They moved forward with their warped version of the truth that Veronica had done this. And as such, the new theory was now locked in stone. There was no turning back. They were now trying desperately to prove Veronica was the killer and weren't about to let their fear of the truth destroy their illusions. So much for their sworn oath of office. Where's the professionalism? Honesty? Integrity? Oh, how quickly they forget.

As previously mentioned, after giving up a crime scene, various problems can occur when trying to return later. And what just happened here is a good example. The first problem started shortly after giving up the crime scene on December 30th. Before releasing Chucky from detention, he was given specific instructions that Veronica's apartment was off-limits and was told not to go back there. However, within minutes after giving up the crime scene, guess who showed up? Chucky. Then strangely, after consulting with investigators, the patrol officer who was still there released it to him. It wasn't even his apartment. So, your guess is as good as mine about what he did there or how long he stayed. For any number of reasons, this could further complicate any future return to the crime scene. But despite any of the possible complications, they felt it was important enough, even after three weeks, to return to the crime scene.

Author's note: Later, we'll learn what happened as the result of my interview with Chucky's friend Max, who surprisingly provided a very plausible explanation as to why Chucky may have been so anxious to return to Veronica's apartment.

It was also previously mentioned that there was a risk of anything newly discovered at the scene being compromised or devalued after a lack of police presence. That exact problem presented itself during this second crime scene search three weeks later. When considering what was done concerning the temperature, any results, even after three days, let alone three weeks, would have no value. Why? Because there was no way of knowing what the temperature was three weeks earlier. You can't just assume it was the same.

On a related note, one of the first patrol officers on the scene the first day was later asked by the DA if he'd noticed anything unusual about the temperature inside the apartment? He answered, "It seemed normal." Clarifying, the DA asked, "Room temperature, in other words?" The answer was "Yes."

During the second search warrant's execution, they again described and reexamined the children's bedroom, including its contents, and took more photographs. Additionally, they noted the entertainment stand with a TV and numerous DVD movies, music CDs, and video games. They also measured and inspected some of the CD jewel cases for any traces of blood or hair but found nothing. I was curious about this but later learned it was only a rumor that Veronica's oldest daughter Haveen had hit Lyric in the head with a CD jewel case.

Later, the hole in the living room wall previously examined was supposedly reexamined and inspected. Stebbins wrote, "*The pieces of drywall that fell into the hole were removed. There did not appear to be anything noteworthy, such as blood or hair.*" There was nothing to support the claim that any pieces of drywall were ever removed from inside the wall, let alone examined. And how do we know that? Because the hole was more than 4½ feet off the floor. Any pieces that fell into the hole would have dropped to the bottom, inside the partition. Therefore, unless Stebbins' arms were five feet long, there was only one way to recover them. By carefully cutting and removing the drywall underneath the hole. That would allow their retrieval from the bottom of the partition. Of course, that whole procedure would have been photographed as well if it had happened. There were no photographs because it never happened. So, those pieces Stebbins claimed were examined? They never were.

Incredibly, Stebbins mentioned nothing whatsoever about the broken pieces scattered on the floor below the hole, even though they remained right where they were three weeks earlier. Once again, physical evidence was simply left behind and ignored. More importantly, you don't just pick up a piece of broken drywall, give it a quick once over with the ole naked eye, and say, "Nope, I don't see nothin'," and toss it back in the hole, throwing away any chance of finding any unseen touch DNA. Another opportunity was lost.

Before leaving, they did take some additional measurements of the entire crime scene, along with a hand diagram. Later, they used it to create a more formal diagram. That was one of the better things they did. But why wasn't that done the first time?

Oddly, other than the newly added measurements, there were still no descriptions of the kitchen, bathroom, game room, Veronica's bedroom, closets, dresser drawers, or any of their contents. From their photographs, even three weeks later, the jean pants Lyric had been wearing can still be seen lying on the floor next to Veronica's bed. Since it wasn't done initially, I was somewhat optimistic they would do a better job this time on the kitchen. If you recall, during their separate interviews, both Chucky and Veronica told investigators about the kids being fed Tater-tots, French fries, and Mac & Cheese before going to bed. But other than recording the kitchen temperature, they did nothing to try and locate any associated food packaging containers that could likely confirm or refute what they were told. Searching through closets, dresser drawers, garbage, and dirty laundry at a crime scene is a fundamental necessity. Yet here, they never did that. What better way to hide or dispose of evidence than to stash it where you think no one will bother to look. Another missed opportunity? Indeed.

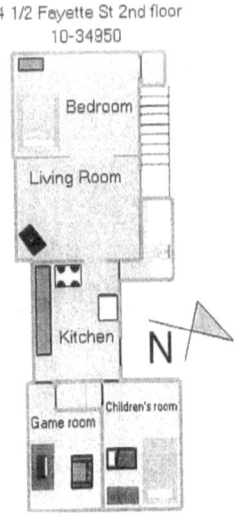

Stebbins reported taking additional photographs during the second search warrant. Later, there were noticeable differences during side-by-side comparisons with the original photos taken on December 30th. This process established that someone other than Veronica had been in the apartment since the first search warrant. Several items depicted in the earlier photographs had been repositioned but were still present. In comparison, other items were missing entirely.

Interestingly, another side by side photo comparison was made of a large black plastic bag sitting on the floor of a small closet in the children's bedroom. It was on top of some other articles of clothing. The earlier photo simply showed a large, unopened, black plastic bag in the closet. In the newest photos, the unopened bag looked nearly identical to the first. However, there was also a second shot showing the top of the bag after being partially opened. The bag was packed full, but only the top-most item could be seen, a pink-colored material with a large, brown-colored stain. Unfortunately, neither this item nor any of the underlying contents were ever emptied and examined. For now, I'll leave it at that. But we will learn more about this later.

Surprisingly, in Stebbins' narrative report, after wrapping up her so-called crime scene investigation, she wrote in a rather bizarre final sentence, *"Due to the unclean status of the apartment and belongings within, nothing noteworthy was located."* Seriously? Did I just read that correctly? Yep. That's what it said. That was one of the most outlandish things I'd ever heard coming from a crime scene investigator. So, from her perspective, if the status of the surrounding area or any belongings are 'unclean,' nothing noteworthy can be found? That's nonsense. Besides, if cleanliness was a requirement or prerequisite in locating anything noteworthy, crime scene investigators may as well pack their bags and go home. I must have reread that at least four or five times because I still couldn't believe she would write that. Although, it might explain some of the abbreviated crime scene work and why she'd abandoned the scene so quickly. Especially if she had a problem with getting her hands dirty. Later, this matter will be addressed further.

Author's note: In case you missed it, Sergeant Stebbins' report of the 'unclean status' of the Taft apartment was entirely contradicted by Traci Reynolds in her CPS report, who wrote, "minimal clutter and did not appear dirty."

Some might argue that I was just second-guessing or nit-picking. But this was not the case. This was a major homicide scene with little or no physical evidence. As such, it was all the more essential to take a closer and more aggressive look at the crime scene in the search for evidence, even if that meant spending several more hours or even days in that effort. Especially knowing that Lyric, an innocent and defenseless two-year-old, had been savagely beaten and killed in that apartment. A very violent murder had taken place. It was now their job to try and find any evidence that may help determine what happened, how it happened, and who may be responsible. As such, despite the challenge, there was a clear, justifiable, and dutiful obligation to do more. The crime scene was theirs for as long as necessary to do the job. So, why the rush? Why all the shortcuts?

Sadly, the real story behind this, which might answer those questions, may never be known and will likely remain a mystery. That being said, by using my own crime scene investigation experience regarding these so-called crime scene searches, I can only offer that there was a remarkable yet strange failure to follow both the fundamental and elementary protocols of crime scene investigation.

For most of us, in our post-modern age of forensic science, we recognize and understand the value of DNA testing. The success stories are endless. Therefore, it should be relatively easy to understand the importance of DNA testing concerning the blood evidence found on Lyric's diaper. That said, you might likely be troubled by what you're about to learn, or perhaps even a bit angry.

Having discovered the blood on the diaper and recognizing the importance of identifying who's blood it was or wasn't should have been a high priority. Typically, a crime lab submission form would have been completed, requesting an examination for DNA. Shockingly, that never happened. After completing her limited examination, Stebbins simply returned the blood-stained diaper to the evidence locker. It is unclear whether she decided this on her own or was instructed to do so.

Author's note: The issue involving the untested bloody diaper did not stop here. It became even more troubling four months later when we learned what happened after the Senior ADA personally reexamined it.

Even though BPD reports did not reveal any interview with Hope Taft, there were a few scant notes in the file made by the ADA. Hope had been located and interviewed at Binghamton General Hospital, where she worked on February 22, 2011, by the ADA and three other investigators. Hope admitted knowing Charles Pratt but not all that well. From what she did know, he seemed to have a good relationship with Veronica's kids. She described Veronica as a good mom and said that they would often speak on the phone. When questioned about the morning of December 30th, she recalled getting a call from Veronica and responding to the scene. When she arrived, Pratt was there, but Veronica had just left for the hospital. Hope never made it to the hospital. Instead, she was taken directly to the police station to help with the kids.

Later, after speaking with Veronica, Hope learned that when she arrived home from work that morning, Veronica had gone straight to bed and didn't check on the kids. Hope added how Pratt had checked on the kids and told her about Lyric. Pratt also told her about Veronica telling him to "bring him to me." Hope also reported what Veronica had told her about Pratt complaining about his foot hurting after Lyric's death. And further, of him telling Veronica that he would tell the police that she'd kicked Lyric and broke his ribs. She'd also heard from

Veronica about Pratt making dinner for the kids as she was leaving for work.

---

1. *Algor mortis:* The second stage of death, involving a cooling of the body temperature postmortem until reaching the ambient air temperature.
2. *NOAA*: National Oceanic & Atmospheric Administration.

18

VERONICA TAFT – INTERVIEW # 3

The DA's office had been anxious to reinterview Veronica ever since she'd stormed out of the interrogation room on January 1st. It was now March 28, 2011, and attorney David Butler had been assigned to represent Veronica. As such, Butler agreed to another interview with Veronica, but only in his presence. Veronica had since moved to the Syracuse, NY area to live with a friend but agreed to the interview. During the interview, a Broome County Senior ADA, one of his investigators, and the BPD lead investigator were present.

The interview started with what she recalled happening when she got home from work that morning. She said Chucky was up in the kitchen, telling her that Zoey hadn't slept all night and was in her bed. She remembered telling him to put Zoey back in her own bed. Which he did, but it seemed like he was gone a long time. So, she'd gone in to ask him what was taking so long. Chucky said he was covering up Lyric. While she was there, she noticed that Amira was in bed next to Lyric. She then explained how Chucky shut the door, and she'd questioned him as to why since it was cold in there. He told her it would still be open a little. They both went back into her bedroom; he started to rub her shoulders, and she fell asleep. When she woke up, she looked over and noticed Chucky was awake, just staring at the ceiling. She'd then asked why the kids weren't up and told him to go get them. When he came back, he said Lyric was cold. She then explained that she'd also noticed how his stomach was raised but not his chest when she first saw Lyric. Then added how Chucky picked up Lyric and said, "Come on, Lyric, come on."

As the interview ended, she mentioned how Chucky complained about his foot hurting for about a week after it happened. Then also mentioned having recordings of Chucky on her phone but couldn't locate them at the time.

Their new theory claimed that Lyric was killed around the 9:00-10:00 p.m. timeframe. Therefore, I found it rather remarkable how she'd never been questioned about what she was doing or what, if anything, was happening before Chucky arrived.

Notably absent from the interview were any questions about using a black spoon to discipline her children. Stranger still was the absence of anything concerning Lyric's blood-stained diaper, stomach contents, or time of death. Those were the key elements of the case. Yet, they were never addressed during Veronica's interview.

Even knowing she was a suspect, Veronica agreed once again to appear voluntarily for another interview. However, she was under no obligation to do so. Once she appeared for the interview, she was open to any line of questioning. Unfortunately, for whatever reason, any questions about the key elements were strictly off-limits.

19

PREMATURE DECISION

Strangely, as I navigated my way through all the discovery material, other than one short paragraph in the CPS report, I had not found anything more regarding Chucky other than his initial interview that first day. I knew he had a criminal history and spent a few years in state prison for drug possession and sale, as well as having a pending assault charge here in Binghamton. I thought I would find his rap sheet, which would have included some of the underlying details. Obtaining that information would have been basic protocol.

During Veronica's first interview, when asked about any of Chucky's prior relationships, she claimed he was previously involved with two other women who had children. Surprisingly, neither of those women had ever been identified or interviewed in the discovery material provided, nor had their children. Even Pratt's mother, who he claimed to have called often, including the day in question, was never identified or interviewed.

Thinking I must have missed something, I returned to the lead log and checked it line by line, from beginning to end. Sure enough, other than lead #3 assigned to interview Pratt and lead

#12 to subpoena his phone records, there was nothing more. In my view, the absence of any other Pratt leads was not only strange but troubling. My fear was, they knew he was their killer but believed they'd lost their opportunity to question him further because he'd lawyered up so quickly. They knew they could never use any statement he made after that against him. And because of that, prosecuting him would be difficult. As a result, DA Gerald Mollen decided to simply drop any further investigation of Charles Pratt.

But there was still an open homicide where someone needed to be held accountable for this brutal murder of little Lyric Taft. So, as an alternative, with Pratt out of the picture, assuming he was no longer prosecutable, Mollen was faced with a second decision on how to proceed. As preposterous and unethical as it was, absent any evidence against Veronica, he decided she was fair game to pursue as Lyric's killer.

So, when I say Mollen's decision was made prematurely, what does that mean? According to the CPS report, Mollen was present at the BPD on day one. He was being briefed by investigators and monitoring the progress of the investigation as it unfolded. During Pratt's interview, he was either watching on a closed-circuit monitor or receiving regular updates. As a result, he learned of Pratt's irrational, angry and apparent drug-induced performance, as well as his early demand for a lawyer. As such, he would have undoubtedly reminded the police that anything he said after that, even if incriminating, could never be used against him.

As we've already learned, the BPD continued to interview Pratt to let him tell his story. As much as they wanted to continue, they were limited by his early demand for a lawyer. At the time, that left them no other choice but to let him go. But, like Eggleston told Veronica after informing her he'd been let go, "It doesn't mean anything." Initially, it seemed as though Eggleston wasn't finished with Pratt and wanted to continue pursuing him. Regardless, even if that was his initial intent, it was short-lived once Mollen decided Pratt could not be prosecuted and dropped the case against him.

This is where the premature part comes in. The investigation was only in its infancy. The autopsy was scheduled but not yet completed, and therefore, they had not yet established the time of death. Equally important was Veronica's work alibi, which had not yet been confirmed. So, they had a lot more work to do. But within the next 24-hours, they had the time of death estimate and confirmation of Veronica's work alibi.

Remember Mollen himself was present during the autopsy when Dr. Terzian, using Lyric's body temperature, calculated his estimated time of death. Shortly afterward, utilizing that information, investigators were able to verify Veronica's work alibi, which confirmed she was at work during that time. At this point, all eyes would have or should have been focused on Chucky as the killer.

Shockingly, less than 24-hours later, despite the time of death estimate and Veronica's iron-clad alibi, absent any explanation, Mollen decided to abandon any further action against Chucky, choosing instead to focus exclusively on Veronica Taft. As troubling as it was, regardless of what any future evidence might bring, he would never look back. Never change his mind and never reopen a case against Chucky.

A week later, it became even more troubling when the discovery of that 'future evidence' became a reality —when the transfer bloodstains were discovered on the *outside* of Lyric's diaper. One of which appeared in the form of a bloody thumbprint. As a result, there was supporting physical evidence, which would likely, directly link Charles Pratt to the killing. All that was needed was a confirmatory DNA test. But incredibly, as we've already learned, they never tested it. Instead, it was simply returned to the evidence locker.

The decision to abandon Chucky and pursue Veronica was a significant turning point in the investigation. Not only premature but unjustified as well. Because, within days, the evidence pointed right back to Chucky, and a more just decision would be in order. Besides, there's no shame in turning back when you discover you're on the wrong path.

20

PRETEND JUSTICE

There was nothing in the leads, but as I continued looking through the discovery material, I stumbled across some handwritten notes dated February 8, 2011. Notes made by DA Investigator Ingrid Segrue, which referenced another interview that had taken place with Charles Pratt at the DA's office on February 8th. Other than her notes, there was no record of this interview in the BPD lead log. Later, however, we learned that Pratt had consulted with his attorney before this interview, and the DA's office drafted a Debriefing Agreement. It was presented for his signature before the interview. After that, it was just a recap of what he'd said back in December for the most part. Since we've already learned what he said previously, I'll just clarify what he said earlier and include some of the new things he added.

Pratt acknowledged knowing Veronica for the past five months and had been babysitting every night while she worked. He remembered that before Veronica left for work, he'd seen her friend Pica sitting on the bed with her. He then claimed that he hadn't seen the kids in the living room or Veronica's room and assumed they were watching a movie. But later, he'd fed all the kids macaroni and cheese and fries after Veronica left. He added that they had all eaten at their little table in the living room. He also remembered getting a call from Veronica while they were eating, later adding that he'd made four plates and remembered hearing Lyric's voice but not seeing him.

When asked who would change diapers, he said, "Me once in a while," but usually Haveen and Veronica. When asked if the kids stayed up late, he acknowledged they did. Then added, "I'm not their father, so I let them do what they want."

When asked about the morning in question, he said Lyric was under the covers on the bottom bunk with Amira. He remembered Lyric having jeans on when he first picked him up. He mentioned how much Veronica loved the kids but then started throwing her under the bus, claiming the kids had become a burden. He said she was always yelling at them, especially Lyric, who she treated as an outsider. Then, he described how she would hit Lyric with a black spoon on his hand and head while calling him names. Later he added, "I don't like kids being abused because I was." As the interview ended, he claimed to have seen Veronica kick Lyric in the chest with her foot.

I wasn't at all surprised to learn that Chucky had been questioned about who would change diapers. There were already four things they'd learned earlier that would have prompted this line of questioning:

- Veronica changed Lyric's diaper before she went to work,
- Bloodstains & bloody thumbprint on the outside of Lyric's diaper,
- Veronica displayed no signs of being injured or bleeding,

- Chucky exhibited bleeding knuckles on both hands.

However, other than the question about who changed diapers, what was surprising was the fact that he was never asked if he'd changed Lyric's diaper that night while Veronica was at work. Incredibly, he was neither shown any photographs nor told about the blood on Lyric's diaper. Presumably, he was never asked whose blood it was or if it was his fingerprint. Or, more importantly, if they were going to find his DNA.

I was sure there was much more to this interview than what was revealed in the scant few notes. But absent any videotape or formal report, we'll never really know.

As we've already learned, DA Mollen had already decided early on against trying to prosecute Chucky for Lyric's murder. But knowing they would still need him to testify, their only purpose now was to see what else they could learn that might strengthen their case against Veronica. They knew that whatever he said, even if incriminating, they could never use it against him. From my perspective, they'd simply crawled into bed with this thug, who they knew was the killer. After that, their questioning was strictly limited and controlled to avoid any incriminating remarks or otherwise to learn what really happened. In other words, with his attorney present, a ruthless baby-killer was being handled with kid gloves. One wrong question and his attorney would say, "Don't answer that."

To make matters worse, even though BPD and CPS knew from the get-go that Chucky was the real killer, they readily embraced Mollen's decision. They agreed that Lyric was the victim of a brutal murder and believed there was a sense of urgency to make an arrest. The citizens of Binghamton and the surrounding community knew it was either the mother or the boyfriend and were likely asking what was taking so long. Therefore, Veronica Taft quickly became their new target. And why not? After all, according to the cry-ladies, she was a prostitute and druggie who cooked crack in her bathtub, screamed at and regularly beat her kids, never bathed them, lived in a maggot-infested home, taught her two-year-old how to masturbate, and more. Because she was branded a "bad mom," that must also mean she murdered her son, right? Apparently so, because soon after Mollen's decision, there was a united team effort to launch an aggressive and unjust campaign to pursue 'pretend justice' against their new target – Veronica Taft. A campaign, which by design, was strategically carried out to exclude, reject or ignore, anything and everything that pointed to Charles Pratt. Instead, their focus was strictly limited to only what was needed to arrest and prosecute Taft.

Pretend justice? That's what it was. Because they knew damn well Pratt was the real killer. But having lost their opportunity to prosecute him, or so they thought, they would just pretend it wasn't him. Then, to make matters worse, pretend it was Veronica instead.

21

A THIRD SEARCH WARRANT

Three months had passed, and it was now March 30, 2011, two days after Veronica's third interview. Previously, the BPD suspected that both Veronica and Chucky might have been physically disciplining the children by striking them with a black plastic spoon. However, during repeated questioning, Veronica denied that she had ever struck them with a spoon. She only admitted to an occasional 'pop' on their hands or butt with her hand. Other than that, she had them do timeout by sitting in the corner.

A little earlier, we learned what happened when, after three weeks, they returned to the crime scene with their second search warrant. Other than a few measurements and some more photographs, nothing of value was accomplished or obtained. So, it was a surprise when they decided to apply for a third search warrant to return to the same crime scene three months later. Three months was a long time, and it did not make a lot of sense. But what was it they were after this time?

Their newest application was nearly identical to the two prior applications, where they had asked for just about anything and everything. Previously, they had requested to search for *"any instrument capable of inflicting injury or other objects that may be forensically examined for blood, hair, and/or human tissues and otherwise compared to the injuries discovered on the body of Lyric Taft."* In the new application, however, they tweaked this paragraph by inserting *"including but not limited to a kitchen utensil such as a ladle, spoon, etc."* I knew immediately that this was coming from the fact that both Veronica and Chucky were believed to have disciplined the children by striking them with a black plastic spoon.

There was also an added paragraph in the new application where they described how members of the BPD and DA's office had met and consulted with Dr. Terzian. At which time, he was presented with the black spoon theory. Trying to be helpful, Terzian felt that some of the injuries could have been caused by a kitchen utensil such as a ladle or spoon. But he said the injuries were more likely to have been caused by the handle. Notably, however, he never identified the specific injuries to which he was referring. And no other suggested means of injury was presented even though it was reported that Chucky had injured his foot. The BPD had been telling Veronica and her mom that Lyric had been used as a soccer ball.

Interestingly, one of the more severe-looking injuries appeared in the form of two side by side, black and blue abrasions located on Lyric's upper left chest, just below his neck. Considering the size of the abrasions and type of clothing he was wearing at the time, it seemed unlikely that the force generated from swinging a spoon handle would be enough to penetrate the clothing and still cause those injuries. From my perspective, a much more powerful force was involved. The damage appeared to be much more consistent with a powerful punch, kick, or perhaps a stomping action. This story might also explain how Chucky injured his foot. But what happened next only helped reaffirm how desperate they'd become in trying to find something they could use to strengthen their case against Veronica.

Continuing with the new application for a third search warrant, they asked once again to search for *"any clothing and footwear, personal effects or other items that may be evaluated for the presence of DNA and other physical evidence common with the scenes being processed and subjected to forensic examination and evaluations."*

Wait! Hadn't they already done that? Admittedly, I was a bit confused but, moreover, suspicious of their actual purpose here. Why would they still be interested in going back to look for a plastic spoon this far removed from the date of the crime? For obvious reasons, even if they found one, it would be of no value after this length of time. Perhaps, the search for a plastic spoon was just an excuse to allow them to return and finish what they failed to do earlier. Maybe they wanted to go back and collect the pieces of broken drywall and have them examined forensically for trace evidence such as blood, hair, fibers, or DNA. Perhaps they also wanted to retrieve Lyric's pants and have them examined. Remember Chucky had just told them during his February 8th interview that Lyric was wearing jeans when he first picked him up that morning. Regardless, three months had passed, and I had no reason to believe they would find anything of value. Besides, Veronica had long since vacated her apartment and moved out of town.

Considering the negative results of their two previous search warrants and the fact that three months had passed, I was a bit surprised that a judge was willing to grant another. Yet after the application was made and approved, a third search warrant was granted. On March 31st, the third search warrant was executed, and entry was made back into Taft's apartment. Before entering, a large piece of plywood fastened over the door had to be removed by the landlord. During a brief search, a black plastic spatula was photographed and collected from the front bedroom floor. Additionally, four black plastic kitchen utensils were photographed and collected from the kitchen counter. That was it – in and out in about ten minutes. The only purpose of the third warrant was to look for black kitchen utensils. Mission accomplished. What was so damn important about the black plastic spoon? Of note was the fact that even though they had been there twice before, they were still asking for a third time to search for *clothing, footwear, and personal effects,* which allowed yet another opportunity to retrieve and examine Lyric's pants that were left behind twice before. Yet that never happened. Their only interest was the black plastic spoon.

My first question was whether the handle of a kitchen utensil, such as a large plastic spoon, spatula, or ladle, would be capable of causing physical injury if used as a weapon? Of course. But the more important question would be whether it was capable of causing a lacerated liver, internal bleeding, nearly fractured skull, swelling of the brain, gouge marks that resemble fingernail marks, or taking a chunk out of an ear? I think not. Obviously, authorities knew this as well. So again, what was the real purpose?

The DA and BPD weren't seriously considering the plastic spoon as the murder weapon. They knew that theory would never fly. Therefore, their only purpose in pursuing the plastic spoon was a rather desperate move to try and disavow Veronica's claim that she'd never used a black spoon to discipline her children. If successful, they could then argue that Lyric done something to anger his mother before he was killed, and she began hitting him with the spoon. It quickly escalated into an angry and uncontrollable fit of rage that led to his vicious beating and subsequent death. In other words, they wanted to argue that Veronica's motive evolved from and was triggered by her spoon spanking.

From my perspective, that argument was a real stretch.

Veronica jumping from a swat on the butt to murder? That's a pretty giant leap. But more importantly, even if that did happen, a search for the spoon three months later would have no value and serve no purpose. Even if examined and found to have Veronica's DNA or fingerprints, it would prove nothing other than having been used legitimately in her kitchen. Besides, Veronica had vacated the apartment long before that.

Eventually, someone realized this because they were never examined further, even though they were collected as evidence. And not to belabor the point, but the black spatula was found on the floor in the back bedroom, Veronica's former bedroom. When comparing their most recent photos with the originals from day one, there was no black spatula. And the black utensils found in the kitchen? They were not in the original photos as well. That's what happens when you give up the crime scene prematurely.

In my view, as incredibly bizarre as it seemed, their emphasis on the black spoon had grown far greater than the bloody DNA evidence on the diaper, which was carefully tucked away and ignored. Let that sink in for a moment. Call it what you will, but for me, it was a rather shameful example of misguided, unprofessional behavior. Perhaps even amusing if there wasn't so much at stake. Therefore, with the 'Black Spoon' vs. 'Bloody Diaper' evidence, the choice between which one to focus on should have been obvious.

22

BLOODY DIAPER – A SECOND LOOK

Fast-forwarding to late April 2011, the Senior ADA, initially overseeing the DA's case, had resigned his position to go into private practice. After that, DA Mollen reassigned Senior ADA Peter N. DeLucia to take over.

Later, in May of 2011, while getting up to speed on the case, DeLucia contacted the BPD and made arrangements to review the physical evidence. He asked specifically to look at Lyric's diaper. On May 24th at the BPD, the diaper was retrieved from the evidence locker and presented to DeLucia, who looked it over for several minutes. Recall that Sergeant Stebbins had examined the bloody diaper but had never tested it for DNA. It was simply returned to the evidence locker. I also mentioned previously that the issue with the untested bloody diaper would become even more troubling after the Senior ADA personally examined it. But what was it that was so troubling?

At the time, the investigation was still ongoing, and no arrest had been made. However, if a future arrest were made, DeLucia would be the prosecuting attorney. In as much, any major decision-making relative to the ongoing investigation involving witnesses or evidence would now fall under his authority. Having observed the blood-stained diaper first-hand, he was now personally and officially aware of the blood evidence, including the bloody thumbprint on one of the closing tabs. It was crucial physical evidence that was needed to confirm the identity of Lyric's killer and make an arrest. Which, in turn, would likely become the lynchpin for the prosecution.

In his pursuit of justice, if DeLucia had any integrity at all, he would have felt morally obligated to do the right thing and have it tested. Unfortunately, he had something more sinister in mind, which had nothing to do with justice. He chose *not* to test the blood-stained diaper for DNA. Instead, it was once again returned to the evidence locker.

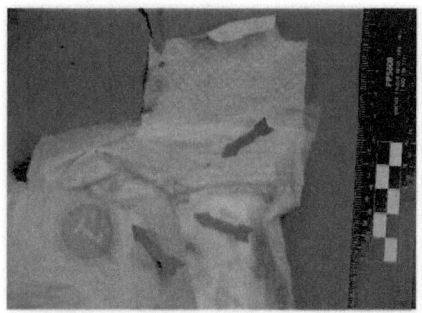

| Blood-stained Diaper

Needless to say, I was blown away by DeLucia's decision not to test the diaper for DNA, asking myself repeatedly how could he *not* do that? How could he simply ignore that kind of game-changing, physical evidence? Given my experience, it was even more troubling. Had I been the one to find the blood on the diaper, its submission to the lab would have been automatic. And knowing its importance, there would be no need to ask or wait for the DA to decide. Besides, what possible harm could there be in knowing who's blood it was?

Then it hit me. And it troubles me to say this. In light of DeLucia's decision, it had become painfully clear that his only objective now was to make an arrest and later secure a conviction against Veronica Taft for the murder of her son. With that goal in mind, he wasn't about to let the truth get in his way. He knew damn well but would never admit that had the DNA testing been done, it was a near-absolute that the profile would match Charles Pratt. Instead, he readily embraced Mollen's overriding decision to abandon any case against Chucky and pursue Veronica instead.

They'd already been actively pursuing her for months. So, if they were to learn now that it was Pratt's blood, it would ruin everything. It's been said that *"A just cause can never be damaged by the truth."* Agreed. Unfortunately, the damage to any 'just cause' was already done by failing to test that blood-stained diaper for DNA. As unethical as it was, DeLucia knew precisely what he was doing, and it had nothing to do with justice. After all, his prideful ego, reputation, and selfish interests were all on the line. He was controlled by his desire to climb the career ladder by adding another murder conviction to his resume, even if it meant convicting an innocent woman and allowing an evil killer to walk free. Reopening a case against Chucky was out of the question. Pretend justice doesn't get much worse than that.

Certainly, Lyric could not have changed his own diaper. Therefore, whoever did change his diaper last, was recently injured and bleeding. Before that, however, Lyric's pants would have to be removed first, then put back on. It increased the likelihood that there might have been blood on his pants as well. That would have been helpful to know. Unfortunately, his pants were never recovered, so we'll never know. But the known evidence clearly demonstrates that sometime *after* Veronica changed Lyric's diaper before leaving for work, someone else removed his pants, changed his diaper, and put his pants back on. Whoever did that was bleeding from a recent injury. Their blood was transferred onto the diaper, including that bloody thumbprint. In as much, even without DNA confirmation, the collective evidence had explicitly pointed to our killer.

23

CRUEL PROSECUTION

Sadly, as the story unfolded, DeLucia became even more aggressive with his selfish interests in what he would describe as the pursuit of justice. His intent was evident, and it had nothing to do with justice. As such, he deliberately ignored and circumvented the more compelling physical evidence. Instead, he adopted more of a "fake-it-till-you-make-it" strategy with arguably, unreliable or pretended evidence, including, of course, the loathsome cry-ladies. And we must not forget the "extremely warm" temperature or the deadly black spoon.

DeLucia's conscious decision not to test the bloody diaper was not only unethical but unprofessional, which would likely fall under the definition of prosecutorial misconduct. Notably, that decision was not exclusively his to make. If you recall, DA Mollen's hasty decision set things in motion against Veronica Taft. Then later, he designated DeLucia to prosecute her.

During my own experience working with the Broome County DA's office under the Mollen administration, one thing was made clear – nothing was done without his approval. In as much that didn't always sit well, especially with some of his senior staff members. Oh, the stories I could tell.

Given Mollen's approval, DeLucia pushed forward in his continued pursuit of Veronica Taft. A cruel pursuit designed and fueled by his fear or denial of the truth. Or, at least, his unwillingness to accept it. Perhaps, even to a level known as alethophobia[1]. In other words, his way of coping with the uncomfortable truth.

As a Senior ADA, DeLucia was a highly qualified and experienced prosecutor. There was no misunderstanding or confusion about his perception of the value of the physical evidence. Therefore, there was no plausible explanation or excuse for his misconduct. Like I said before, it was all being controlled by his selfish interests. Most assuredly, this was *not* the result of some simple mistake.

If that wasn't bad enough, his misconduct only worsened when he later pursued and added a desperate jailhouse snitch to his war chest who had asked, "What's in this for me?" I'll share the disturbing details of that scenario a little later. By now, he had gathered just about everything he needed to present his case to a grand jury to seek an indictment against Taft. However, there was still that one major stumbling block – the time of death.

Previously, Dr. Terzian, using the standard Glaister Equation[2] formula, applied to Lyric's recorded rectal temperature of 86 degrees Fahrenheit, had calculated and estimated the time of death between 3:00 and 4:00 a.m. Based on the swelling of his brain, he further estimated that he may have lived up to an hour after being injured, which would place the time of his actual assault about an hour earlier.

As noted, the Glaister formula uses a dead body's natural cooling rate of approximately 1.5 degrees per hour. However, that rate is based on an average size adult weighing about 155 pounds. Lyric weighed less than 33 pounds: in other words, nearly five times smaller. Logically, a smaller body mass would cool much faster. More likely in the neighborhood of two degrees per hour, perhaps more. So, at the very least, applying a conservative modification to the formula would be required for a more accurate time of death. So, more realistically, it could be as much as two or more hours *later* than Dr. Terzian's original estimate. In other words, closer to the 5:00 or 6:00 a.m. time frame.

Equally important was the issue involving rigor mortis. If you recall, the onset of rigor starts to appear within the first 2-4 hours after death, becoming maximal within 6-12 hours. The math doesn't work when you apply those figures to Lyric being killed *before* his mother left for work.

Briefly, according to their theory, Lyric was killed sometime between 9:00 and 10:00 p.m. When he arrived at the hospital the following day and had his temperature taken, it was 11:15 a.m. In other words, more than 13 hours had passed. So, as I said, the math doesn't work. Not to sound too morbid, but frankly, if their theory were correct, by the time Lyric arrived at the hospital, after more than 13 hours, he would have been ice-cold and stiff as a board. As it was, however, his core was still a little warm, and they only detected the earliest onset of rigor.

Additionally, the contents of Lyric's stomach created yet another factor for consideration when estimating the time of death. According to the autopsy report, evidence of regurgitated food matter was found in his esophagus and aspirated vegetable matter in his lungs. Also, evidence of vomit was found on the sleeve of his sweatshirt and on the bottom mattress cover where he was found. Despite all that, there were still 50 grams of an unidentifiable food substance in his stomach. Veronica's understanding was that Chucky had fed all the kids after she went to work. Before that, their daytime babysitter, Ray Ramos, had fed them nearly six hours earlier, around 5:00 p.m.

Accordingly, this raises a couple of equally essential questions. First, what food substance was present in Lyric's stomach? Second, how long after eating does food remain in the stomach? The answer to one or both of these questions should help narrow down the time of death.

As a reminder, Investigator Minor had previously informed Veronica that Lyric's stomach contents were consistent with potatoes. However, when she later reminded him of that, he tried back-peddling away from what he said. Notably, during that same interview, she'd also asked about how long food remains in the stomach. She was asking all the right questions and was clearly on the right track. And didn't we learn from CPS back in early January that the stomach contents had been sent out for analysis? It had been four months. So, where were the results?

During the autopsy, as we have already learned, the contents of Lyric's stomach, consisting of 50 grams of food matter, were recovered and frozen for further examination. Furthermore, when estimating the time of death, stomach contents can be used in addition to the rule of thumb formula of body temperature. Using them together can help tighten up the estimated time.

We've all seen autopsies played out on television or cinema where pathologists analyze stomach contents to establish what was eaten and when. Despite what you think, it's not just entertainment. In reality, it's a handy tool in a pathologist's arsenal – a valuable means of evidence. It makes it possible not only to identify any types of food present, but it can also identify foreign substances such as poisons, drugs, etc. Therefore, the stomach contents, specifically their condition at the time of the autopsy, can help further estimate the time of death. Unfortunately, the stomach contents recovered from Lyric were never used for that purpose. Later, we'll hear Dr. Terzian's answer as to why that was never done.

1. *Alethophobia*: A fear or dislike of the truth; an unwillingness to come to terms with truths or facts.
2. *Glaister Equation*: A formula used to approximate the post-mortem interval, (PMI) or time since death. Using a body's natural cooling of 1.5 degrees per hour, to approximate the number of hours since death.

24

LIE DETECTOR

On May 26, 2011, Senior ADA DeLucia sent a letter to attorney David Butler inquiring whether his client, Veronica Taft, would be amenable to taking a PSE lie detector test. In a follow-up phone call, Butler advised DeLucia that Veronica was interested in taking the PSE[1] test but needed more time to discuss it with her further.

On July 10th, after not hearing back from Butler, DeLucia sent another letter, reminding him of his understanding that Veronica was willing to submit to a PSE test. He then offered two dates when his examiner would be available to conduct the test. He explained that his Chief Investigator would be conducting the examination, adding that the test would be videotaped, and the length of time required would be 4-6 hours. In his next paragraph, he stated that they would agree not to use anything Veronica stated during the interview in a potential grand jury presentation stemming from the investigation. But then added, *"We would, however, reserve the right to use anything your client says during the examination against her in cross-examination should she choose to testify either at trial or in grand jury."*

In his final paragraph, he wrote, "*The results of this testing would simply be a matter for our consideration in furtherance of this investigation. In other words, even if your client were to 'pass' the examination, she could still be charged with criminal activity as a result of the outcome of our investigation. Whether or not she is charged as a result of this investigation, therefore, is <u>not</u> contingent on the results (pass or fail) of this examination.*"

Considering what was written above, should Veronica take the PSE test or not? Before answering that, let's back up a little and place ourselves back in her shoes for a moment. If you recall, during her very first interview, she said, "I'll take a lie detector. Do you guys do that here? I'm willing to do that." And their reply, "Well, we'll keep that in the back of our mind. Do you think we should give you one?"

Think about that for a moment. At the time, Veronica was a major witness or suspect who had just volunteered to take a polygraph. She'd also explained how it might help clear their heads about what she knew or didn't know about what happened to her son. In response, they said, "I don't know – I'll be honest, I don't have a crystal ball right now. I don't know if you know or you don't know." Wasn't that precisely what she was trying to clear up by offering to take the polygraph? It was the perfect opportunity to do just that. But for whatever reason, even though a polygraph was just a phone call away, it never happened. Another lost opportunity? Indeed. In hindsight, absent a crystal ball, perhaps they could have used an Ouija board. Sorry. I couldn't help myself.

By the time Veronica completed her second interview two days later, she knew Chucky had killed Lyric. And during her first interview, even without a crystal ball, the police had been crystal clear in their belief that Chucky was responsible for Lyric's death. But suddenly, like one of the investigators said later, "The tides turned," and everything flip-flopped. Veronica was stunned, dumbfounded, confused, and very frightened. She was struggling to understand how things could have changed so quickly. And just like that, like the flip of a switch, Chucky was gone, and there was no interest in pursuing him further. Instead, they targeted her as the number one suspect. She kept repeating to herself, "This isn't real. This can't be happening. How can this be happening? Why me?"

I've never been a big fan of the polygraph. Mainly because its reliability is often challenged, and there are many valid reasons why it's not accepted in a court of law. Despite its flaws, it can still be an effective tool during an investigation. As such, had the police followed through with Veronica's offer to take a polygraph, it could very likely have steered the investigation down the right path – away from her and back on Chucky. Unfortunately, that never happened. Yet, after five months of pursuing her as a suspect, there's this sudden renewed interest in having her take the test?

When considering all that was done to hide the truth thus far, one would have to question their real agenda now. Was there a sudden interest to discover the absolute truth? Or were they simply looking for something more to use against Veronica? Even though it troubles me to say this, but from my perspective, it was the latter. So, the question remains. Should she take the test or not?

Despite Veronica's suggestion to do the test early on, after reading DeLucia's letter and subsequent discussions with attorney Butler, they both agreed there was no longer any practical advantage. If anything, the only benefit would be theirs. And apparently, that's all they were interested in. Therefore, DeLucia's request was denied.

---

1. *PSE*: Psychological Stress Evaluator – also known as VSA - Voice Stress Analysis.

25

JESSE NOEL

Shortly after moving into her apartment at 4½ Fayette Street, Veronica met a handsome black man named Jesse Noel, who was nine years older than her. He was often seen frequenting a neighboring apartment a couple of doors down at 8 Fayette Street. A mutual physical attraction led to a brief tryst together before she met and started her relationship with Chucky. But unbeknownst to Veronica, she became pregnant. After that, over the next two or three months, she continued her two-timing relationship between Noel and Pratt.

During that time, Noel was involved in a long-term relationship with another woman named Jackie Dillon. They had three children together between one and eight years of age. It was Dillon who lived at 8 Fayette Street. So, Mr. Noel was doing a little two-timing of his own. However, there were significant problems in his relationship with Dillon, involving several ongoing and repeated instances of domestic violence. He'd been arrested several times. Not only for domestic assaults but for Criminal Contempt for violating the Family Court Orders of Protection Dillon had issued against him.

Later, after learning about Noel's relationship with Dillon, Veronica began distancing herself from him, wanting to work on her relationship with Chucky. Noel, however, wasn't quite ready to let go entirely and continued to call and speak with her. But mostly, just when he wanted sex.

A few days before Christmas 2010, Veronica began experiencing severe cramping and heavy bleeding. As the tough woman she was, not knowing what was happening, she thought the cramping and bleeding would soon ease up and stop. But it never did. As a result, she began feeling woozy and started having fainting spells. Not knowing what was wrong, she called and spoke with her mom, who insisted she go right to the hospital. Taking mom's advice, Chucky took her to the hospital, where she learned she was pregnant and had a miscarriage. Later, when she admitted to Chucky that Noel was the father. It didn't go well, and he was furious.

Over the next few weeks after Lyric's death, not wanting to return to her Fayette Street apartment, Veronica bounced around from place to place, staying with family, friends, and occasionally, an overnight in a local motel. Then, near the end of February, after being threatened and assaulted by Chucky, she left Binghamton and moved in with a friend near Syracuse, NY. After that, she only returned to Binghamton for her supervised visits with her children at DSS. And the only contact she had with Noel was by phone, which had become less frequent.

Then, on June 11, 2011, Noel was again arrested after violating another Order of Protection against Jackie Dillon. Only this time, the charges were much more severe, including two Class E felony counts of Criminal Contempt in the First Degree. Count one was violating two prior Orders of Protection, both of which were still active, and count two was due to his previous conviction of Criminal Contempt Second. In addition, he was also charged with Criminal Mischief, Endangering the Welfare of a Child, and Criminal Obstruction of Breathing or Blood Circulation.

In brief, shortly after arriving at Dillon's apartment, an argument ensued, which quickly led to an assault on Dillon, where he punched and choked her in front of the children. When the police arrived, Dillon was seen with bruising on her face and legs and finger impressions around her neck. A criminal history check revealed that Noel had a prior felony drug conviction for the Attempted Sale of a Controlled Substance.

After his arrest at Dillon's apartment, Noel was taken to BPD headquarters. After being booked, he sat down for an interview with Investigator William Martino. Interestingly, his interview had nothing to do with why he had been charged. Instead, it was about what he could tell them about his relationship with Veronica Taft. They'd already learned well before his arrest that he'd been in a relationship with Veronica. In as much, they were anxious to learn whatever he could tell them about her.

Knowing of his prior record of convictions and now facing more serious felony charges, Noel knew he was at risk of being sent to state prison. Therefore, to reduce that risk, he revealed his relationship with Veronica and what he knew about Charles Pratt and Lyric Taft's death.

During the interview, Noel disclosed his prior sexual relationship with Veronica, explaining that there were times when he would meet her on the job while working nights at the school. He claimed at one point, her boyfriend Chucky found out and got upset. He also claimed to know who Chucky was and was familiar with him from the Bronx where they grew up and that he babysat for Veronica when she worked.

Noel said he was shocked when he learned about Veronica's little boy getting killed. He'd heard that Chucky had something to do with it. About three weeks after Lyric was killed, Noel and his two friends, the Johnson brothers, Dwaine and Devon, a.k.a.,

"Weezy" and "Lips," went over to Chucky's apartment on Henry Street. When they got there, Noel asked what had happened. Chucky admitted to killing the little boy, claiming that Veronica was screwing around on him, and she was a crack-smoking whore. He'd also admitted to slamming the boy into a wall and kicking him. Then shortly after his admission, he threatened all three of them, and they took off.

Martino's notes revealed that Noel had been interviewed the next day again. During this interview, he added a little more to his story, where he claimed that Chucky had told Veronica that he would kill her son if she went to work that night.

Sometime later, after being arraigned on his charges, he was remanded to the Broome County Jail to await further court proceedings. Meanwhile, the DA and BPD were faced with the dilemma of how to handle this stunning new revelation of Chucky's admission to killing Lyric. After all, they'd been actively pursuing Veronica for the past five months and were strategically lining up their case against her. She was on the verge of being arrested. On the other hand, they had long since abandoned the case against Chucky. So, in light of this newest development, they were likely asking what did they do now? From my perspective, the answer seemed clear. But would they do the right thing?

The next reported interaction between Jesse Noel, the DA, and BPD took place at the Broome County Jail on June 28, 2011. In the interim, however, undocumented interviews with Noel and other witnesses continued behind closed doors. None of which appeared in the BPD leads. Further discussions were being held regarding Noel's disclosure between the DA, BPD, and later, Noel's attorney. As a result, a meeting was held on June 16, 2011, and a Debriefing Agreement was prepared for Noel. It stated, should he elect to provide assistance and cooperation to the DA or law enforcement, consideration could be extended to him on the charges he currently had pending. It added that the extent of any consideration would be solely up to the DA's Office.

Earlier, I mentioned sharing some disturbing details regarding a desperate jailhouse snitch who had asked, "What's in this for me?" And as we've just learned, his name was Jesse Noel. So, let's jump forward a few days to June 28, 2011, to learn what happened when Senior ADA DeLucia and his team of investigators interviewed Noel at the Broome County Jail. This time, though, the camera was rolling.

When DeLucia and company made their entrance, Jesse Noel, dressed in an orange jumpsuit, was seated at a small table across from his attorney, Mark Rappaport. After brief introductions, DeLucia asked, "Have you had enough time to talk?" Noel answered, "Yeah, basically I have." DeLucia added, "Cause there's no rush." Then mentioned having spoken to him earlier and said, "I have a general idea of what you're going to say." DeLucia then reviewed and explained the Debriefing Agreement. After reading and signing the agreement, DeLucia continued with, "So, basically Jesse, tell us again what you had to say." Before answering, DeLucia added, "Obviously, be as honest as possible, as painfully honest as you can. Because obviously, we do our homework on things so, you've got to tell us the god's honest truth, okay?" Noel nodded and explained:

| Jesse Noel – Jail Interview

"One night after this happened, she calls me, right? She says Chucky came over here and forced his way in. He'd told her if she don't come back to his home, he was going to kill her. So, she called and told me that. The next day, me, Lips, and Weezy go over there. My intent was to beat Chucky up. However, when I got there, I said, dude, what the hell happened? Like, what happened? Why you threatening her? And what happened to little junior? Chucky said, 'I don't know, she was cheatin' on me, so I was upset with her.' I'm telling you this is what he said, 'The kids were always whining and crying and stuff at night, and I couldn't take it.' He said he got upset, picked the little kid up, and said, 'shut up, shut up,' and slammed him into the frickin wall and then said he just lost it and kicked him. And after he realized what he did, he put the little boy back to bed. I know that's what I know and was told. That was at his house, on Henry Street in the hallway."

A question was asked, "Weezy and Lips were with you?" He answered, "Yes."

The next question they asked was, "Anybody else?"

"No," Noel replied.

DeLucia followed up with, "Yeah. I gotta tell you, I mean, look, I'm not trying to give you a hard time, but obviously, we don't usually ask questions we don't already know the answers to. I mean, we've done our homework when it comes to Weezy and Lips and stuff like that." Noel said, "What are they sayin'? They sayin' I'm lying?" DeLucia again said, "I mean, it's just not making any sense. The first thing that comes to mind is if Chucky is the guy with Veronica and you're the guy with Veronica, and I'm Chucky, why tell me?" Noel said, "I can't explain that." DeLucia added, "But then you told Veronica Taft?" Noel replied, "I did tell Veronica, Deanna, and the Spanish girl downstairs. I said, yo, you need to explain it to the authorities. She said, I know, but I'm scared, man. Like, that's what I know."

Investigator Wagner jumped in and said, "We talked to Weezy. He said, don't be making up lies about me to save your ass." Then added, "Veronica Taft, I'm not going to get into all the details, but I'm gonna tell you. We've been talking to her with her attorney about this. She never made mention of your admission. Veronica knows we're on to her. We talked to Deanna. I'm going to tell you exactly what I think here, Jesse. I know how these things go sometimes. You tell a story to the police. You gotta stick with it. Today's your chance. From right now to move forward. My exact feeling is from talking with everybody, and I have a good feeling for this case. My partner and I have worked this every day. We talked to a hundred people on this. You and Veronica. This is what I'm absolutely 99.9 percent sure. Veronica, and this is coming from our conversations with her and everybody else, Veronica has sometime approached you to alibi her." Noel quickly replied, "No. No. No. No."

Wager continued, "Your story is not jibing with everybody here. People that want to see an arrest made. These people have been cooperative." Noel replied, "I can see where you're coming from." Wagner came back saying, "These girls have no reason...," but doesn't finish before saying, "Veronica knows she's about to get arrested. She knows that. It's never been, hold on, or time out. Jesse told me that Chucky made admissions to him and what happened. Nobody can sit in the hot seat and go down for it if they know someone else did it on a murder." Noel replied, "I understand. I'm just telling you what I know, man. I'm not that much in love with her that I'm going to alibi her for a murder. I know of Chucky's admission to myself. I know for a fact that Weezy and Lips was there. I'm not trying to alibi her."

Wager asked, "Why would you sit on an admission of a two-and-a-half-year-old who was killed – murdered? Why would you sit on that? Why would anybody sit on that?" Noel replied, "Because I told her, like I said before, where I come from, that's like snitching. Nobody ever came to me, and I told her what to do."

Wagner said, "You and I went over that, Jesse, when we talked. You know better than I do. There isn't one person in the Broome County Jail or any prison in New York state or anywhere that's going to look at you as a snitch for a two-and-half-year-old being murdered."

By now, Noel was already starting to realize that they didn't believe his story. But they kept hammering away and made it crystal clear that nothing he was saying made any sense. But he was desperately searching for a way out that could still save his deal without admitting he'd been lying. Recognizing his vulnerability, DA investigator Ingrid Segrue gave him the out he was looking for when she asked, "Did *she* tell you that's what happened? Is that what *she* said happened?" For a brief moment, Noel just stared straight ahead with a stunned look on his face but didn't say a word. He then turned and looked at Mr. Rappaport but still didn't say anything. Finally, Wagner broke the silence and asked, "Do you want to talk to your attorney?"

After that, Noel and Rappaport stepped into an adjoining private room to talk, shutting off the camera. Just over four minutes later, the camera came back on as they reentered the interview room. Rappaport said, "I think Jesse wants to change his story a little bit here." Someone said, "That's fine." Then Wagner added, "Well, we need the truth, Jesse, okay? We understand how things are, and that's why we're giving you a clean slate." Rappaport turned to Jesse and said, "All I can say, Jesse, is I'm not one of them. I'm over here with you, but I'm also saying to you, they don't want the wrong person to go upstate. They're not just trying to get a conviction to say yeah, we got somebody. They want to get the right person. If they don't get the right person, then they haven't done their job, you know? I'm often on the other side, but I do know that most of them, and these guys, in particular, try to do the right thing and not just the easy thing, especially in a serious case like this. Tell them what you know and what happened. And be honest with them."

As a reminder, Noel had already been in dialogue with the BPD and DA's office for over two weeks, where he stated consistently, on three or more occasions, including just minutes earlier, that Charles Pratt was the one who admitted to killing Lyric. And DeLucia made it clear from the very beginning that he needed to be as honest as possible. As painfully honest as he can. But now, the pressure was on for the "real" truth.

As a result, knowing he'd been lying all along, Noel found himself between a rock and a hard place. Because no matter how hard he tried, his interviewers made it clear they didn't believe him. Initially, he thought he would receive consideration for the charges pending against him by telling them about Pratt's admission. But now, they had him by the short hairs, and if he didn't tell them what they wanted to hear, the deal was off, and he'd be going to prison.

Faced with the ultimatum of prison vs. freedom, Noel opted for his freedom. But now, there was only one way he could make that happen. He already knew what they wanted to hear because they'd just told him that Veronica was about to be arrested. So, all he had to do was flip his story.

Therefore, Noel offered the following:

> "Veronica told me that she just couldn't take it. Just couldn't take it. CPS all her life. She'd been up all night and just couldn't take it. The kids were getting on her nerves, and he reminded her of his father, who was a

cantankerous ass. That was her words. And she just lost it. She was the one that picked him up and slammed him against the wall."

Later, when questioned further, he claimed she had called him late one night at his girlfriend's house and told him everything. He thought it was in mid-January but wasn't sure of the exact date. As the questioning continued, he was asked if she had said anything about what she may have done afterward? He said, "I don't know, man. I didn't get into that." Wagner asked, "What did she say the other kids were doing?" He replied, "They were in their room." Wagner again asked, "So, to kind of get this straight. What you told us originally is the truth, except it was Veronica. Okay so, Veronica slammed him into a wall and kicked him?" He answered, "And she was the one who put him in bed." Wagner again asked, "What did she tell you about that night? Did she tell you anything about the next day? About discovering him? Well, did she say he was dead or..." Noel replied, "No. All she said was that she ran across the street to the neighbor's house, and they came back over there to do CPR or something. And Chucky got upset and punched the wall. I don't know, man."

Continuing, Wagner asked, "After that, how often did you talk to her?" He replied, "After that, I didn't speak to her again until February 22, when I was moving to Eldridge Street." Later, he said she'd called him again for his birthday in mid-March. Then he advised that he had seen her in person on March 21st at a bowling alley but didn't talk to her. He then added, "I think the last time I spoke to her was about two days before I got locked up." Continuing, he claimed that Veronica had told him, "I know I'm a suspect, and I know they're looking at me."

Later, Wagner asked, "Did there ever come a point in time where she said she needed your help?" Although it wasn't clear what he was trying to ask, it seemed as though he was interested in knowing whether Veronica had asked him to lie for her by saying that Pratt did this. But it didn't seem as though Noel had answered his question. So, in following up, Wager asked, "I don't mean to beat a dead horse, but I don't think I got the answer. Did she ever tell you to lie to the police about this, or did she ever say I would like you to go to the police, either or?" Noel replied quickly, "No."

Considering Noel's answer to that last question, I think Wagner's bubble busted. If you recall, he'd said earlier, "This is what I'm absolutely 99.9 percent sure. Veronica has sometime approached you to alibi her." Yet, during my review of all police reports provided, I hadn't found a single witness who told the police that or even suspected it. So, where that 99.9 percent figure came from is anyone's guess. Perhaps, it was simply a pressure tactic used to try and get Noel to change his story. But most likely, it was nothing more than Wagner's speculation or wishful thinking. Regardless, with Noel's sudden "epiphany," DeLucia and company now had what they needed to continue their pursuit of Veronica Taft, which would ultimately lead to her arrest. After that, Wagner sat down and obtained Noel's formal statement as DeLucia looked on.

Shortly into his statement, Wagner commented, "We want to make sure this is the truth." Then added, "We've looked at everything." While writing out Noel's statement, Wagner asked a few questions to help clarify what he'd said earlier about what Veronica had told him. Noel added, "She told me he's crying. Won't stay where she put him. Wouldn't stay in his bed or his room." Then later, after describing Veronica's admission to slamming him into the wall, he said, "If you look at it, it's like a child's size hole there too." Continuing, Wagner couldn't let go of his 99.9 percent figure and asked again, "Are you sure she never told you to tell the police Charles Pratt, did it?" "Right," he said.

Initially, believing that Chucky was responsible for Lyric's murder, I wanted to believe Noel's earlier story that his admission to killing Lyric was the actual version. Furthermore, I wanted to believe that he'd only changed his story out of fear of losing his deal and going to prison. Then selfishly threw Veronica under the bus to save himself by telling the police what they wanted to hear. Later, however, under closer scrutiny, I found several reasons to believe that Noel had lied, not only about Veronica's admission but Chucky's as well. For many reasons, I was not overly impressed with the way this investigation was being handled. However, in my assessment of Noel's claim about Chucky's admission, I did find myself agreeing with DeLucia and Wagner, who were telling Noel his story wasn't making any sense. DeLucia had challenged Noel by saying, "The first thing that comes to mind is if Chucky is the guy with Veronica and you're the guy with Veronica, and I'm Chucky, why tell me?" Good question. And I didn't like Noel's answer either when he replied, "I can't explain that."

DeLucia was right. Chucky and Jesse were not friends. They didn't even like each other. But it was more about Chucky not liking Jesse. If you recall, Chucky had just learned a few days earlier, when Veronica had her miscarriage, that Jesse was the father. And he was pissed. Therefore, I agreed with DeLucia because it seemed highly unlikely that Chucky would ever admit murder to Noel. In addition, Wagner had challenged him by asking why he would sit on an admission of a two-and-a-half-year-old who was killed – murdered? Why would anybody sit on that? To which Noel replied it was like snitching. Nobody ever came to him, and he told her what to do. Wagner had also challenged him when he claimed to have told Veronica and two others about Chucky's confession. Then explained having talked to those people, including Veronica. None of them knew anything about it.

Furthermore, there were even more things that led me to believe he was lying. If you recall, one of the first things he said after changing his story was that Veronica had been up all night and just couldn't take it. Up all night? Agreed. But she was up all night at work – not at home. Then later, when Wagner was taking his statement, they talked about the hole in the wall when he tried to improve his story by adding that it was like a child-size hole there – making it sound as if he'd been there and seen it. When in fact, he'd never been there after it happened because Veronica wasn't there. So, from where did that description come?

Also, there was a discrepancy in Noel's timing regarding the day he'd gone to Chucky's place with Weezy and Lips. Initially, he claimed it was mid-January, about three weeks after Lyric was killed. But in his final interview, he claimed they had gone over there after Veronica called to tell him about Chucky forcing his way into her apartment and threatening her. But that didn't happen until February 22, 2011. He was just making stuff up as he went along.

The bottom line was that there was no confession by Chucky or Veronica. Noel just made up the story to save himself. But was anything truthful? Or was everything just one big lie? It's hard to say for sure. However, what I learned later, led me to believe that perhaps part of his story was true.

III

THE ARREST

ARRESTED FOR MURDER

By mid-August 2011, nearly eight months had passed since Lyric's brutal murder. DeLucia's team was entering the final stage of their investigation, tightening up any loose ends in preparation for Taft's arrest. Previously, Chucky had been threatening Veronica on various occasions. But after their most recent encounter in late February, where he broke in, assaulted, and threatened to kill her, Veronica packed her things and moved to Syracuse to live with a friend. She only returned to Binghamton for her one-hour visits with her children at DSS, which were limited to once every other week.

On August 25, 2011, a Felony Complaint was prepared by the BPD, accusing Veronica Taft of the criminal offense of Murder in the Second Degree, a violation of section 125.25 sub. 4, of the Penal Law of the State of New York, a Class A-1 Felony.

The Felony Complaint alleged that on the 30th day of December 2010, Veronica became upset with her two-year-old son, Lyric Taft, at which time she picked him up and banged him into the wall, causing him to sustain severe trauma, which eventually caused his death.

During my review of the complaint, a few things jumped out at me right away. Right off the top, they got the date of death wrong. Or did they? And notably missing was any estimated time that it allegedly took place. According to their new theory, they alleged Veronica had killed Lyric *before* she went to work on the 29th. Thus, the wrong date.

In contrast, according to the estimated time of death, it happened on the 30th. If that's the case, it wasn't Veronica. But somewhere along the line, I figured they would likely recognize their mistake and amend the date.

The second part of their complaint was a bit more troubling. Its claim that Lyric had been killed after Veronica became upset with him was nothing but speculation. There wasn't a single witness, not even her own children, or any evidence whatsoever, absolutely nothing, to support that theory. I was somewhat surprised there was no mention of the deadly "black spoon." Incredibly, they further alleged that she'd picked him up and banged him into the wall. That wasn't true either, and they knew it.

So, what *did* they know? During Chucky's interview on day one, he admitted punching a hole in the wall with both fists and bloodying his knuckles, which he showed to investigators. Similarly, during Veronica's interview that day, she explained how she'd witnessed him punching the wall. Additionally, Sergeant Stebbins claimed to have examined the hole and found no evidence linking it to Lyric's death. They'd known all this for eight months. But suddenly, that version disappeared. Only to magically reappear eight months later, with a completely different version. One where it was Veronica who was banging Lyric's head into the wall. It was ludicrous. Perhaps the saying is true: "Desperate people can make themselves believe anything."

Four days later, on August 29th, the Felony Complaint against Veronica Taft was presented to a Binghamton City Court Judge, who subsequently issued an arrest warrant charging her with Murder in the Second Degree.

Meanwhile, when she was living with her friend near Syracuse, NY, Veronica received a phone call from a young friend named Deanna Bryant, who used to babysit for her. Deanna was crying and upset, telling Veronica she was frightened and had something important to tell her but didn't want to talk about it over the phone. Veronica explained that the soonest they could meet was September 1st, when she would be in Binghamton visiting her children at DSS. Deanna wanted to meet sooner but agreed to wait and meet right after she visited her children.

As fate would have it, as soon as Veronica walked out the door from DSS on September 1st, she was arrested. So, whatever it was that Deanna was frightened of and didn't want to talk about on the phone remained a mystery. The mystery deepened after Deanna was found dead in a friend's apartment just over two months later.

Veronica had been cooperating with the investigation since day one and staying in regular contact with her attorney, David Butler. But suddenly, now that an arrest warrant had been issued, she apparently had become a flight risk. So, rather than arrange to have Butler surrender his client, they preferred a more dramatic, high-profile approach for the arrest. Choosing the element of surprise, they contacted CPS and learned that Veronica's next visitation with her children was scheduled for 9:30 a.m. on September 1, 2011. Armed with her arrest warrant, a team of five investigators and one uniformed officer sat outside the DSS building, waiting for Veronica to make her exit after visiting her children. Then, right on schedule, at 10:30 a.m., she was seen exiting the building and was quickly taken into custody without incident.

While being searched, her cell phone was seized and later logged in as evidence. She was hustled to BPD headquarters, where she was booked on the charge of Murder in the Second Degree. Then shortly after that, she appeared before a City Court Judge to be arraigned. A technical plea of "not guilty" was entered on her behalf, and she was immediately remanded to the Broome County Jail without bail to await a grand jury proceeding.

| Veronica Taft – Arrest Photo

Author's note: Before her arrest, while living in Syracuse, Veronica became pregnant again. At the time of her arrest, she was in her 2nd trimester.

Two days later, on September 3rd, the first report of Taft's arrest appeared in the local *Press & Sun-Bulletin* newspaper. Staff reporter Nancy Dooling wrote the headline, "Mother charged in death of her child," with the sub-headline, "Zikuski: Boy suffered from multiple traumas." Dooling reported that, according to neighbors, Veronica Taft had loud parties in her apartment in the days and weeks after her son Lyric died there. Neighbors also claimed that she left her apartment a few weeks after her son died.

Other than a day or two in late February, Veronica never went back to her apartment in the days following her son's murder. Therefore, if there was any partying going on, it didn't include her. Also, it was Chucky who went back to her apartment after being instructed not to.

Dooling further reported interviewing BPD's Chief of Police, Joseph Zikuski, who declined to say why the investigation took so long. He said only that it was "a difficult investigation" with "difficult witnesses" and long hours. He praised his detectives and the Broome County DA's Office staff for their work on the case. "Difficult witnesses?" Indeed.

Less than a week later, on September 7th, a Broome County grand jury handed down an eight-count indictment against Veronica Taft. Now formally charged with two major felonies, including Murder in the Second Degree and Manslaughter in the First Degree, as well as six misdemeanor counts of Endangering the Welfare of a Child. As a result, she had to appear before a Broome County Court Judge for an arraignment on the indictment. Where once again, a not guilty plea was entered on her behalf. Bail was set at $100,000/$200,000. In other words, $100,000 cash or $200,000 property bond. But bail for Veronica was not an option. She couldn't have scraped up $1,000, let alone $100,000. Therefore, she was remanded to jail once again. This time, to await her trial.

Interestingly, however, shortly after Veronica's indictment was announced, Jesse Noel called Butler's office inquiring about bail. Was he feeling a bit guilty, perhaps? Rest assured, we will hear more from Jesse Noel. But for now, let's back up a bit for a brief look at what took place in the grand jury.

27

GRAND JURY

As we just learned, Veronica had been arrested on September 1, 2011, and less than a week later, a panel of grand jurors was seated to hear the case against her. After that, Senior ADA DeLucia presented his case by calling several witnesses. Some testimony was more pertinent than others, so I'll focus more on some of the highlights rather than repeating much of what we already know.

Author's note: In New York State, by law, any witness who offers evidence to a grand jury, unless waived in writing, automatically receives Transactional Immunity, also known as "blanket" immunity, which legally protects the witness from any future prosecution of any crime related to their testimony.

DeLucia set the stage by calling the first patrol officer to arrive at the Taft apartment, followed by the neighbor who did CPR, then the EMTs. Interestingly, when Patrol Officer John Taylor testified, he was asked for his impression as to the warmth or coolness of the Taft apartment. As mentioned earlier, he answered, "It was normal temperature." Following up, DeLucia asked, "Room temperature, in other words?" Taylor answered, "Yes."

Next up was Dr. Terzian, who described his autopsy findings in graphic detail, with the supporting photographs. More specifically describing the two fatal injuries. Those being the head trauma which caused a swelling of the brain and the lacerated liver. The laceration in the liver, he said, "was about two inches long and one inch deep, just split open like a ripe tomato." When asked if he had reached any conclusion about the cause of death, he said, "Yes, the cause of death was multiple blunt traumatic injuries to the head and abdomen. The mechanism of death was exsanguination or bleeding to death from those injuries."

Later, he identified some of the things used to determine the time of death, such as cooling of the body (*algor mortis*) and stiffening of the muscles (*rigor mortis*). Then, he described some of the things that could interfere with those findings: body size, humidity, clothing, or a hot or cold temperature at the scene. Then added, "It's really a pretty inexact science, I'm afraid."

Continuing, he was asked how long it takes the stomach to empty after a meal. He answered, "In general, as a rule of thumb, the stomach will empty a regulation size meal in an hour or two at most.

From there, the questioning turned to Lyric's rectal temperature taken at the hospital. DeLucia asked, "Given what you know about the injuries to Lyric, is it conceivable that he could have died on the evening of the 29th of December?" Dr. Terzian answered, "Yes, that's possible." DeLucia went a step further and asked, "So, for example, is it within the bounds of possibility that he could have died at least maybe 12, 13, 14 hours prior to his arrival at the hospital?" He answered, "That is possible." After finishing his questioning, DeLucia opened it up for questions from the grand jurors.

Author's note: Unlike trial jurors, grand jurors are permitted to ask questions of the witnesses.

A grand juror asked, "You were asked about if the time of death could have been like 12 to 14 hours or whatever. Could it also have been a wider range than that?" Terzian replied, "The range is really difficult to pin down in this case. I mean, I would say it's less than 18 hours. That doesn't help too much, I know. But I can't say beyond that with any degree of certainty because of all of the compounding factors here. As I understand, Lyric was originally found in his bed under covers, clothed in a warm environment. I mean, so that changes all the parameters that we just talked about. It slows down the drop in body temperature. Normally, the body temperature post-mortem drops about one-and-a-half degrees per hour for the first several hours. I was told the body temperature was 86 degrees. If we assume he started at 98.6, you've got a 12.6-degree drop. You divide by one-and-a-half. You know, that just creates a few hours. Then you have to account for the situation where he was found, the ambient temperature, the clothing, the bedding, which slows it down."

The juror asked, "You don't think it's any less than 12, or 12 to 18?" Terzian answered, "Well, it could be less than 12, and it could be perhaps up to 18, but I just can't say for sure in this case."

As a final question, the juror asked about the 50 grams of food in Lyric's stomach and how fast food would empty from his stomach. Terzian explained it would take between one and two hours to empty from the stomach itself but not entirely from the abdominal cavity. Then he explained further, saying, "That suggests to me that he died within an hour or two of his last meal."

Not surprisingly, DeLucia had steered entirely away from Terzian's original 3:00 to 4:00 a.m. time of death estimate. In other words, the eight-and-a-half hours he initially calculated from his rule of thumb formula. By having Terzian agree that it could be "within the bounds of possibility," as much as eighteen hours, he'd just created an error rate of more than 100 percent. I found it troubling that Terzian was still using his rule of thumb formula for an average size adult of 1.5 degrees per hour. When initially, he'd told the BPD, due to Lyric's small size, it was more like two degrees per hour. Or perhaps even more.

Also, Terzian testified about all of the compounding factors here that could change the parameters of his calculation: specifically, being clothed and under covers in bed in a warm environment. The only problem with that was that it wasn't a warm environment. The kids' bedroom was cold. Besides, nothing was ever found to suggest that it was anything other than average room temperature. But for the sake of argument, let's say that it was warmer than average. Even though Terzian mentioned the stiffening of muscles (rigor mortis) as one of the means used to help determine the time of death, he failed or avoided mentioning what effect a warm environment would have on rigor. Unlike the body's cooling (algor mortis), which can be slowed due to abnormally warm conditions, that same effect on rigor mortis is just the opposite. A warm environment will speed up the onset of rigor. But as we've already learned, only the earliest onset of rigor was described by the ER doctors. It can't be both ways.

Needless to say, I was anxious to read through Chucky's grand jury testimony. For the most part, it was as bizarre as I suspected. The following were a few of the highlights. After establishing his relationship with Veronica and the children and a few other details, Chucky testified about going over that night to babysit and what happened after Veronica left for work. He explained that his brother Jemel was there and how he had fixed macaroni and cheese and Tater-tots for the kids and his brother. He said, "First I made the kids a plate, four plates, then I made him a plate." He then went on to explain how he was getting tired and had already gotten undressed. Later, he was asked, "When you started getting ready for bed when Veronica called you, at that point, had you seen any of the children?" He answered, "At that point, no. At that point, when I was making the food and cleaning up, I put on three movies. I had the movies rewinded for them. That would be *Mean Girls, Winnie the Pooh,* and *Mrs. Doubtfire.* So, I had everything ready for them, prepped to go to bed and watch TV." He was asked, "At that point, did you see Lyric at all?" "No, I haven't, but I knew his plate was empty."

For those who remember, rewinding VHS tapes can take a while, even more so when you have three to do. Considering what he just said, he would have spent that time standing in front of the TV stand, in the kids' bedroom, with Lyric lying on the bed right next to him, no more than two feet away.

| Kid's Bedroom

Moving on to early the following day, he explained that Zoey had woke up crying around 5:30 or 6:00 a.m. He'd picked her up and brought her into Veronica's room. Then, when Veronica came home a little after 7:00 a.m., she'd told him to fix her a bottle and put her back in bed. He said, "So that's what I did. From there, I tucked everybody in besides Lyric. Lyric was already tucked in."

From there, his testimony about what happened after Lyric was discovered was reasonably consistent with what he'd said earlier, including his punching the wall and claiming that it was done in frustration of the situation with Lyric.

Later, he claimed to have ended his relationship with Veronica after hearing that she had been cheating and prostituting. Even though he'd just said, "I was in the midst of trying to get her to stay." Then added, "Basically we ended it when she moved out to Syracuse."

"Trying to get her to stay?" He certainly had a strange way of doing that. If you recall, what caused Veronica to pack up and move to Syracuse on February 22, 2011? It was because Chucky had forced his way into her apartment, threatened to kill her, and physically assaulted her. That's a hell of a way to try and get someone to stay.

Continuing, DeLucia ended his questioning by asking if he knew a person named Jesse Noel. He answered, "Jesse Noel. Jesse Noel. Jesse Noel. It sounds familiar." DeLucia again asked, "So you don't know that person?" He answered, "No."

The questioning was then turned over to the jurors. The first question was, "I thought you fed him?" Chucky answered, "I did feed him. I made four plates." The next question was, "Did you actually see Lyric eating food?" He answered, "No, I haven't because I was busy cleaning." At this point, I knew the juror wasn't buying his story, but it got worse.

The juror asked, "You didn't find that odd that the other kids were eating?" He answered, "I know the other kids was eating."

The juror asked, "So, Lyric was the only one that you didn't see that night?" He answered, "I don't know because I was busy cleaning up." Okay, so let's think about that for a moment. Didn't he just admit to seeing Lyric's empty plate and all three of the other kids eating while he was cleaning up? But he never saw Lyric?

Later, another juror asked, "Had you ever noticed any bruising the day before?" He answered, "No because Lyric stay – he have pajamas on." The juror asked, "He what?" Chucky replied, "He stay – he having pajamas on." His answer was a bit confusing, but apparently, DeLucia knew what he was trying to say and asked, "He kept his pajamas on?" He answered, "Yes, pajamas." What Chucky was trying to say was that Lyric stayed in his pajamas. Isn't that interesting. So, why was Lyric in his street clothes? And where were his pajamas?

Nearing the end of his testimony, without being asked a specific question, he felt compelled to offer a statement saying, "You know, this is not the first family I've been with kids. Do you understand what I'm saying? I'm good with kids. My business, you know. I want to go back to college for business and accounting. I want to run a daycare center. These are my goals. I love kids, but I don't have kids, you know."

Occasionally, between juror questions, DeLucia would jump back in with more of his questions. At one point, he'd asked Chucky whether he'd ever checked on Lyric that night. Using the example, "Like checking on their covers?" He said, "No, I don't go in their room. You know, everybody know how kids are with their room. They leave a mess. I usually clean up their room, but I'm saying to myself, what's the point of me keep on cleaning it when they're going to keep dirtying it. So, I don't go in their room." I don't think DeLucia was prepared for that answer when he said, "That's the subject for a long conversation, but we can't get into that."

But continuing, he asked, "So, in other words, during the night of the 29th, the morning of the 30th, until you found Lyric, you hadn't checked him or seen him?" His odd answer was, "No, because, like I said, I don't go in their room because it's three females, one male. I always been brought up saying never go in their room where there's kids at." Call it what you will but for me, considering everything he'd said earlier, that made no sense whatsoever – utter nonsense. For now, I'll just leave it at that.

After Chucky finished with his testimony, his brother, Jemel Fields, was called. For the most part, Fields backed up his brother's testimony regarding the evening of December 29th at Veronica's apartment. Like his brother Chucky, he claimed that he, too, had only seen the girls and had never seen Lyric. He confirmed that Chucky had fixed plates of macaroni and cheese and Tater-tots for the kids, including a plate for himself that he took into the game room to eat while watching a movie. He remembered the two older girls being in the game room when he first went in and later coming out to eat. Later, after he'd finished eating, he brought his empty plate out to the kitchen, at which time he saw Chucky in his pajamas.

Jemel was also asked if he'd ever seen Chucky disciplining the children in any way. He answered, "No. Like I wouldn't call it – like telling them that they can't be in a certain place like because they smoke cigarettes and stuff like that." DeLucia asked, "Who smokes cigarettes?" He answered, "Like Chuck. Chuck smokes cigarettes, and he usually tell them not to be around. He's like, oh, you can't be in the room. I'm smoking right now. So, you have to leave. Like that's the only discipline I actually have witnessed myself."

Chucky smoked cigarettes? Okay, but we already knew that from his interview on December 30th. We also learned that Veronica was not a smoker. In and of itself, that doesn't mean much. Interestingly, however, recalling earlier when Lyric was being examined and treated at the hospital, ER doctors discovered and described what appeared to them as a possible burn mark on his left ear. Considering what Fields just said, if it was a cigarette burn, absent any other explanation, was that just a coincidence? Maybe. Maybe not.

Investigator Matt Zandy's testimony focused on the photographs he'd taken during his examination of the crime scene on December 30th and later on January 19th. Consistent with what Sergeant Stebbins had written in her report, he testified that Taft's apartment temperature on December 30th was extremely warm. Later, he was asked what the temperature reading was when they returned to her apartment three weeks later? He answered, "74 degrees Fahrenheit." Initially, however, he never offered what room that temperature was taken from, or was he ever asked. It was only after his testimony about the single space heater in the living room when a juror asked, "It wasn't central air?" He answered, "That one unit, to my understanding, supplied the heat to the entire apartment. The juror added, "That would make the back bedroom, the children's room really much cooler."

From my perspective, the juror's question was right on target. Without central heating and the only heat source being that space heater in the living room, it would logically be much cooler in the rooms furthest away. But in response, Zandy said, "I don't know if I would say that."

We've already learned the story behind Jesse Noel. But now, he would have to tell his story before the grand jury, under oath. After establishing his brief relationship with Veronica, the questioning turned to the call he allegedly received from Veronica on January 10, 2011, around 2:00 a.m. From there, he went on to testify about Veronica's alleged confession. For the most part, he described a similar scenario to what we learned earlier. He claimed Lyric kept crying and screaming, so she grabbed him, shook him, and slammed his head into the wall. Explaining further that after he fell to the floor, she kicked him.

Continuing, he claimed she had told him how upset she was with all types of things, especially with child support in her life. DeLucia asked, "You mean Child Protective?" He answered, "Yes, Child Protective agencies were at her. Also, they were there that day, they had been coming there harassing her about the children, and she just lost it. You know, she just lost it. I mean, she lost her control of herself."

Not surprisingly, Noel had just added another lie to his story. He was trying to strengthen it by claiming that Veronica's ongoing issues with CPS, including that very day, were what pushed her over the edge – causing her to "lose it" and kill Lyric. That's what he wanted the grand jury to believe. But the truth was, CPS was not there that day, the day before, or the day before. In fact, according to their records, CPS had closed their family services case on Veronica more than two months earlier. Nice try, Jesse.

He admitted when talking to the police earlier that he hadn't been truthful and told a different story – it was Chucky who had confessed. When asked why, he answered, "Well, I also had feelings for Veronica, too, and then it was like I assumed it was – I just – I don't know. All I can say is I did that, but then I realized, hey, I can be putting the wrong person in jail." Wow! By the way, just one month after Veronica was indicted, Noel was released after spending less than four months in jail. Not a bad deal for a second felony offender.

At the time, Investigator Wagner had about 14-years of experience with the BPD. He was called to testify about his interview with Veronica on December 30th, moments after learning of her son's death. DeLucia had asked him to describe her demeanor. He said, "It's hard for me to describe. I don't – I guess everybody's different, but I don't think she acted like I would have if I lost a child. She seemed pretty calm." DeLucia asked, "Was she crying at all?" He answered, "No. No." Apparently, Wagner never watched the videotape.

Interestingly, however, when they were later reviewing the videotape of her interview, DeLucia, referring to the video, asked, "We are now seeing a person on the left crying. Is that Veronica Taft?" He answered, "This is Veronica Taft." So, she was crying. And it wasn't just that one time. She can be seen crying quite often. Later, Wagner even admitted during the latter part of his testimony that "Every now and then she would cry."

From there, Wagner testified how Veronica had changed her story a few times – specifically regarding her explanation about the last time she saw Lyric and where he was in bed. Nothing was ever mentioned about her being distraught, in a state of shock, or the emotional crisis she was in, having just learned of her son's death. Equally important was Wagner's failure to mention how Veronica admitted to being confused and may have gotten her days mixed up.

Near the end of his testimony, questioning was turned over to the jurors. One of them asked, "On December 30th, at this instance, she was not arrested?" Wagner answered, "No, she wasn't, sir." The juror asked, "Is it correct for me to understand that she volunteered to sit with you for three-and-half hours?" "That is correct," Wagner answered. "What was the last date that Child Protective Services paid a visit to her apartment?" the juror continued. DeLucia quickly interrupted and said, "We can't ask the investigator." He had Wagner explain how he played no role with CPS. In response, the juror said, "I thought I heard someone say that they were there that morning."

The juror was right, of course. It was Jesse Noel who testified that CPS had been at Veronica's apartment that day. The juror was doubtful about whether that was true and was looking for confirmation. Even though Wagner could have answered his question, DeLucia wouldn't let him because he wasn't part of CPS. That's understandable. But it was still a valid question and the grand jury, being an investigative body, had a right to know. It could have and should have been easily resolved by calling a witness from CPS. But DeLucia knew if he did that, it would have undermined Noel's testimony. Which, in turn, would likely have destroyed his credibility and ruined everything.

As a final witness, Investigator Anthony Diles was called. For the most part, his testimony was about the second interview of Veronica he conducted along with Investigator Corey Minor on January 1st. Shortly into his testimony, he was asked to read Veronica's written statement – the one he had taken from her during the first part of her interview. After that, his subsequent testimony focused on the remaining portion of Veronica's interview after she'd given her statement. He explained, "During the time that we were speaking at the first portion with her that morning, other investigators were speaking to other witnesses or locating people to interview them. More information was being discovered. It happened that the tides turned." They did indeed.

Continuing, he added, "At the time we got done, and I'd taken the statement from her, some of the detectives came in with further background information about Ms. Taft and her family to us from other detectives." In other words, the cry-ladies. After that, he explained how her Miranda rights were read to her, which she signed, and then agreed to continue speaking with them.

Later, DeLucia asked him to describe what happened after her Miranda rights. Then, he asked whether or not there was any change in her demeanor or topic of conversation. He answered, "During the first portion of the interview, she seemed kind of flat, not necessarily overly interested or emotional certainly. Soon into the second portion, she seemed sort of defensive right away to me. I wouldn't say completely argumentative, but certainly, I would say defensive. In asking questions, she did eventually become sort of upset with us at the nature of the things we were asking about."

Kind of flat? Not overly interested? How can he say that? Wasn't it Veronica who was telling them, on two or more occasions, that once they establish the time of death, they would know it wasn't her? Why would she offer that if she thought it might point to her? And wasn't it Veronica who mentioned Lyric's stomach contents and said, "Cause you can tell how long it's been there, can't you?" She was trying to encourage them to do their job. Yet she's flat and not overly interested? Nonsense. Or, as Veronica might say, "bull crap."

Near the end of his testimony, DeLucia inquired about the earlier portion of the interview. Then asked if she'd ever used any language during that interview that she was sorry about what happened to her child or was she upset? Did she vocalize about being upset or distraught? Having repeatedly watched her interview, I knew what his answer should have been. As such, I found it troubling to hear him say, "I don't remember specific statements. I guess the best way I can say is, I don't recall seeing any tears from her, any over-the-top emotion. I know how I would react if my child passed away. She seemed emotionally flat." Wow! He must still be wearing those reality blinders. For someone who's supposedly a 'trained observer'– well, enough said. I'll just leave it at that.

IV

PREPARING VERONICA'S DEFENSE

28

IN DEFENSE OF VERONICA

A little over a month after Veronica's indictment, attorney David Butler received and started reviewing the first batch of discovery material, including copies of all the pertinent information the prosecution intended to use at trial. After spending another month studying the material, I received a call from Butler's office. Dave and I had worked together on several different cases previously and had a good working rapport. During the call, I learned he had recently accepted a new murder case involving a young woman named Veronica Taft, who'd been charged with murdering her two-year-old son back in December of 2010. I remembered a little something from what I'd read in the newspaper. After giving me a very brief run-down of the case, the first thing that caught my attention was the eight-month delay before an arrest was made. He then asked if I would be interested in the case. I said, "Well, it certainly sounds interesting, but I'd like to learn more." He said, "I was hoping you'd say that. Let's meet at my office, and we'll go over everything."

Later, I met with him at his office for a more thorough case briefing. After learning about all the various issues involved, including the time of death, Veronica's alibi, and more, it didn't take long to decide I was interested and agreed to adopt a case. I was anxious to get started right away. Shortly after that, Butler's paralegal made copies of all the discovery material for my review in preparation for my subsequent investigation. I had my work cut out for me.

In the days and weeks that followed, I spent many long, painstaking hours getting up to speed on every aspect of the case by thoroughly reviewing every piece of discovery. Including, but not limited to, police reports, photographs, videotapes, witness interviews, witness statements, CPS reports, hospital medical records, EMT reports, autopsy reports, phone records, ID reports, evidence logs, diagrams, search warrants, and more. Along the way, making notes, observations, cross-referencing, fact-checking, and identifying any and all witnesses, evidence, and investigative leads to follow-up. Then, repeating the same process as needed.

After reviewing everything in the discovery materials, I already had a pretty good grasp of everything. However, I was still left with more questions than answers. Therefore, I knew I still had a lot of work ahead of me. And ordinarily, a good place to start is with the accused. But before I did that, I wanted to see what I could learn from a few of the other known characters.

Previously, we learned about the CPS interview of Hope Taft at BPD headquarters on that first day. So presumably, there would be something in the BPD report regarding their interview with Hope. But I found nothing. Although, I later found a scant half-page of notes of a Hope Taft interview near the end of February 2011 conducted by the Broome County ADA and three investigators. Generally, a narrative summary of a witness interview appears in a formal report along with notes. The absence of a more detailed written narrative made it difficult to interpret what Hope had said during her interview accurately.

Even though a few notes proved helpful, the majority were simply too vague, requiring further explanation. It was time to speak with Hope myself.

Author's note: The following is a compilation of three interviews I had with Hope Taft leading up to the trial.

It was now January 20, 2012. Veronica had already given Dave Butler her mom's number and told her I would be calling. She was still at work when I called but said she was anxious to speak with me. Within minutes of my interview with Hope, I recognized many similarities between her and Veronica – that same, no-nonsense, strong-willed character as her daughter.

Hope recalled the hysterical phone call she received at work that morning from Veronica. She said, "Ronnie was hysterical. I could hardly recognize it was her and couldn't understand a thing she said, and the only thing I could make out was that Lyric was blue, and I needed to get over there right away." She rushed right over, but the ambulance with Lyric and Veronica was just pulling away by the time she got there.

She remembered seeing Chucky at the scene and speaking with him, but he didn't know what had happened. She approached one of the uniformed officers at the scene, identified herself as Veronica's mother, and asked what happened to her grandson. The officer just told her, "He's gone." Initially, after speaking with the police, attempting to learn more, they'd offered to take her to the hospital and placed her in one of their cars, and started heading that way. Then suddenly, without explanation, they reversed course and took her directly to BPD headquarters. She spoke up and told the officers that her husband Tom was on his way to the hospital and asked if she could call and let him know there was a change in plans. Her request was denied, and they continued to BPD. There, she was met by more BPD investigators and CPS workers and learned that she was brought back to the station was to help with the children. Hope added, "My primary concern was for the children. I just wanted to get them out of there and take them home, away from all that was happening right in front of them. But when I tried leaving with the children, I was stopped. And one of the officers screamed at me and threatened to take the kids, so I just stayed with them. I was there for what seemed like several hours. There was another officer screaming at me that he'd been beaten to death and another telling me that Lyric had been beaten before and abused all along. Later, I went with the girls for their interview at CAC but wasn't allowed to be present. Considering how young they were, I didn't feel that was right."

I then asked, "I know it's been a while, but what can you recall about your first in-person conversation with Veronica after this happened?" She replied, "Veronica – we call her "Ron," told me that when she got home that morning, she was tired, and Chucky insisted she just lay down and he had just put Zoey down, who had been up all night." Then added, "I had actually spoken to Ron before she left for work that night because I was worried about her going to work. Just the week before, she'd had a heavy bleeding problem, and I made her go to the ER. I thought she may have been pregnant, but when I asked, she said no, or at least didn't think she was. I was concerned she wasn't ready to go back to work because she tired so easily. But when I talked to her that night, she said she just woke up and had to rush to get ready for work. Later, she called me from work and told me that Chucky had to make them dinner because she had fallen asleep and got up late. She sounded pretty normal – nothing unusual in her demeanor. She was tired but always tried to keep the kids on her schedule. It was very normal for her to call me from work at any hour. But her call that morning? I've seen Ron upset in the past, and I can tell when she's upset about something but never – never to that extreme."

Continuing, I asked, "Anything more you can recall about your conversations with Ron?" She replied, "Well, I'd been trying to rationalize as to what may have happened before I knew any details. Initially, I didn't suspect that anyone had done anything to intentionally harm Lyric. It was only after talking with the police and CPS at the Crime Victim's building where I had gone with the children for their interview, where I learned from one of the detectives who told me that Lyric had been used as a soccer ball. But the turning point for me was when Ron told me about Chucky turning his ankle. It was right after that when she ended her relationship with Chucky, who didn't take it well and began threatening her. He started acting crazy. Threatening to tell the police that she'd come home during the night and went back to work."

Later, she added, "A few weeks after this happened, Ronnie had gone back to her apartment on Fayette Street for a short time before she went to live in Syracuse. She called me one night, screaming after Chucky broke down her door and forced his way in. She was screaming and fighting with Chucky. My husband Tom and I went right over. Tom got into a heated argument with Chucky. It was intense and almost got physical. Someone called the police, but I think Chucky took off before they arrived. Ronnie was terrified of Chucky, who physically assaulted her by throwing her to the floor and then threatened her with a gun. As far as I know, Chucky was never arrested or even questioned. It was that same day that Ronnie moved up to Syracuse."

Continuing, I asked Hope what she could tell me about Ron as a mother. She said, "All of her pregnancies were difficult, but she was a good mom. She nursed all of her kids. Ron and I talked every day, and I would see the kids often. They were always well cared for. Even though she wasn't the greatest housekeeper, her kids were well fed and always had clean clothes to wear. Admittedly, like most kids that age, they could be a bit rambunctious at times. For the most part, however, they were all well behaved." Following up, I asked, "What about discipline? How did she discipline her kids?" She said, "Well, it didn't happen often, but ordinarily, she used the timeout method. But there were times when she would swat them on the butt. I did too."

During a later follow-up interview with Hope, I had brought along some of the police photographs of Veronica's apartment and the clothing Lyric was wearing the morning he was discovered. She quickly pointed out the clean kitchen and was adamant that it had never looked that neat in all the times she was over there. She also recognized the unhinged door and explained that it was always on its side whenever she had been there, not standing up. Then recalled telling Veronica that it was dangerous and too easy to fall on one of the kids.

Then I showed her the photographs of the clothing Lyric had been wearing that morning. She was adamant that Veronica would never put her kids to bed in street clothes. Then added, "A T-shirt maybe when it's warm, but never street clothes." When I showed her the picture of the hole in the wall, she said, "Well, I was there on Christmas, and I know it wasn't like that then."

I asked if Veronica had ever mentioned whether she'd ever found Haveen's pink Barbie comforter? She said, "Yeah, she did ask me, but no, I looked for it, but it wasn't there." Continuing, I asked, "How about Lyric's SpongeBob pajamas? Did you ever find them?" She said, "Oh, he loved them. They were his favorite. I think he'd just gotten them for Christmas. I did go back into the apartment to gather up clothing for the other kids, but I never saw SpongeBob either." I said, "By the way, speaking of clothes, that reminds me, when you first went in there that morning gathering up clothes for the other kids, how were they dressed?" She said, "They were all still in their pajamas, but it was chilly outside. That's why I needed some other clothes."

I couldn't leave without asking her what she could tell me about those complaining witnesses who had been making all kinds of allegations against Veronica. She knew them all and provided even more details about their poor relationships with Veronica and many of the causes which led them to make their allegations. Briefly, while babysitting for Veronica, one had stolen her iPod, MP3 player, and rent money. And previously, she was caught stealing from a store. Veronica took the blame so she wouldn't get in trouble. Another was known to be involved as a prostitute as well as in drug sales and use. And another had her own two kids taken away by CPS.

About two weeks after my first interview with Hope Taft, I located and interviewed Ray Ramos. He was a high school friend of Veronica who had babysat during the day on December 29th while Veronica ran some errands and, later, some grocery shopping with Chucky. Ramos confirmed what he had told the BPD: he did babysit that day, just as he had done on several prior occasions. He'd never seen any signs of abuse or neglect in all the times he knew Veronica and babysat her children. The kids always seemed to be clean, appropriately dressed, well-nourished, and for the most part, well-behaved. Certainly, nothing out of the ordinary. He recalled feeding the kids twice that day. Once around lunchtime and then again around 5:00 p.m. just before Veronica and Chucky returned from shopping. I asked Ramos, "Do you recall what you fed them at 5:00 p.m.?" He replied, "Yeah. It was just peanut butter and jelly sandwiches."

During my interview with Hope, she had given me the name of her other daughter, Veronica's younger sister, Roxann. Then explained that for a few days after Lyric was killed, Veronica and Chucky had stayed with Roxann and her live-in boyfriend. I located and interviewed Roxann and her boyfriend at their apartment in nearby Johnson City, NY. They had been living together for about 11 years. They both confirmed that Veronica and Chucky had stayed with them for a few days shortly after Lyric was killed. Both distinctly remembered Chucky having a problem with his right foot. He never said how he had hurt it, but it was swollen. Roxann recalled his foot being swollen and giving him a bag of frozen vegetables to help the swelling.

As a friend of Chucky, I wasn't sure whether Martin "Max" Rodriguez would speak with me or not. But when I told him who I was and why I wanted to talk with him, he welcomed me into his apartment. He claimed that Chucky and Jemel had been at his apartment most of the day on the day in question, smoking pot and playing video games. He recalled Veronica having called Chucky several times during the day to remind him about babysitting and to make sure he wasn't late. He also recalled how they left his place around 10:30 or so to go to Veronica's.

The following day, Jemel came to his house and told him that after they got to Veronica's house last night, Chucky fixed the kids something to eat and put them to bed. He was claiming that Chucky had only seen the two oldest girls but not the little boy. Jemel had told him further that he and Chucky were drinking and playing X-box after the kids were in bed. Then, after that, he left and went back to Chucky's apartment for the night.

Max also mentioned speaking with Chucky on the phone the next morning – some time "after they found the young boy dead." During the call, he said Chucky was very vague about what happened, simply saying that the young boy had died, and Veronica was very upset. He recalled speaking with Chucky again later that same morning when he was at the police station. Adding that, "I was the one that told Chucky not to say anything and ask for an attorney." Then, the following morning, Chucky showed up at his place wearing a sling on his arm and said he got mad and punched the wall after he found out the young boy was dead. He'd further stated that he thought the boy may have fallen out of bed and had told the cops that. While attempting to question him further about what happened, he refused to talk about it and appeared nervous. However, he did say that when Veronica came home that morning, he'd told her the kids were fine and that she should just go to bed and get some sleep. He'd spoken to Chucky several times by phone after the incident, but he'd long since moved back to the Bronx.

Before leaving, I gave Max one of my business cards, thanked him for speaking with me, and said, "If you think of anything more that might be helpful, give me a call." He replied, "Well, for obvious reasons, I never told the police this. But just so you know, Chucky should've had ten baggies of heroin on him that night. Because just before he went over there, I'd given them to him to sell, and I have no idea what happened to them." I said, "Thanks, that's good to know. But did you ever ask him what happened to it?" He said, "Well, all he said was, the police probably found it." Hmm!

Let's rewind here for a moment and go back to day one. If you recall, just before Chucky was released, he'd been given a direct order by Sergeant Eggleston not to go back to Veronica's apartment. After explaining that it was considered a crime scene. Chucky agreed. But instead, as we know, he went over and hung out near the apartment. Then within ten minutes after they'd finished at the scene, Veronica's apartment was released to him. Considering what I just learned from Max, it might just explain why Chucky was so anxious to get back into the apartment. He wanted to recover whatever heroin was left from wherever he stashed it. Hoping the police hadn't found it. But notably, no heroin or any other illicit drugs appeared on the police evidence log.

My repeated attempts to find Charles Pratt or his brother, Jemel Fields, were unsuccessful. Pratt had presumably returned to an unknown location in the NYC area and Fields to parts unknown.

It took some time, but I finally tracked down Lynette Pica – Veronica's downstairs neighbor who had gone up to Veronica's apartment on the night in question and had spoken with Veronica. She had been interviewed by the BPD on two occasions and had given contradictory statements. When I located Pica at her new residence on Ackley Avenue in Johnson City, I learned that she'd just been released from jail. She was somewhat reluctant and defensive but did agree to speak with me. I was particularly interested in what she'd told the BPD during her second interview, when she had mentioned having seen the kids when she went in the apartment, including Lyric, who had spoken to her. Unfortunately, she denied having any knowledge of that, and the rest of what she said during the interview was in further contradiction to all she said previously. So much for calling her as a witness.

VERONICA TAFT - JAIL INTERVIEW

Previously, Dave Butler received approval from the Broome County Jail, permitting me one on one interviews with Veronica as needed, which I took full advantage of on several occasions. But there were many occasions when two of us spoke with her together, especially when preparing for trial.

I'd been reviewing the discovery material since mid-October of 2011, but it wasn't until early April of 2012 when I first met and interviewed Veronica at the jail. I learned that Veronica was pregnant when she was arrested and recently gave birth to a son in the interim. In the brief moment she was allowed to hold him, she named him Omari Taft. He was then quickly whisked away by authorities and placed in foster care.

By this time, sixteen months had passed since Lyric's death, and Veronica had been sitting in jail for nearly half that time. Other than seeing her in videotaped interviews, I had never met her before, so I wasn't sure what to expect or what my first impression would be. Yet, I was anxious to find out. Not that it matters, but I don't get too many female clients. Even though I've worked numerous murder cases, this was only my second with a female defendant. Dave Butler had already told Veronica who I was and that I would be coming in to speak with her. She just didn't know when.

Earlier, having received the court's approval for my services, I was allowed to use the same contact interview rooms used by attorneys to conduct private interviews with Veronica. Each room is about ten feet squared and surrounded by clear, sound-proof glass for privacy and safety. I was already seated in my assigned room when Veronica walked in and said, "You must be Mr. Beers. I've been expecting you." I said, "Yep, that's me. Nice to finally meet you. Please, have a seat."

Before diving into the details, I wanted her to feel comfortable speaking with me, so I told her a little about myself and why I do what I do. I then asked her to tell me a little about her background and history. She seemed rather anxious for someone to talk to and willing to listen even though she had never met me before. As such, she began to tell all openly. Sensing her comfort level in speaking with me, I could tell it was time to turn to the matter at hand.

After learning of the death of her son, Veronica was an emotionally distraught mother in crisis. Previously, she'd explained the details of what happened with the police several times. But sixteen months had passed since then. Hopefully, it wouldn't be as painful to relive it again.

From the discovery material, I learned that to avoid some ongoing issues with the father of her two youngest children and CPS, Veronica and her children had moved to the state of Maine to live with a friend. Then later, she moved back to Binghamton in August of 2010. I asked her to pick up the story from there. She explained, "Shortly after coming back from Maine, I found a job and started working at the Binghamton High School. It was the night shift, doing maintenance work. Before that, I worked in food service at two different Binghamton school cafeterias." I then asked her to tell me about Chucky. She'd met him late that same summer, shortly after her return to Binghamton. He'd been introduced to her by a friend. By November, he began babysitting the kids at night while she worked. Later, she added, "I was only making $200 a week, and I was giving him $90 a week to babysit." Before that, she said, "My girlfriend Deanna had been babysitting for me. She was only 17, but my kids loved her, and she loved them. She was really good with them. I never learned what really happened, but she mysteriously died shortly after I was arrested."

Continuing, I asked, "What can you tell me about Jesse Noel?" She'd had a brief fling with Noel around the same time she was seeing Chucky. She didn't know it at the time, but she'd become pregnant and only learned of her pregnancy after being hospitalized for bleeding issues and having a miscarriage. She added, "It was just a few days before Christmas." She said she knew Noel was the father. Then said, "And when Chucky found out, he was pissed." "I'll bet he was," I said.

I then shifted to the night in question before she went to work. She'd been grocery shopping with Chucky earlier that day and returned home around five o'clock. Her friend Raymond, who she knew from high school, often babysat during the day. He'd been there babysitting and had just fed the kids. Shortly after she and Chucky arrived, Ray went home, and Chucky headed for Max's house to smoke pot and play video games. "Other than babysit, that's about all he'd ever do," she said. Then after he left, she was home alone with the kids until he returned to babysit so she could go to work. She said, "I was tired from running all day, and the kids were all being good, in their room watching movies. I knew it was going to be a long night, so I decided to lay down and rest for a few minutes before work. It was probably around 9:00 p.m. or so. I must have fallen deep asleep because I woke up in a panic, thinking I'd be late for work.

I knew the kids needed to eat again, so I hustled into the kitchen to pre-heat the oven for some Tater-tots and French fries and then went to get dressed. At some point, Lyric wandered in because he needed his diaper changed, and I did that." Tearing up a bit, she added, "That was the last time I saw him, just walking back to his room." She stopped for a moment to wipe her tears, then added, "I just assumed he was headed back to watch the movies with his sisters."

Continuing, she said, "Not long after that, Chucky arrived, followed shortly after by his brother, Jemel. My neighbor downstairs walked in behind Jemel and sat on my bed, and we talked briefly while I was getting dressed. I'm not sure if I was putting the food in or taking it out of the oven before I left or not. But I did remind Chucky that he needed to feed the kids. I then ran out the door to catch my ride to work. My friend from downstairs was right behind me."

Before moving on to the following day, I asked her how long she'd been working the night shift, what type of work she did, and specifically about the night in question. She explained, "Before this all happened, I'd been working there for six or eight weeks. I got the job through a temp service. Usually, it was simple maintenance work like sweeping floors, emptying trash, that type of thing. But when this happened, the schools were closed for Christmas break. So, our workload got a lot busier because we had to strip and wax all the floors. We were on a pretty tight schedule to get it all done before school reopened. Really working our asses off that night."

Before I could ask my next question, she said, "Do you want to know what happened when I got home?" "Of course, that's why I'm here. I want to hear all about it – everything," I said. Then added, "Look, I've read all the reports, watched all your videotaped interviews, so I know what you've said and how many times you've been over this with the police and CPS.

Undoubtedly, this has been playing out hundreds of times in your own mind." She said, "Ain't that the truth, but it's good to hear you say that." Then added, "Yeah. I remember talking with them and maybe some of the things I said but not everything. To be honest, it's kind of a blur cause I don't think my mind was in the right place at the time." I said, "No doubt. That's perfectly understandable. I was thinking the same thing."

Continuing, she added, "But you're right about this playing out in my mind because I've been over this like a thousand times. It's always on my mind. But what I'm trying to say is, now that I've had more time to think about all this, I have a much better recollection of things that happened. Things I couldn't remember at the time or understanding their significance." I said, "Well, I'm not at all surprised because that's been my experience in other situations like this. But I'm anxious to hear any new thoughts. So, let's pick it up on that morning right after you finish work at 7:00 a.m." She explained as follows:

"Okay. I finished work right at 7:00. Usually, the same coworker that drives me to work would also drive me home after. But that morning, he had an early doctor's appointment, so I had to hoof it, which takes about 15-20 minutes. So, I got home around 7:15 or 7:20. I was exhausted. I'd had a long day the day before, a very busy night at work, and then the walk home. Plus, I was still sorta weak from my miscarriage. As soon as I walked in, Chucky met me at the door immediately. I didn't think anything of it at the time, but that was unusual. And the other unusual thing that also didn't register with me at the time was that he was already dressed. Because usually, whenever I'd get home from work, he would still be in bed in his sleep clothes. But that's not all. As I walked into my bedroom to get out of my work clothes, my youngest daughter Zoey was lying on my bed with her bottle. So, I asked him, what's Zoey doing up? He told me she'd woke up crying, so he fixed her a bottle and brought her in my room so she wouldn't wake the other kids. Zoey seemed content with her bottle, and I wanted to check on the other kids anyway, so I told him I was going to put her back in her crib. He immediately grabbed Zoey and insisted on doing it himself, saying something like, 'No, no, no, just relax. I've got this. I'll check on them. It's your vacation. Just relax. You gotta get your rest.' Then reminded me how tired I was and insisted I go right to bed. So, when he left with Zoey, I crashed on the bed and waited for him to come back. But it seemed like he was gone a long time, and I was thinking, what's taking so long?

Finally, I decided to go and see what the holdup was. When I looked in the door, he wasn't near Zoey but was standing over by Lyric and Amira holding Lyric's Transformers blanket. When he saw me, he sorta froze and was acting a little sneaky. At first, I thought maybe his brother was still there, and he was hiding him. So, I asked if his brother was still here, and he said no. I stepped over and looked into the game room to check. When I turned back, he was putting the door up in front of the kid's room, which is something we don't normally do. So, I asked him why he was putting the door up, and he said, "Oh, so the kids don't bother you." I just accepted that and headed back to my bedroom to lay down. He came in right after me and stood there and made this big sigh as if he was about to say something but didn't. He then came over and started rubbing my shoulders. That was strange too. But again, I was so tired I didn't pay much attention and just rolled over and fell asleep. I'm not even sure how long I slept, but when I woke up, I looked over, and he was just lying there starring at the ceiling. I then heard the girls talking in their room, and since he was fully awake, I said, "Why haven't you let them out?" So, I started to roll out of bed to go get the kids myself. When, all of a sudden, he just flew over me and headed towards the kids' room."

Later, she added, "I wish I could have remembered more of these things at the time, but like I said, my mind wasn't quite right." I said, "No, I understand perfectly, but these are good things to know. However, the problem is, and I think you know as well as I do, if the prosecution was to hear of these things now, they'd just say, well, you never told us that before. Then argue that you're just making things up to save yourself to make it look like Chucky did it." "Yeah. I figured as much," she said.

She then explained what happened when Chucky returned from the kids' room and back to tell her that Lyric was cold and not breathing. Although still emotional and crying whenever mentioning Lyric, her explanation about what happened was remarkably consistent with what we've already learned. However, she did add an interesting new revelation about what she was thinking after the EMTs arrived and started working on Lyric. She said, "I've given this a lot of thought. I know, I know I was in denial at the time, but here's the thing. I know I wasn't thinking clearly at the time, but as we stood there watching the EMTs, I knew he'd done something. I could tell by the look on his face and the way he was reacting. Even though I wasn't in my best mind, I can remember him starting to rub my arms up and down like this (indicating) with a strange look on his face. At that point,

I think I just shoved him away from me. I may have even said, "Just get away from me." "Feeling a bit guilty perhaps," I said. "Probably, but at the time, I was in deep denial, not wanting to believe he could have done this. Where in the beginning, I was actually trying to defend him. Go figure. The police probably figured I knew something and was covering for him." I said, "During your interview, you were telling them you weren't in denial, but now you realize you were. So, they probably were thinking that."

Continuing, I said, "Let's back up for a moment. You said you remembered changing Lyric's diaper in your room before you went to work. Do you remember if your friend from downstairs was with you at the time?" She said, "I'm really not sure. She could have been, but she may have come in right after, so I'm not sure. What does she say?" I answered, "Well, I haven't spoken to her yet, but the police interviewed her twice. Her second interview contradicted her first. But in her second, she admitted coming up the stairs behind Jemel and seeing the kids. She even remembered Lyric saying something to her. She also admitted sitting and talking with you on your bed but nothing about seeing you change Lyric's diaper." She said, "Yeah. I remember talking with her. We were talking about doing something together for New Year's." "Yep. She said that as well," I said.

I already knew of Veronica's interview history with BPD and her prior history with CPS. But I wanted to hear directly from her about those complaining witnesses. You know, the cry-ladies. I was already of the opinion that they were not credible witnesses. But after hearing directly from Veronica, who identified even more reasons for their lack of credibility, there was no longer any doubt.

Near the end of the interview, I asked her to explain what happened in the aftermath of Lyric's death up to the day of her arrest. She explained that initially, right after it happened, she didn't want to go back to her apartment. It was too painful. She'd spent a night or two in a motel and then stayed with her sister for a few days. Other times, she jumped from place to place, staying with friends. For a while, she'd stayed with her grandmother, who lived close to her mom. But from time to time, she and Chucky still saw each other. She explained that she was still trying to get him to talk and hoping he might say something about what happened so she could tell the police.

Near the end of February 2011, she somewhat hesitantly decided to go back to her apartment for a day or two until she could find a new apartment. The rent was paid, but she hadn't been back since the day it all happened. She'd asked a friend to stay with her. She wasn't planning on staying long but wanted to gather whatever belongings remained behind before moving out permanently. Before that, her relationship with Chucky had fallen apart due to a series of repeated threats he'd made – threats that ended their relationship. Somehow, however, he learned she was back at her apartment and showed up at her door, forcing his way in by breaking down the door. A rather nasty verbal altercation started immediately. It quickly turned physical, with him throwing her to the floor and wailing on her. Because Chucky was much stronger, Veronica was getting the worst of it. She received injuries to her head, arms, shoulders, and knees. He'd also brandished both a knife and gun while making repeated threats to kill her. She said, "When he hit me in the head and knocked me to my knees, I thought he was gonna fuckin' kill me."

In the midst of all this, one or more of her neighbors had called the police. Veronica herself called her mother and friend in Syracuse, screaming that Chucky was threatening her with a gun and beating the crap out of her. Later, we'll learn some additional details. Notably, when it was all over, despite Chucky's overt acts of criminal mischief, assault, menacing, and burglary, there was no arrest. After that, the police sent them their separate ways. With Chucky heading to parts unknown and Veronica gathering up a small bag of her belongings to move to Syracuse to live with her friend. A place where she remained until her arrest in early September.

Before leaving, I told her I would be back to follow up on my investigation from time to time. In the meantime, I encouraged her to jot down any questions or concerns she had and anything else I should be looking into. I advised her that if there was anything urgent, to call Mr. Butler. She agreed. But as I was leaving, I asked, "Anything else you want to tell me before I leave?" She replied, "Well, it's probably no big deal but remember those complaints about me being a prostitute and pimping other young girls? Well, that's a bunch of crap, and the cops know it."

I asked what she meant, and she said, "Because they know who all the prostitutes are. I've seen them talking with them many times. Because a lot of them 'worked' in my neighborhood." "Good point," I said. "I hadn't thought of that, but you're right. It's been some time, but the last I knew, they kept a list of their names. So, if ever there was a crime in the area, they could turn to their list of street-walkers for information." She replied firmly, "Well, there's no way my name was on that list or the other two girls they claimed I was pimping. That's crap. Besides, I'd been living there for five months. If I was one of them, don't you think the cops would have known? Besides, the other prostitutes would have known. Were they ever interviewed? Of course not."

By now, she was both angry and crying. While wiping away her tears, she added, "But here I am, with their bullshit accusations still hanging over me." Other than telling her that I understood, I didn't know what else to say. Just then, the jail desk buzzed in and said our time was up. So, as I walked to the door, I just thanked her for speaking with me and sharing her story and assured her I would be back again soon.

My first interview with Veronica went very well. Despite being locked up for eight months, she seemed very upbeat, high-spirited, and held her head high. I was impressed with her positive attitude and level of intelligence. Not only was she smart, but she was well-spoken, strong-willed, and energetic – all woven together by a level of street smarts. In the poverty-stricken, cut-throat world she was living in, her very means of survival was a daily challenge. Her survival depended on her ability to stand up for herself and not take any crap from anyone. Something she'd become well accustomed to since her days in school. Yet, that attribute of her character angered those who later sought their revenge by making malicious complaints against her.

When considering the sixteen months that had passed since Lyric's death and my knowledge of the case before the interview, I found it rather remarkable how consistent her story remained between then and now. She'd been giving it a lot of thought and was still able to articulate what happened accurately. Her truth was supported further by looking me straight in the eye and providing forthright answers to all my questions while presenting a strong desire and determination to play an active role in her defense.

After learning about the altercation between Veronica and Chucky on February 22, 2011, at 4½ Fayette Street, I wanted to see what more I could discover. Accordingly, I filed a FOIL[1] request with BPD for any and all police reports involving any dispute or disturbance calls at that location between January and March of 2011. A week later, I received a copy of 17 different complaints filed at that address. Unfortunately, the one I was interested in was marked "sealed." Initially, I was a bit confused about why it was sealed. It was only listed as a criminal mischief complaint. According to both Veronica and her mother, no arrests had been made. So why was it sealed? But then I realized that each party involved, Veronica Taft and Charles Pratt, were still part of an ongoing homicide investigation. That must be the reason, right? In my view, it should not have been because, other than the parties involved, nothing happened that had anything to do with the ongoing homicide investigation. Regardless, my FOIL request for that specific matter had been denied by its sealing.

When I started writing this story ten years later, I renewed interest in learning what was in that file. Assuming that the file would no longer be sealed after ten years, I filed a new FOIL request. Strangely, it was still sealed.

---

1. *FOIL*: Freedom of Information Law

30

DEANNA BRYANT

Remember that strange phone call Veronica received from Deanna Bryant, who was frightened and didn't want to talk about it on the phone? And how she was found dead two months later? As I muddled through the discovery material, I uncovered some interesting new details about Bryant, both before and after she died.

Interestingly, Bryant had been interviewed by the BPD and DA on at least three occasions between January and March of 2011. She was not one of the cry-ladies. In January, she was interviewed by Investigators Wagner and Cornell. She explained that she had lived with Veronica and did some babysitting for about a month during October and November of 2010. Since then, however, her mother hadn't allowed her to speak with her. When asked whether she had any suspicions or concerns about how the children were treated, she hadn't seen anything abnormal. When asked about discipline, she said Veronica would spank the children mostly with her hand but at times, with a wooden spoon on the butt, but nothing excessive.

Later, on February 22, 2011, Bryant was reinterviewed by

Wagner and Cornell, along with the ADA and his investigator. It was during this interview when she told them that Veronica had broken up with Chucky. Then added that she'd previously dated a man named Jesse Noel. Notably, this was the same day Veronica moved to Syracuse after being assaulted and threatened by Chucky at her Fayette Street apartment. Bryant further mentioned having personally seen Chucky dealing drugs. She had also seen one of the cry-ladies hitting the children while babysitting. Then, she also claimed to have overheard Chucky saying, "I don't know why they keep asking people things since they're not going to find anything else out."

What prompted the third interview with Bryant was unclear, but on March 2, 2011, she was interviewed again by the same team. She claimed that her new friend, Ray Ramos, had heard and told her that Veronica killed Lyric because he reminded her of his father. From what was noted during the interview, she had obviously disobeyed her mother and spoke with Veronica. According to Bryant, when speaking with Veronica, she was told that Chucky kept going into the kids' room that morning. And further, that Chucky had been abnormally nice to her that morning. She added that she felt she would get in trouble because she'd left Lyric with Chucky.

Initially, I hadn't placed too much significance on the information obtained from Bryant. This was supported by the fact that she had never been called as a witness during the grand jury. Later, however, I discovered there was some significance. During her second interview in late February 2011, she'd identified Jesse Noel as a former boyfriend of Veronica. Yet strangely, even though the BPD learned of this back in February, it wasn't until his arrest in June before he was ever interviewed.

From a logical and investigative perspective, failing to interview Noel was remiss and another lost opportunity. The point being, if you know someone who's in a relationship with a suspect, who may possess valuable inside information, why wouldn't you talk with him? I found myself struggling to understand why that never happened. Equally important was to question whether Noel may have said anything different if he hadn't been under arrest and facing time in prison.

Yet, considering everything else that had gone wrong, the thought did cross my mind that perhaps Noel had been interviewed earlier, and they didn't like what he had to say. Either that or maybe he'd said nothing at all. I reviewed the lead log earlier but decided to double-check to make sure. Nope, there was nothing there. Strangely, however, for a reason(s) unknown, the lead log mysteriously ended on January 22, 2011, after only 26 leads. It was strange because ordinarily, during a homicide investigation, there are hundreds of leads. And it was mysterious because, as we've already learned, at a minimum, the investigation continued until Veronica's arrest in September. Therefore, the obvious question was, how do you keep track of what's being done, when, and by whom without a controlling lead log?

Also strange was the BPD narrative report itself. Other than two single pages documenting Noel's first interview in June and Veronica's arrest in September, the final entry in their report was dated January 7, 2011. So, had nearly eight months of investigative work gone unreported? Of course not. It was reported alright. The only problem was it was never disclosed.

As an example, remember what Wagner told Jesse Noel during his jail interview? The fact that they had talked to a hundred people on this? If that's true, who were they, and what did they have to say? Because they identified only a handful in their report.

It appeared as though Bryant's last involvement had ended back in March, but it resurfaced again in November, just over two months after Veronica was arrested. Only this time, it was not for another interview but instead another death investigation – her own death investigation.

Briefly, on the evening of November 8, 2011, a 9-1-1 call came into the Broome County Emergency Call Center, reporting an unconscious 17-year-old female. Immediately after that, the BPD and BFD Fire Medics were dispatched to an address in a six-unit apartment building on Binghamton's Southside. Upon arrival, first responders were directed to a second-floor bedroom, where the 17-year-old female had been found lying in bed, unresponsive. All subsequent medical efforts used to try and revive her failed, and she was pronounced dead. Later, after speaking with the three other adults who were present, the young woman was identified as Deanna Bryant.

Since Bryant was a potential witness in the Veronica Taft case, a supplementary investigative report prepared in connection with her death was included in the discovery material turned over to attorney Butler. However, the narrative report authored by lead investigator Robert Fimbres was only preliminary, consisting of just three pages and a few notes.

The incident classification was listed as "Undetermined Death." The investigation revealed no apparent trauma to the body or any signs of a struggle. Other than an ashtray, with signs of marihuana use, there were no other drugs or drug paraphernalia reported. Two of Deanna's friends had been in the apartment all evening and hadn't noticed anything unusual about her. A third friend claimed to have arrived just before she was discovered. Later, Deanna's mother and aunt were called to the scene and interviewed. Investigators learned that Deanna had been in rehab for marihuana and alcohol use, but she'd recently been cleared for early release to start college. According to her mother, Deanna was a troubled child and habitual runaway who was recently petitioned as a PINS[1] with an assigned probation officer. Furthermore, she had been diagnosed with depression and was prescribed medication.

Later, during my interview with Deanna's mother, I learned that Deanna had been living at home with her at the time. I also learned that Deanna's mother had numerous types of medication in the house that Deanna had easy access to, but none were ever discovered missing. In fact, she said, "Deanna hated taking medication and, more often than not, refused to take it. I couldn't even get her to take an aspirin."

According to the report, she'd also told the police she was holding on to Deanna's meds because she wasn't taking them. She said further that other than depression, there were no other known medical issues. Interestingly, just the day before, she also told the police that Deanna was visibly upset about something during a conversation, and she was crying. When asked why, all she said was, "You wouldn't understand."

In the report's final paragraph, Fimbres wrote that the coroner had ordered Bryant's body to be taken to the morgue at Wilson Hospital for an autopsy the following day. He also noted that investigators from the ID Unit would be in attendance. Then added, "See ID supplementals" for further details. The discovery material we received never included the autopsy report, BPD's final investigative report, or any of those supplementals from the ID Unit.

By the time I first spoke with Deanna's mother, nearly ten years had passed since her daughter's death. I was surprised to learn that she'd never learned anything further from the BPD during all that time, other than the night it happened. Nearly ten years, and she still doesn't know what happened to her daughter or the final results of their investigation. Interestingly, however, she had received a call from the pathologist who performed the autopsy, advising her that Deanna had died from a massive overdose of OxyContin – more than four times the lethal dose.

. . .

Author's note: OxyContin (oxycodone hydrochloride) is a highly addictive prescription painkiller, which has become one of the most abused prescription drugs in the US. It is commonly misused by ingesting it after it's been crushed or diluted. In doing so, its built-in time-release function is disabled, releasing the entire drug all at once. It gives the user a potentially fatal dose. (WebMD)

Interested in learning more about what happened to her daughter, I offered to assist Deanna's mom in filing a FOIL request, seeking a copy of the final police, autopsy and toxicology reports, and any witness statements. To look for anything new that might help explain how Deanna's case was closed and what more, if anything, was done that led them to that conclusion. Unfortunately, the returned FOIL results failed to answer either question. There were no witness statements or any autopsy or toxicology reports. Instead, there was just a couple of new pages with a few notes from the ID Unit. Investigator Matt Zandy authored the ID report – the investigator called to process the scene. After reading his report, a couple of things jumped out at me right away. Noticeably absent was any mention of anyone being present during the autopsy. Moreover, when comparing his report with the one written by Fimbres, there were some discrepancies.

Before Zandy arrived at the scene, Fimbres described having seen male and female clothing on the floor next to the bed where Deanna was found. He'd also described a male's pair of pants on the floor with the wallet and ID of a man named Sequan Thompson.

Strangely, even though Zandy offered a complete description of everything in the room, including a detailed description of the bed and its contents, he never reported any of the clothing on the floor described by Fimbres. Stranger still was the fact that during Zandy's examination of the body, he wrote, *"Bruising is noted on the inside of both upper arms and on her legs."* Then just two sentences later, he contradicts himself, writing, *"Deanna has no visible injuries or signs of trauma."*

I wondered why bruising is no longer considered an injury. I thought that it must have been a mistake. I needed to see the autopsy report. So, I reached out to Deanna's mom to suggest an alternative method of getting that report. Anxious to learn more herself, she agreed and wrote to the Broome County Coroner's Office. In response, she received the complete autopsy and toxicology report. In addition to the fatal overdose of OxyContin mentioned earlier, the pathologist also reported bruising on her arms, chest, and left side of her face. Then, it suggested that she may have been held down at some point. Notably, other than the pathologist and his assistant, no one else was in attendance. It also indicated that Deanna's fatal level of oxycodone was 365 mcg/L (micrograms per liter) and the normal therapeutic level of 20-99 mcg/L. Interestingly, even though the examination of the stomach revealed particles of digested food material, no pills or any odor of alcohol were present.

Unfortunately, other than those couple of added pages from the ID Unit with a few notes, nothing more was revealed about further action. There was not even a closing paragraph as to how the case was closed, leaving Deanna's mother, family, and friends in the dark, not knowing and still wondering what happened.

Adding to the mystery and further suspicion were Deanna's so-called friends, who were present when she was discovered. They were identified in the report as Sequan Thompson and Jemel Fields. Remember Jemel? Chucky's half-brother. Of course, the BPD would have known that as well. Anyway, he was the one who told police that he was just visiting from the Bronx but often visited because he had other family in the area. They would have known who that was as well – Mr. Chucky.

After Fields explained that he arrived just before it happened, he added that he didn't "really know who Bryant was." So, if he didn't really know who she was, why was he there? And who is this Sequan Thompson? He'd been right there in the apartment for at least 4-5 hours before she was discovered. As noted earlier, Thompson's pants and wallet were found on the floor, right next to the bed where Deanna was found. Yet, at least according to the report, Thompson was neither asked nor offered any explanation. Then later, we learn that Deanna did have bruising on her arms and legs.

I learned from my investigation that Fields and Thompson were both several years older than Deanna. But more importantly, they'd both spent time in prison as convicted drug dealers. So, what was their real purpose in being there that day? Later, Thompson was convicted on Robbery and Assault charges and returned to state prison. He's since been released but remains on post-release supervision.

All things considered, including Chucky's previous threats to kill Veronica, even without knowing the final results of the Bryant investigation, attorney Dave Butler and I were both in agreement. We were wondering and questioning whether this was just a bizarre coincidence or was something more involved?

Later, I learned from a reliable source that Jemel had been a suspect in her death. But supposedly, he'd been offered immunity because his testimony was needed to corroborate his brother in Veronica's trial. This might very well explain why we never received any of those final reports.

What happened here regarding the missing reports in connection with Deanna's suspicious death was strikingly similar to what happened back in February. After Chucky forced his way into Veronica's apartment, where he assaulted and threatened to kill her, the BPD was called to the scene. But as we've already learned, despite his apparent crimes, he was never arrested. Why? Because they knew, even though Veronica hadn't been arrested yet, they would need Chucky's testimony once she was. So, they just let him go and sent Veronica on her way. Later requests to review that report were denied. Furthermore, because Jemel was a suspect in Bryant's death, they did the same thing again. What didn't they want us to know?

Later, when asked, Deanna's mom had no idea who Jemel was. She had never heard of him. She was clueless as to who he was or why he would've been there that night. She did know Chucky but was shocked to learn that Jemel was his brother. After that, she immediately understood the connection to Veronica Taft and agreed that Jemel's presence was indeed suspicious. And even though the death certificate was marked "Accidental," she agreed that Deanna's death may not have been accidental.

---

1. *PINS*: Person In Need of Supervision

31

LYRIC'S GOD MOTHER

Continuing with my investigation, I located and interviewed Rita Sherifi at her home in Brewerton, NY. We'd talked earlier on the phone, but I wanted to follow up with a face-to-face interview. I learned that Veronica was best friends with Rita's sister, Rillyria Sherifi, better known as Ria or Lyria. Lyric was named after her. Veronica and Ria were best friends in school when she lived in Whitney Point. She was currently residing in the state of Maine.

Rita explained that she was the Godmother to all of Veronica's children. She had moved to the Syracuse area about six years earlier and worked as a nurse in a nearby hospital. Veronica would often bring her kids up to visit. She'd never seen any signs of abuse and said, "The kids loved their mom." Then added, "Veronica was a very loving mother and didn't discipline her children much and usually gave them what they wanted."

Even though it was a year-and-a-half after the fact, knowing that Rita had witnessed some of what happened between Veronica and Chucky back in February of 2011, I asked her to describe what she could remember happening. She explained that Ria had come down to her house when Veronica called from her apartment. She was screaming, telling them that Chucky was threatening and assaulting her. They could hear a lot of banging going on. Fearing she was in danger, she and Ria immediately left for Binghamton. Veronica had told them that she thought a neighbor had called the cops. It was already dark, and she thought it was somewhere between 8:00 and 9:00 p.m. when they arrived.

The police had just arrived also and started asking people what had happened. Some were upstairs talking to Chucky. She noticed Veronica had a welt on the back of her head, with another noticeable hand mark on her upper right arm and bruises on her knees. Rita wasn't allowed upstairs, but she saw Chucky at the top of the stairs. She recognized who he was because she'd met him after Lyric died. She remembered asking the police if they were going to arrest him but was told, "Just wait downstairs." Later, because Chucky agreed to leave and Veronica was going to leave with her, no arrest was made. Unfortunately, this was just another example of Chucky being handled with kid gloves.

While waiting for the police to finish talking with Chucky, she spoke with the downstairs tenant, who had also witnessed Chucky beating the crap out of Veronica. She learned that she was the one who called the police. When it was over, Veronica just grabbed a few of her things, threw them into a small bag, and they took her back to Baldwinsville, where she stayed until she was arrested.

Later, she took Veronica back down to Binghamton on three occasions for the supervised visits with her children at DSS. The first time she had just dropped her off, but Veronica told her the caseworker was giving her a rough time and asked her to sit in on the visit the next time, and she did. She identified the caseworker as a black female by the name of Nicole Vaughn. She was always giving Veronica a hard time during visitation, even when trying to schedule them. Vaughn was very critical during visitation and often reprimanded Veronica for the words she chose when speaking with her children. But not as much judgment when Rita was with her. According to Veronica, Vaughn had also said, "When you admit what you did to your son, you'll be able to see your kids more, but not until then." Then described her as being very mean. Remember that Veronica had not yet been accused of anything.

Continuing, she said Vaughn had even cut one session short by 15 minutes for no good reason. Sessions were supposed to be an hour. Later, Vaughn told Veronica that Rita could no longer come in with her. Another time, they drove down there, arriving five minutes late, and they wouldn't let her visit her children. Rita then explained that Veronica had taken the bus the last time she went for visitation, and that's when she was arrested. She said, "They set her up because they knew she was coming."

While I was there, I asked her to tell me about the summer of 2010, when Veronica had taken Lyric and Zoey to Maine to live with Ria while her two oldest stayed with Hope. She explained that Veronica was trying to distance herself from Lyric and Zoey's father, who had been abusive to her, and to escape the wrath of CPS. She explained further that Hope brought the other two children to her house, and she took them up to Maine to see their mother. Then added, "The kids were really excited and happy to see their mother." She went on to explain how, when Veronica learned she was having a boy, "she was thrilled." Then added, "She named him after Ria, whose full name is Rillyria. She'd always called her Lyria, and that's where she came up with the name Lyric."

Toward the end of the interview, she explained that she went right down to be with Veronica after learning of Lyric's death. She said, "When I first saw her, it looked like she was suffering from a severe case of PTSD but trying very hard to cope." Then added, "We went out one night together, hoping it would help her cope with the situation, but she couldn't stop second-guessing herself."

One of Rita's more interesting comments came near the end of the interview when she said, "I don't know how important this is, but when Hope brought the two older girls up here to visit, somewhat out of the blue, Haveen said something about knowing that Chucky had killed Lyric and had given him a bath that night." From my perspective, considering Haveen's tender age at the time, as well as the length of time that had passed, even if true, her current recollection may have been influenced by any number of stories she heard from a variety of sources. I also knew from her CAC interview that she hadn't said anything like that. More interestingly, however, was her comment about Chucky "giving Lyric a bath" that night. Where did that come from?

During my trip back to my office in Binghamton after my interview with Rita, I couldn't stop thinking about what Haveen told her about Chucky bathing Lyric. Initially, I was inclined to dismiss what she said as perhaps a rumor she'd heard somewhere along the way due to her young age, knowing that rumors are pretty common in murder cases. Yet, I couldn't stop thinking about it, wondering if there might be something more to it. Besides, I'd been examining every aspect of this case for several months, including several of those documented rumors. However, Chucky bathing Lyric was not one of them. So, my question was twofold: was this just an overheard rumor or direct knowledge? I know. I know. She's only five, and she'd never said anything like this before to anyone, including her mother. But the more I thought about it, the harder it was to believe that this little five-year-old girl would say something like that, just out of the blue, without any prompting. The more I thought about it, the more curious I became. If it were true, I wondered why Chucky would have been bathing Lyric in the middle of the night. I wanted to see what more I could learn and pursue this a bit further. I wasn't overly optimistic, but I was anxious to get started.

As it turned out, it didn't take long to find what I was looking for. The BPD and ID Unit reports were of no help at all, but fortunately, they took many photographs. There was never any description of the bathroom or its contents. However, a closer look at the photos revealed something I'd overlooked earlier. Something that, at the time, didn't appear relevant. There, scrunched up on the floor in front of the tub, was a large white bath towel – a wet bath towel. It appeared to have some kind of stain on it. And lying right next to it was a blue washcloth, which also seemed to be wet. The towel rack on the wall opposite the tub was empty.

My first thought went immediately to what Haveen had said, keeping in mind, of course, that there could be another explanation. But I wanted to explore this a little further. And I wanted to start by going back to speak with Veronica. Besides, I had a few other things I needed to cover with her as well. I had her full attention after filling her in on Haveen's comment to Rita and showing her the bathroom photos. But then again, she was always paying attention. Her answers to the slew of questions I asked provided some helpful insight, which started opening up a plausible new theory about what may have happened. But at the time, I wasn't quite ready to share that with her.

After learning about Haveen's comment to Rita, Veronica seemed somewhat surprised and said, "What do you make of that?" I said, "That's just it. I'm not sure." I explained my thoughts about whether it was something she may have just heard along the way, or perhaps she actually did witness something. She asked, "What does Rita think?" I said, "Well, she seems to think it could be true because it just kind of came out of nowhere. And I have to admit. It does seem like a pretty odd comment to make." She nodded in agreement.

Veronica had answered all of my related questions. I learned that none of her kids had baths that day. She also reminded me of what she'd told me earlier. How she'd fallen asleep and woke up in a panic, thinking she might be late for work. There was no time to shower. She just dressed and went to work. She also felt the wet towel and washcloth on the floor was strange because it was customary to hang them on the towel rack to dry. Later, she said, "I'd never just leave it on the floor all wet like that."

As far as whether Chucky would ever shower at her place, she couldn't rule it out, but it didn't seem likely. To her knowledge, in the five months she'd known him, he was never known to shower there.

The wet towel on the bathroom floor was really bugging me, especially in light of Haveen's recent comment. Nothing I had learned so far provided any reasonable explanation. Veronica's answers to my questions only helped reaffirm the suspicion I already had – Haveen's revelation was true, and Chucky did bathe Lyric that night. She'd either heard it or watched it happen. Either way, she would have been one terrified little girl. Afraid to tell anyone, even her mother and grandmother, and indeed no authority figure. Then only recently, she mustered up enough courage to tell her Godmother.

By now, I was convinced that Lyric's late-night bath by Chucky was in some way related to his murder. But there were a few missing pieces to the puzzle. My next objective was to determine *how* it was related and whether he was killed before, during, or after his bath.

From the beginning, I'd been brainstorming different scenarios when trying to understand or figure out what may have caused Chucky to kill Lyric. In other words, some type of motive.

There didn't appear to be any evidence of pre-mediation. Unless, of course, you want to believe Jesse Noel, who claimed Chucky had threatened to kill Lyric if Veronica went to work that night. I think it's safe to say we can rule that out. Therefore, it seemed more likely that there had been some type of unknown event that led to some interaction between Lyric and Chucky. An event that ultimately turned violent – then deadly. But my question was, what kind of event could have triggered such a violent reaction if that did happen?

There was already one vital clue supporting this unknown event – one that came right out of Chucky's mouth. If you recall, during his detention that morning, he'd placed a phone call to his brother, Jemel, and was heard telling him, "This little nigger be running around doing mad shit. And that ain't right." What exactly did Chucky mean by "running around doing mad shit?" It meant Lyric was running around doing something that made Chucky angry. Really angry. So angry that he felt compelled to try and stop whatever "mad shit" Lyric was doing. He was quickly overcome by his own madness in that effort, turning him into a ruthless, rage-filled madman.

In addition to the clue just mentioned about the unknown event, other clues came out of Chucky's mouth as well. Earlier, he was heard talking to himself, and he said, "It was on my watch." Then later, during a phone call with Traci Reynolds from CPS, he said, "I'm not getting the death penalty for no accident. People are talking shit, and my attorney's guns are loaded." Also, in the summary notes from his second interview, he described having fed all the kids after Veronica went to work. Then he remembered getting a call from Veronica while they were eating, telling her that he'd made four plates. Then he added that he remembered "hearing Lyric's voice" but not seeing him.

Conceivably, some might argue, myself included, that Chucky's comments could be construed as a tacit admission to killing Lyric. Otherwise, it was at least an admission to it being on his watch. With added admissions of hearing Lyric's voice and describing him as "running around doing mad shit." Both of which had taken place *after* Veronica went to work.

Despite all that, I still wanted to know and was struggling to understand, what a defenseless little two-year-old could have done during this unknown event that was so infuriating, he would be savagely beaten and killed for it. But I was sure it had nothing to do with the dog peeing on the bed. Strangely, however, that same theory would later help to establish a more plausible one that we'll learn about later.

32

WHERE IS SPONGEBOB?

Admittedly, when I first saw the photographs of Lyric's clothing that morning, I never gave much thought that he'd been wearing street clothes rather than pajamas. The police didn't either. That would have been a good line of questioning for both Chucky and Veronica. It just never came up. In fairness, however, it should also be noted, from your own experience as a parent, there may be times when a child falls asleep in their street clothes, and you just let them sleep. Evidently, that was the assumption here. However, it would've been helpful to know not only what the usual bedtime routine was, but more importantly, whether it was any different that night. I can't even tell you how long it was before this issue finally sunk in. But when it did, I wanted some answers. Hopefully, Veronica would have the answers I was seeking.

Veronica hadn't yet seen the photographs of the clothing Lyric had been wearing. I just assumed she would have known what he was wearing, having seen him that morning. But before showing her the photo, I asked if she could remember what he was wearing that morning? She said, "I'm assuming his pajamas, but to be honest, I don't really remember. All I do remember, his lips were purple, and he wasn't breathing. That's it. Sorry." I said, "So the police never told you or asked you what he was wearing when you left for work?" "Nope. That never came up." I said, "Okay. So, let me ask you now. Do you remember, or can you say for sure what Lyric was wearing before you went to work?" She said, "Yeah. Sure. He was in his PJs. His yellow SpongeBob PJs. All the kids were in their PJs. They're always in their PJs before I go to work." I said, "So, just to clarify. When you changed his diaper before you went to work, he was already in his pajamas?" "Definitely," she said. Then asked, "What's this all about?" I said, "I'll explain in a moment but let me ask you this. Did you ever put the kids to bed in their street clothes?" She replied, "No. Never. They always wore their pajamas to bed." Then quickly added, "Wait a minute! Are you trying to tell me that Lyric wasn't wearing his pajamas?" I nodded, then showed her the photos.

As soon as she recognized his clothing, she became quiet, and her eyes teared up as she continued staring at the photos. Finally, while shaking her head back and forth slowly, she broke her silence and said, "Yeah, these are his clothes. But he wasn't wearing these before I went to work." She stopped briefly to wipe away her tears, then added, "He was wearing his SpongeBob pajamas. The ones he just got for Christmas. He wore them every day." She then turned away as more tears started streaming down her cheeks.

| SpongeBob PJs (similar)

A definitive answer about what clothing Lyric was wearing and when was a turning point in helping to understand better what may have happened. My subsequent interviews with Veronica's mother and friend Chelsie helped to support and reaffirm what I'd learned from Veronica about putting her kids to bed in pajamas. If you recall, during one of my interviews with Hope, she'd been asked whether she'd ever found Lyric's SpongeBob pajamas? To which she said, "Oh, he loved them. They were his favorite. I think he'd just gotten them for Christmas. I did go back into the apartment to gather up clothing for the other kids, but I never saw SpongeBob." Later, after speaking with Veronica, I had also asked Hope if she'd ever found Haveen's pink Barbie comforter? She hadn't found that either.

Police interviewed Chucky's brother Jemel, and he mentioned being over to Veronica's apartment just the day before. He recalled seeing all the children that morning, including Lyric, who was wearing, you guessed it, a SpongeBob outfit.

Later, in a follow-up interview with Ray Ramos, Veronica's

daytime babysitter, he also remembered seeing Lyric in his SpongeBob pajamas.

But it wasn't just SpongeBob and Barbie that were missing. Recalling what Veronica had told me earlier when she said, "The other unusual thing that also hadn't registered with me at the time was that Chucky was already up and dressed in his street clothes. Usually, whenever I'd get home from work, he'd still be in bed in his sleep clothes." And recall that before Jemel Fields left to go home that night, he'd seen Chucky in his sleep clothes. So, why had Chucky changed out of his sleep clothes so early? But more importantly, where were they?

Therefore, I think a few fair questions might be in order, starting with: where the hell is SpongeBob? Why was Lyric wearing street clothes instead of his PJs? What happened to the pink Barbie comforter? And where are Chucky's sleep clothes? In all likelihood, they were right where Chucky left them. In other words, right where he stashed them after killing Lyric and cleaning up the evidence of his crime. But the bungled crime scene search failed to find them. More about this later.

33

CONTINUED INVESTIGATION

Earlier, I mentioned not being able to locate and interview Chucky's brother, Jemel Fields. Later, however, I learned that he had left the area and moved back to Ohio. I found his original phone number in the police reports and dialed it up. Surprisingly, he answered and agreed to speak with me. Jemel said he had been staying at his brother's place at the time but could no longer remember the address. He recalled waking up on December 29th and going over to Veronica's apartment, explaining further that Chucky had just spent the night there. He remembered going inside and staying for a while, and the kids all seemed fine. He left there with Chucky and went to his friend Max's place. Then explained that they remained there all day, playing video games.

Later, he remembered going back to Veronica's place with Chucky because he had to babysit so she could go to work. Continuing, he explained that Chucky made the kids Mac & Cheese, French fries, and Tater-tots after Veronica left. Then claimed to have seen the girls but not the young boy. He then fixed himself a plate of food and took it to the game room, where he ate and played video games with Chucky. Then, somewhere around 12:00-12:30 a.m., he left to go back to Chucky's place to sleep. Before leaving, he noticed Chucky had changed into his sleep clothes.

The next morning, Chucky called him from outside Veronica's apartment and told him the boy was injured, wasn't breathing, and may have fallen out of bed. He added further that the police were there treating him like a suspect. Jemel also mentioned that he was with Max when Chucky called from the police station. And also recalled Max suggesting to Chucky that he get an attorney. Then later, when Chucky called back, he was given the attorney's number.

Notably, Fields' version of events he just described was reasonably consistent with what he'd told the police earlier. But the suspicious part of me wondered why he just happened to be in town from Ohio visiting Chucky when all this happened. I wanted to see what more I could learn about him.

My suspicion paid off. As it turned out, Fields had a lengthier criminal history than Chucky. All drug-related. Most of which had taken place in Hudson County, NJ. Briefly, he'd been arrested for drug manufacturing and distribution, obtaining controlled substances by fraud, dispensing and possession in a school zone, possession and distribution within 500 feet of public housing, conspiracy to sell drugs, and manufacturing and distribution of heroin and cocaine. Additionally, he'd also been arrested in NYC for Criminal Sale of a Controlled Substance and did some time at Rikers Island. So, he wasn't just a small-time drug user. He was a major manufacturer and distributor of illicit drugs, including cocaine and heroin, and who knows what else. So again, why was he in Binghamton? Just a friendly visit with his brother? Perhaps. But my suspicious mind was telling me it was more than that.

Similarly, I wanted to learn more about the Johnson brothers,

Dwaine and Devon, a.k.a. "Weezy" and "Lips." If you recall, they'd both been identified by Jesse Noel as having gone over to Chucky's apartment with him after Lyric's death. Initially, I'd assumed they were just a couple of low-life crackheads because Veronica had told the police earlier about chasing a guy off her porch for dealing drugs. A guy she only knew as "Lips." But my criminal background search revealed something more. They were actually major, career drug dealers.

At the time, Dwaine "Weezy" had previously been convicted of Attempted Criminal Sale of a Controlled Substance and was still on Felony Probation. His brother Devon "Lips" had a more colorful criminal history. He'd been convicted of Robbery in 1996 and did time in state prison. Then convicted again in 2004 for Attempted Criminal Sale of a Controlled Substance and sent back to state prison for another 4-8 years. He was then released on parole in 2007, only to be convicted again in 2008 for Criminal Possession of a Controlled Substance and sent back to prison. He was released on parole just days before Lyric was killed. Later, well after Lyric's death, I learned he had been convicted again as a key player involved in a major trafficking operation that was funneling thousands of dollars worth of heroin into the community. He was sent back to state prison for another 5-10 years.

Needless to say, neither Weezy nor Lips can be considered reliable or trustworthy witnesses. Therefore, had they been interviewed by Investigator Wagner about their alleged trip to Chucky's apartment that day with Jesse Noel, it's not likely they would have been truthful. Especially if their real purpose in going over there wasn't to help beat up Chucky or confront him about killing Lyric. But instead, the more likely purpose was another drug deal. Considering all I'd learned about the current and former drug histories of Chucky, Jemel, Max, Jesse, and more recently, Weezy and Lips, the drug dealing scenario seemed very plausible. It might also explain why Weezy would deny knowing anything when speaking with Wagner.

Admittedly, none of this had any direct connection to Lyric's murder. However, as mentioned previously, I had already rejected Noel's claim of any murder confession by Chucky or Veronica and then questioned whether he had fabricated his entire story. But at the same time, I also wondered if any part of it was true. In my view, there was a slight chance that at least part of Noel's story may have been genuine – that he and his drug-dealing buddies had gone over to Chucky's apartment. Not to beat him up like he claimed but instead for a drug deal.

Fast-forward to June when Noel gets arrested, and it was much more serious this time. He was facing some major prison time. Perhaps even state prison. The gears in his head were turning fast, trying to think of something he could offer in exchange for a deal – a deal that might just keep him out of prison. He was desperate and knew that whatever he came up with would have to be something big. Big enough to perk a few ears and raise some eyebrows. Something that couldn't be ignored.

From speaking with Veronica and others over the past few months, Noel had already developed a reasonably good understanding of how Lyric had been killed, believing Chucky was responsible. After that, during his custodial interview, he decided he could use the story of his trip to Chucky's place with Weezy and Lips, knowing that it actually happened. However, for his plan to work, he'd have to tweak his story just a little. It was relatively simple. Just remove the drug part and insert Chucky's murder confession.

Noel, however, was clueless, never realizing how he was being played big time by the DA and BPD. They knew he was lying from the very beginning and just played along, pretending to believe his story. Right from the get-go, they easily could've said, "Sorry, Jesse. We know you're lying. No deal." Then haul him off to jail. Instead, after learning of his relationship with Veronica, the perfect opportunity presented itself to use him to get to her. Ordinarily, with a more viable suspect, this would have been a pretty clever strategy. Unfortunately, something more ominous was at work.

They knew how desperate Noel was for a deal that would keep him out of prison, which allowed them to maintain their needed control over him. So, the first part of their plan was to lock him into his fake story by having him repeat it a few more times. Which would also help build his confidence in getting his deal. The stage was set.

Jesse Noel was desperate and willing to do whatever it took to stay *out* of prison. Equally desperate were the authorities, also willing to do whatever it took to put Veronica Taft *in* prison.

After more than two weeks of strategic planning, they put the final phase of their plan in place. The dramatic finale was to take place at the jail with the camera rolling, which started by having Noel retell his story of Chucky's confession once again. So far, so good. The plan was coming together nicely. But once he was locked in on camera, it was time to make their move to confront him with his lies. Like DeLucia said, "We've been doing our homework." The stunned expression on Noel's face said it all. He was caught off-guard and quickly realized that any hope for a deal was slipping away fast.

A moment later, his hope was restored when Wagner offered him a second chance by saying, "That's why we're giving you a clean slate." Thus, opening the door to save his deal. To make it even easier, he'd just been told, "Veronica knows she's about to get arrested." He faced the dilemma of choosing between his freedom or tossing his innocent friend to the wolves. That dilemma was very short-lived when he quickly decided to change his story, cowardly sacrificing Veronica in exchange for a deal that would keep him out of prison.

Author's note: Jesse Noel was a perpetual liar, far from being trusted as a credible witness. Unfortunately, we haven't heard the last of him.

34

A LIFELONG FRIEND

Chelsie Snyder was a lifelong friend of Veronica. They had known each other since childhood and were practically "joined at the hip." They grew up together and attended Whitney Point Schools. Sharing similar interests, they later became varsity cheerleaders together with Chelsie's mom as their coach. It was also Chelsie who had been summoned and arrived to pick up Veronica at the BPD after her first interview on December 30th. Notably, Chelsie was in possession of a great deal of valuable knowledge, which could have been very helpful during the police investigation. Apparently, it wasn't the type of information the police were interested in because she was never interviewed.

A LIFELONG FRIEND | 265

| Chelsie & Veronica

When I reached out to Chelsie and her mother, Mary, they were both anxious to speak with me. I later met and interviewed them in their Binghamton home. Chelsie started by telling me that Veronica was always being picked on at school by her classmates and school officials. Then added, "She was very small in school, but she never backed down from anything and never hesitated to speak her mind." "Well, nothing's changed there," I said. She smiled and continued saying that she'd been with Veronica during all of her pregnancies and the births of her children. She added that "Her deliveries were always very quick." Also recalling that Lyric had been born in a car before getting to the hospital. Also adding, "She was always a good mother and very excited to have Lyric since it was her first boy."

Continuing, she recalled Veronica having been involved in abusive relationships with her boyfriends and how she'd once told her about being abused by a relative. She further explained being present with Veronica on one occasion after Lonell Barnes had assaulted her. Then added, "The police were called, but they just let him go." She was also aware of Veronica's problems with some people in Whitney Point and Lisle but couldn't offer anything specific. However, she did agree that they had little or no credibility. Both Chelsie and Mary spoke up about one of the families in the area with who Veronica had issues. Then added, "They were nothing but trouble, a lot of drug use."

Not unlike what I'd learned earlier from Veronica's mother and sister, Chelsie agreed, saying, "Veronica was never into using drugs and only limited alcohol."

She explained having been at Veronica's home on several occasions where she'd witnessed Veronica's interaction with her children. Then added, "She rarely raised her voice and at most would swat a child with her hand." When asked, she said, "I've never seen any signs of bruising that concerned me." However, she did agree that Lyric was very active and liked to climb and jump. She'd seen some minor bruises on knees and elbows, but on the girls also. After being told what Lyric was wearing that morning, I asked her specifically, "Do you know how Veronica would dress her children for bed?" She answered quickly, saying, "Her kids always wore pajamas for bed." Then added, "She'd never put them to bed in street clothes."

I then asked for her assessment about how the children were cared for. She said, "Well, she wasn't always the best housekeeper, but as far as her kids, they were always clean and well cared for. Clean clothes to wear and plenty of food to eat." Then added, "You know. She would take any job she could find to support her kids." When questioned further, she said, "It wasn't unusual for the kids to be up late, on Veronica's schedule." I said, "Yeah, her mom told me that too." Continuing, she said, "Veronica would often call me from work. Actually, she called me that night, around 12:30, I think. Everything seemed normal. I know her pretty well. If anything had been troubling her, I would have known something was wrong."

Chelsie then described how she and her mom were at the

BPD when Veronica finished her interview and how they had taken her back to their house. She said, "Veronica was very upset. She was trying to hold it together for the benefit of her other children. She kept saying, "I don't know what happened. I was at work." Later, she mentioned speaking with Veronica by phone that first day. Then added, "She was hysterical and distraught but kept saying she had to hold it together for the other kids."

When asked if she knew any of Veronica's neighbors, she said, "I didn't know any of them personally, but I do know they weren't very friendly and always critical of Veronica."

During the interview, I found both Chelsie and her mother to be very credible and would make good witnesses if needed. So, near the end of the interview, I asked Chelsie if she would be willing to testify if needed? Without hesitation, she immediately said, "Yes." Mary jumped in and said she would be willing to testify as well if it would help. In wrapping up, I said, "You know how to reach me if you think of anything else that might be helpful." Then asked, "Any final comment before I leave?" Like others before her, Chelsie said, "In all honesty, Veronica is a good mom but wasn't always the best judge when it comes to boyfriends." "Agreed," I said. Then added, "But unfortunately, she had to learn that the hard way."

35

MEETING WITH CPS

At times, it seemed as though we were getting more valuable information from the CPS reports than the police reports. Especially with those matters involving the cry-ladies. As mentioned earlier, most of the CPS reports involving complaints filed against Veronica were investigated thoroughly. The results of which were unfounded. The reports also included the specific reason(s) as to why they were unfounded.

In preparation for the trial, Dave Butler and I were interested in speaking with the respective caseworkers (CWs) who had reported those findings. After cutting through a little red tape, eventually, we were able to set up a joint meeting with all the CWs involved to discuss their reports. However, they would only agree to meet as a combined group, and their CPS legal counsel would have to be present. Our earlier request to meet with each CW individually, as you would usually with any other witness, was denied. But despite the rules, we still wanted to meet with them to discuss their reports. After that, we met in a conference room at the DSS building, with a total of five CWs, one supervisor, and CPS legal counsel.

We had given them advanced notice as to what we were interested in discussing. The group had their respective reports in front of them, which they had reviewed beforehand. For the most part, without too much objection, we just went around the table, questioning each CW about their knowledge and involvement. Then we asked if they could offer anything further that wasn't in the reports. Other than acknowledging and confirming what was in their reports, they had little else to offer. Understandably, they kept any unreported opinions to themselves, being very careful not to say anything that might jeopardize the prosecution of Veronica. And despite having firsthand knowledge of the lack of credibility of the individuals who'd filed those malicious complaints against her, they didn't mention it.

For the most part, our little meeting was productive. While some were polite and friendly, others seemed standoffish or a bit defensive, as if they didn't want to be there. Regardless, we thanked them for their time but, before leaving, informed them that one or more of them may be subpoenaed for trial.

During our elevator ride back downstairs, Dave and I talked about the impending testimony of the credible CPS workers and the loathsome cry-ladies. We both agreed, the CPS workers could undoubtedly be used to impeach the cry-ladies. With the trial only a couple of weeks away, we were feeling confident.

36

PREP FOR TRIAL

Before we met with CPS, Dave and I were actively engaged in our preparations for trial. By now, we were meeting almost daily, and several meetings included lengthy sessions with Veronica at the jail. ADA DeLucia had turned over a list of potential witnesses he intended to call at trial. There were no surprises. However, noticeably missing from his list was Detective Sergeant Tom Eggleston. When Dave called to confirm, he learned that Eggleston had recently retired and was not being called to testify. Dave said, "Well, I don't care if he's retired or not. If they're not calling him, we will." I said, "For sure. We know why they're not calling him, so yeah, we'll need him. And I know how to find him." Moments later, a subpoena was prepared and later served on Eggleston for his testimony.

Veronica's trial was just a few days away and scheduled to start on Monday, August 13, 2012. Broome County Court Judge, the Honorable Joseph Cawley, would be presiding. Judge Cawley and I had a long history of working together, dating back to years earlier when he worked as a defense attorney. We had a great working rapport, and there was mutual respect between us. Later,

I worked on his campaign to become a County Court Judge. Undoubtedly, a man of great integrity and a true professional. Therefore, from a judicial perspective, I was confident that Veronica would get a fair trial.

I had been working with Dave Butler and conducting my independent investigation since mid-October of 2011. During one of our pre-trial work sessions, Dave asked if I'd be willing to assist him during the trial due to my extensive knowledge of the case. I immediately said, "Absolutely, I'm glad you asked because I was going to suggest that, but we'll need court approval." "I'll take care of that," he said. Later, with Judge Cawley's approval, permission was granted for me to assist Dave at the defense table.

Veronica's trial opened on schedule, starting with jury selection. Dave and I met in a cafeteria across the street about an hour before the court opened to prepare for jury selection. We'd been given a lengthy list of prospective jurors ahead of time. Once the court opened, we took our seats at the defense table as jurors filled the seats behind us. Senior ADA Peter DeLucia, and his assistant, Senior ADA Joshua Shapiro, took their seats at the prosecution table. After making sure both sides were ready to proceed, the Court Clerk called for Judge Cawley, who entered and took the bench. After confirming that both sides were ready to proceed, he called for Veronica Taft. A moment later, court officers escorted her into the courtroom, where she took her place at the defense table.

Ordinarily, jury selection in a murder case can take several days. Assuming that would be the case here, we were prepared. As it was, jury selection moved along rather quickly and, for the most part, uneventful. As a result, there was a full jury by day's end. Opening arguments would begin first thing in the morning, followed by the first witnesses.

V

THE TRIAL

37

THE DRAMA BEGINS

In his opening, DeLucia wasted little time in his character assassination of Veronica. Several graphic and racial slurs she was alleged to have used when referring to her mixed-race son were rattled off to the jury. Then he said, "Those aren't my words. Those are the words of this woman," pointing to Veronica. He then laid out his theory as to motive by claiming that she hated Lyric. Adding that, she was a reckless and abusive mother who had pushed Lyric off the couch, taught him how to masturbate, held his face in a pillow, and beat him with a spoon. He also included how a host of former friends had accused her of being a prostitute, drug user, and a host for crack dealers. Notably, everything he just said had come from the loathsome cry-ladies even though none of their bizarre allegations had ever been substantiated by authorities.

Conversely, Dave Butler's opening was relatively brief, saving the specifics for cross-examination. He basically summarized the lack of evidence and unreliability of witnesses and argued that the evidence would not support a guilty verdict.

Opening arguments ended shortly after 11:00 a.m., taking

much less time than expected. For the most part, the testimony of witnesses during the trial just formalized what they had disclosed earlier during the investigation. Rather than repeating what we already know, I'll offer a summary of some of the highlights, focusing on the key players.

DeLucia opened his direct case with testimony from the loathsome cry-ladies. They offered their allegations in support of the misdemeanor endangering charges. However, their real purpose was to lay the groundwork for the forthcoming accusation of murder. In as much, they held nothing back, often adding to or bolstering what they'd said before. In the end, they'd successfully portrayed Veronica as an evil monster, an unfit and physically abusive mother to all her children but especially Lyric. They added further that she was a prostitute, taught Lyric how to masturbate, saw marks and bruises on Lyric "all the time," cooked crack in her bathtub, used drugs, hosted other drug dealers, and more. Then, under cross-examination, they exaggerated their stories even further.

The first material witness was Dr. Terzian. After testifying about his 3:00 a.m. time of death estimate, DeLucia had him describe some of the factors that could effectively shorten or extend the estimate. He mentioned the ambient air temperature, humidity, body mass, clothing, and whether or not the body was in contact with water or a heated surface. Using some of Terzian's examples, DeLucia asked, "Assuming he did eat, assuming he was in a warm apartment and clothed in a bed under a cover and had suffered some sort of trauma, would that or could that alter that 3:00 a.m. finding backward?" He answered, "Yes, I mean, just throw in for the sake of argument a fifty percent error in this calculation of eight hours, then that would make it twelve hours under those circumstances."

I couldn't believe he had just said that. Just throw in a "fifty percent error?" Where did that figure come from? What was it based on? Obviously, by now, he knew what their theory was, and this was his way of trying to help push back the time of death. If you recall, when Terzian testified at the grand jury, he agreed it was possible to be as much as eighteen hours. In other words, an error rate of more than 100 percent. Somewhere between then and now, he'd cut that figure by half.

Regardless, DeLucia wasn't entirely satisfied with the twelve hours and asked, "Could it even be more than twelve?" He answered, "It might be. But if we just argue 50 percent, twelve hours, then we are back around technically possibly 11 p.m. as the time of death. If you work backward, it will be about 10:00 for the trauma and about maybe 8:00 for dinner." DeLucia again asked, "So one possible way of looking at it is whatever trauma could conceivably have occurred, may have occurred at 9:00 in the evening on December 29, 2010?" He answered, "Yes." Next, he asked, "Or obviously at a different time, but that's one possibility, in other words?" He answered, "That is within the realm of possibility here."

As in any criminal case, it's the sole burden of the prosecution to offer proof, which by definition means "*evidence sufficient to establish something as true.*" Yet here, DeLucia asked Dr. Terzian, a forensic expert, to offer a professional opinion based on assumptions and possibilities. Ordinarily, defense attorneys use those not as a means of proof but rather as reasonable doubt. Offering them as some form of proof just doesn't cut it. Not in a murder trial. Incredibly, however, Dr. Terzian, who should be a neutral, impartial witness, instead turned into an interested team player to provide the answers they needed. Then took it a step further by pulling a 50 percent error rate out of the wild blue to help push back the time of death to the desired time of the prosecution.

While still on the topic of his original 3:00 or 4:00 a.m. estimate, Terzian was asked if he told anyone in attendance about his estimated time of death at any time during the autopsy. He claimed, because it was a year-and-a-half ago, he couldn't remember. However, he did say, "If I did that, it might have been just a simple calculation based on the body temperature." After that, Dave Butler took over with his cross-examination.

Referring to his direct testimony, Dave asked, "There's a lot of assumptions made, correct?" He answered, "Yes." Next, he was questioned about the assumption as to whether or not the temperature of the room, be it warm or cold, could change the cooling period? He said, "That's correct." He also answered yes, as to whether the size of the person would make a difference. He agreed further that an infant cools much faster than an adult.

The questioning then turned to his knowledge of any of those 'compounding factors' he mentioned during the grand jury. Dave asked, "And you were never provided with any temperature with regard to the apartment of the bedroom or anything for that matter, were you?" He answered, "No, I was not." Later, Dave followed up with, "Were you ever given reports advising you or showing you what this child was wearing?" He answered, "No." Then Dave asked, "Were you ever given any reports as to the temperature of the room?" To which he replied, "No."

So, as far as he knew, there were no 'compounding factors.' At least none of which he was ever made aware. In other words, there was no logical or justifiable reason to change his original estimate.

Dave then followed up with what he'd been asked on direct about whether he'd told anyone during the autopsy about the time of death. He asked, "Did you give them a verbal time of death?" He answered, "I don't remember giving them a specific time of death, no." Dave questioned, "Okay. In an investigation where it's determined to be a homicide, would that have been a normal question they would have asked?" He answered, "They often ask that question." Continuing, he asked, "If you did answer it, would it have been done along the lines of at least the calculation ninety-eight point six minus the temperature you had, divided by one-and-half?" DeLucia quickly objected, claiming he'd already said he didn't recall. His objection was overruled. Terzian answered, "I don't remember giving them a specific time. I did do the calculations with the time to tell them without considering any other factors. I estimated it eight hours before the 11:00 time when the temperature of eighty-six degrees occurred."

As his cross continued, Terzian once again testified about the 1-2 hour clearing rate of the stomach after a meal. Then testified that the trauma Lyric suffered occurred within an hour or two after he ate.

Let's stop here for a moment. Terzian just agreed, with his new calculation, that it was possible the time of death may have been around 9:00-10:00 p.m. and 8:00 p.m. for dinner. However, Lyric's last known meal before that was 5:00 p.m. when he had a peanut butter & jelly sandwich. In other words, not one or two hours but instead four to five hours before he was killed. So once again, using Terzian's testimony, knowing that any food would be gone within two hours, the math doesn't work.

Dave continued his questioning regarding the stomach contents, which, by design, led to a question about what, if anything, had been done to try and determine what the food substance was. Terzian realized where the questioning was headed but didn't wait for the final part of the question before saying, "I couldn't even tell what the food was. I mean, I tried to find someone who would analyze that and tell me because I wanted to know what he ate to figure out when he ate it, but I couldn't do it." He then admitted that when he did look at the contents, he couldn't identify anything visually. Then Dave asked, "And, as you indicated, the next step would have been to analyze it, and you couldn't?" He answered, "I couldn't find anybody who could do that for me."

Terzian's claim that he couldn't find anyone to analyze the stomach contents was troubling – very troubling for a couple of reasons. First, if you recall, back in January 2011, during a case briefing with CPS, Sergeant Tom Eggleston reported that the stomach contents had been sent to the Medical Examiner's Office in Onondaga County, NY, for analysis. Further, there had been a consult with the Chief Medical Examiner, Dr. Stopiker [sic]. In as much, there would have been a chain of custody receipt, bearing Terzian's signature, upon leaving the morgue evidence locker, where the contents had been stored for further study. Secondly, several accredited crime labs and private labs throughout NY state and across the country are all well-equipped with the technology to identify both known and unknown substances. This is something that's done routinely. Therefore, as an expert forensic medical examiner, who routinely utilizes the services of those labs himself, I found it extremely troubling to hear him say, "I couldn't find anybody." It was nonsense.

Author's note: For clarification, the correct name of the Chief Medical Examiner for the Onondaga County Medical Examiner's Office was Dr. Robert Stoppacher.

Later, Dave's questioning turned to *rigor mortis*, where he had Terzian first explain what it was. Then, while referring to the ER hospital records, Dave asked him to comment about the early onset of rigor observed and documented by the ER doctors while Lyric was being treated. After his review and acknowledgment of the content in the ER records, Dave asked, "Okay. Now, if these notations were made between 11:00 and noon on the 30th and the boy died at 10:00 p.m. the night before, that would be over thirteen hours, correct?" He answered, "Yes." The next question asked was, "Would you see signs of early rigor at thirteen hours, or is that more along the lines of rigor would be done, fixed, and you would be…." Terzian interrupted and said, "You would still be developing rigor. It wouldn't be the beginning of rigor; it would be well into the rigor."

Thank you, Doctor T. You just destroyed their theory and reaffirmed precisely what was mentioned earlier. Again, the point being had Lyric been dead for thirteen hours, by the time he arrived at the hospital, he would have been ice-cold and stiff as a board.

Based on his most recent answer, Dave pressed a little further, trying to get him to admit that his original estimation was more likely than an estimation going back several hours earlier. Terzian responded by saying, "Boy, I don't know if I could make that conclusion." Later, he claimed that the rigor and all the other factors considered were not enough for him to make a conclusion. Referring to the ER observations of rigor, Dave asked, "Well, you don't discount them, right?" He answered, "No, I mean, I think somebody was seeing some rigor. It wasn't maximal yet. It clearly was present. It should be after at least eight hours, we calculated. From the temperature, I mean." Dave followed up with, "You have your initial three-to-four a.m. You've now indicated on direct that there were other factors that came into play, that if they're all true, could allow you to extend the time of death farther back, okay?" He answered, "That's right." Dave asked, "Take away any one of those factors or all of those factors that then brings it back this direction to the rule of thumb?" To which he answered, "That's right." Continuing, Dave asked, "So your time of death is all based upon assumptions of what the information you're given is, correct?" He replied, "That's right. I have to base it on the assumptions."

Dave kept hammering away on the time of death issue when Terzian finally admitted, "I really have no way of knowing for sure when the time of death was in this case." Considering his direct testimony when he said it was conceivable that the time of death was twelve hours earlier, Dave asked, "I'll use the same word that he did, that this happened early in the morning hours of December 30th as opposed to back there?" He answered, "I really can't tell." Then Dave asked, "So, you're saying it's just as conceivable this happened three-to-four as it happened back then?" He replied, "That might be a fair statement." Somewhat frustrated, Dave asked, "How is that possible, Doctor?" He answered, "It's just that we don't have enough data and enough good ways to make that measurement in this case." Dave again asked, "Well, you do." "No, we don't," he said. Dave responded, "You had the data. You had the rule of thumb. The other data was given to you before you testified at the grand jury nine months later?" He answered, "Um-hm." So, Dave continued, "Take away that data. If none of that data was present, what would your estimate be today?" He answered, "If we only had one thing to go on, it would be three or four in the morning." As a final inquiry regarding the time of death, Dave asked, "So, I understand your position, you know, it all depends, and you agree with me that unless you have solid facts which are actually established facts, it's a guessing game?" He answered, "I'm afraid it is in this case."

Questioning then turned to some of Lyric's injuries. Specifically, the fingernail marks when Dave asked, "A lot of attention was brought to the fingernail marks. You saw three on the right side?" He answered, "Correct." When asked, Terzian agreed that the fingernail marks had formed an abrasion, where the skin had been scraped off. Dave asked, "So, if I had nails and abraded myself here, I would have transferred it under my nails, wouldn't I?" He answered, "You probably would have, yes."

DeLucia came back with a minor redirect about the fingernail marks. Interestingly, Terzian testified that the orientation of the fingernail marks was on the right side of Lyric's neck whereas, the marks under his left ear were from a thumb. This was interesting for two reasons. First, Veronica was left-handed. During both of her interviews, she can be seen using her left hand to sign her Miranda rights and, later, her written statement. Second, during her second interview, she told the police she was a nail-biter and then showed them how short her nails were.

Investigator Matt Zandy followed Dr. Terzian. Senior ADA Josh Shapiro led him through his direct testimony, which was quite lengthy, so I'll try to be brief. Early in his testimony, he talked about taking pictures of Lyric at the hospital and seeing the fingernail marks on the right side of Lyric's neck.

Later, when questioned about his experience as a crime scene investigator, he was asked approximately how many crime scenes he had been to. He answered, "Oh, at least a thousand." Adding that, he had been in the ID Unit for eight years and was in his 15th year with the BPD.

Once again, consistent with his prior testimony at the grand jury, he testified that the temperature in Veronica's apartment on December 30th was extremely warm. Notably, that would be needed to help back up Dr. Terzian's assumptions.

As expected, since Zandy was present during the entire autopsy taking photographs, he was asked, "During that autopsy, did Dr. Terzian ever tell you the time of death was between 3:00 and 4:00 a.m.?" He answered, "No." They followed up with, "Did you ever hear Dr. Terzian tell anyone the time of death was between 3:00 and 4:00 a.m.?" He answered, "No. I didn't." Thereafter, Dave Butler began his cross.

It didn't take long before he got to the topic of the fingernail marks Zandy had seen and photographed at the autopsy. While showing him the photographs, he asked, "Right there looking at these apparent fingernail marks, what significance is that to you as a crime scene investigator?" He answered, "Well, no significance at the time." During further questioning, Zandy continued to downplay any significance to the fingernail marks. Later, however, he finally admitted the injuries were consistent with a beating. Continuing, Dave asked. "Okay. So, if the injuries supported a beating and there are significant marks on his face which are apparently fingernail marks, what significance would that have in association with a beating case and death of a small child?" He answered, "Well, it could have significance. It may not have significance." Following up, he asked, "Again, you know what evidence is. When somebody puts their fingernail marks into somebody's face like that and leaves cuts, where does that stuff go?" He answered, "It goes under the fingernails of whatever made the mark." Dave again asked, "Exactly. It's possible, right?" He answered, "It's possible, yeah."

Dave's questioning was rather aggressive and rightfully so, especially when challenging him. Not so much on what he did but rather what he didn't do. Dave's questions were all legitimate, all about standard investigative protocol. Zandy's answers, however, were anything but legitimate and were making him look foolish. As a crime scene investigator myself, I found it hard listening to him.

Zandy's cross went on for a lengthy period, but his answers never improved. After reminding him of the few things he had done and the short one hour and four minutes he spent processing the crime scene, Dave asked, "Is that a significant amount of time in there for this type of case?" His bizarre reply, "I believe at the time, sir, we were not aware that it was a homicide investigation at that point." Yes, he actually said that, and I couldn't resist rolling my eyes.

Dave pushed on further by showing him the photograph he'd

taken of a wet towel on the bathroom floor and asked if that had any significance at all, and he said no. Continuing, Dave asked, "People don't wipe blood up with towels or wipe off blood with towels or clean up scenes with towels?" He answered, "There was no indication of that to me." Dave pointed out, "It looks like it's got some dark coloration in it, doesn't it?" He answered, "Yes, it does." So, Dave followed up with, "Still no significance?" "No," he said.

There was much more to his testimony, but I'm jumping ahead here with just a couple more things. Referring to his search for evidence, Dave asked, "Is it normal procedure to look in trash bags, closets, and drawers for those things?" He answered, "I guess it would depend on the situation." Dave asked, "Well, you didn't know what the situation was?" He replied, "Right." Dave continued, "So, in that situation, would it be normal to look?" He answered, "Yeah, we would look." He then went on to try and explain why he hadn't done any of those things. Dave then identified each area one by one, asking if he'd searched there. His answer was no to everything. Dave even asked if he'd ever gone outside on the balcony. Nope. Hadn't done that either.

As one of his final areas of questioning, Dave returned to the time of death issue and asked, "And it's your testimony there are no discussions during or after the autopsy regarding the time of death"? He answered, "No." Then he asked, "Not even an estimated time of death?" He replied, "No. The time of death was never discussed, no."

Sticking to this line of questioning, the next question was, "When was the first time that you learned about the time of death?" He incredulously answered, "I still don't know the time of death. Dave asked, "You're kidding me?" He replied, "No." Dave pressed a little further, asking, "And you're saying in none of those meetings was it discussed what the time of death was?" He answered, "No." Dave continued, "And in none of those meetings did anyone else?" To which he answered, "I don't remember having a meeting." Shortly after that, Zandy was turned back over to Shapiro for a few redirect questions. For the most part, he just skirted around the issues.

Sergeant Michelle Stebbins had nineteen years on the job, but she was the ID Unit Supervisor for the past eight years. According to her testimony, she was off duty the day Lyric was killed, and her first involvement wasn't until January 7th.

For the most part, her testimony focused on her examination of various physical evidence and her involvement during the search warrants that took place after December 30th. Her first official involvement included the examination of the three articles of clothing Lyric had been wearing. Item one was the diaper collected from the hospital. Referring to her examination, DeLucia asked, "Did you notice anything unusual about it when you looked at it in January of 2011?" She answered, "Initially, when I looked at it, I noted there were several small areas of blood-like stains on the exterior, and there was some red-like blood staining on the inside of the diaper in the front area where the urine seemed to be." Referring to the outside of the diaper, DeLucia asked, "Can you describe and show us what that looked like?" She answered, "Yes, they're just small areas. They look like transfer stains. It's consistent with this object touching another object that might have some blood-like staining on it. It doesn't appear to be droplets like from a spatter incident. It just looks like it's transferred from another area."

Similarly, DeLucia had her identify the other two articles of clothing in the same way. When asked if she had done any type of fingerprint analysis, she said no – explaining that clothing does not yield fingerprint evidence.

From there, his questioning turned to her experience with DNA. He asked, "Have you submitted items for DNA analysis?" She answered, "Yes, numerous times." He continued, "In this case, did you submit any of these items for DNA analysis?" She answered, "No, we did not." He asked, "Why not?" She answered, "There was no evidentiary value to it in our opinion." He asked, "Why do you say that?"

That was a good question, but you better brace yourself for her answer. "Well, any DNA left on those items would have been predominantly from baby Lyric. They were his clothing items taken from him, and the outside part of it would have been from anybody in that household that would have touched it. You would have gotten small areas of trace DNA, if possible, but since baby Lyric was the major contributor to those items, most likely he would have the only profile that would have been obtained from those items."

She could not have been serious. Even more troubling was how she could say that with a straight face. I would agree that Lyric's DNA would likely be present on his own clothing. However, to claim there was no value in finding DNA in the form of blood on the outside of Lyric's diaper was absurd. Especially in light of what they knew at the time.

Before Stebbins examined the diaper, she was already aware of three critical things:

1. That Veronica had changed Lyric's diaper before she went to work,
2. Chucky was the only one in the household that was bleeding,
3. Chucky claimed he'd never seen Lyric all night.

Logically, if that's true, any fingerprint or DNA from Chucky, in any form, shouldn't be anywhere on that diaper. Yet, Stebbins says, "There was no evidentiary value to it in our opinion. It could have been anyone in that household." Then she added, "Most likely he (Lyric) would have the only profile that would have been obtained from those items." Sadly, I can't even begin to describe how difficult it was to sit there and listen to her shamefully bogus testimony.

The questioning then continued regarding her involvement during the second search warrant on January 19th. DeLucia asked, "Did you take note of the temperature in the apartment itself?" After answering yes, he asked, "How did you do that?" She replied, "There was a thermostat on the wall in the kitchen." Adding, "Initially walking into the apartment, it was very, very warm – it seemed to be very, very warm." He asked, "And what was the reading?" She said, "I believe it was seventy-four degrees Fahrenheit." Thereafter, Dave Butler began his cross-examination.

Dave started by showing her the series of photographs she took during her examination of the diaper. The photos were then offered and received into evidence and published to the jury on the big screen. After displaying the first photograph, he asked, "Take a look at the picture. There's red arrows depicted in the picture. What do those indicate?" She answered, "Those arrows signify the areas where I saw the blood-like transfer stains on the exterior of the diaper." He followed up, asking, "And how many blood-like stains did you see on the exterior?" She replied, "Five."

During her direct testimony, she claimed the diaper's fastening tabs were made of cloth material. Following up on that, Dave asked, "You indicated that the tabs were cloth-like, is that right?" She answered, "They're cloth-like paper material, yes." He asked, "Isn't the other side of it adhesive, a sticky material?" She replied, "Right." He then asked, "Is that conducive to a fingerprint?" She answered, "It can be at times." So, he asked, "Did you check the sticky side?" To which she replied, "No, I did not."

Continuing, Dave asked her to explain what a blood transfer

stain was. She said, "A transfer stain is caused by an item coming into contact with another area with blood-like staining." Dave said, "Okay. For example, if I had a cut on my hand and I put diapers on, if I had any blood on my fingers, I could transfer that onto the diaper?" She answered, "You could, right." Following up, he asked, "Now, the fact that you indicated this is a transfer, that was of no significance to you?" She replied, "It didn't appear to be of any significance to me, no."

During further questioning, she agreed that it was possible that if a person had a cut on their hand and they changed the diaper, it could have been transferred from their hand to the diaper. Dave then asked, "So, you didn't consider that the possible assailant had transferred this blood onto the diaper?" DeLucia objected but was quickly overruled, and she answered, "The person who put the diaper on baby Lyric, it doesn't indicate who would have beat baby Lyric, in our opinion. Anybody could have touched that diaper in that household. If the same person did cut their finger and bleed on the diaper, it wouldn't necessarily mean that that was the person who beat him." Dave again asked, "But your job is to rule that out, isn't it, not just say I'm not going to look at it?" She answered, "Like I said, anything on that diaper wouldn't have necessarily pointed to the suspect." The next question was, "So, why do we do DNA anyway then?" She answered, "Because sometimes it does. It depends on the case and the item."

Dave was hammering away with all the right questions, and so far, her answers were awful. And that was putting it politely. By not examining the diaper for DNA, DeLucia had placed Stebbins in a difficult position, where she was forced to explain why that step was never done. Fortunately for him, she was a team player who was more than willing to help protect their bizarre theory. In so doing, whether she realized it or not, she was making herself look foolish.

Moving ahead, Dave began questioning her about her involvement during the second search warrant, three weeks after the first one. He asked, "Did you really expect to find anything there nineteen days later?" She confidently answered, "Absolutely. You know, we don't go there and look anywhere and not find something. So, we just wanted to be thorough. So, we went back to double-check to make sure we didn't miss anything the first time." She was also asked if they had found anything of significance that would help the case? She answered, "No. After the postmortem exam, there was nothing in that apartment that could have helped us evidentiary wise."

They wanted to be thorough and double-check, to make sure they didn't miss anything. Okay. No argument there because that's precisely the right thing to do. However, that needs to be done *before* giving up the crime scene. Attempting to do so three weeks later is exactly the wrong thing to do. Besides, as we've already learned, being thorough and double-checking had nothing to do with their return to the scene.

The questioning then turned back to the diaper and the day she pulled it out of the evidence locker to show to DeLucia. She confirmed that it did happen, and DeLucia had examined the diaper for eight minutes before she returned it to the evidence locker. Later, she said no when asked if she'd ever been provided with any DNA samples or fingernail scrapings from Charles Pratt or Veronica Taft. Following up, he asked, "If you have a suspect, would it be unusual to have that person's hands examined to determine whether there's a transfer from the child's face from the person wherever it came from onto the suspect's nails?" She answered, "That has happened on occasion, correct, yes." He asked, "And if you looked under Charles Pratt's nails and it came back DNA of Lyric, would that have any significance to you?" She answered, "No, it would not." He followed up, asking, "It wouldn't?" "Let me explain," she said. "If somebody is in the same household as somebody else by me, if I went over and hugged Pete DeLucia and, you know, touched him on his skin anywhere I would get possibly trace evidence under my fingernails or on my hand from Pete and so people that live in the same household that consistently touch each other doesn't really give too much evidentiary value. It just shows that those people are going to contact." Dave commented and asked, "All right, but we are not talking about trace – there's going to be actual skin of this child underneath the nails that caused that?" DeLucia objected but was overruled.

The answer that followed was even more bizarre than the one she just gave. Offering an excuse similar to that of Zandy saying, "It wasn't yet determined that this was actually a homicide." Then she added a second excuse, saying, "Or, it may have been a SIDS case. And, anybody in that household would have had Lyric's skin or DNA under their nails." She was clearly trying to squirm her way around legitimate inquiries with bogus answers. A SIDS death? That theory was absurd. One look at Lyric's injuries would rule that out immediately. I could only hope that the jury was paying attention.

Briefly, let's back up to the "hugging of Pete DeLucia" scenario she described. Agreed, touch DNA can be transferred from one person to another through direct contact, such as the hug she described. However, as Dave pointed out in his questioning, this wasn't about 'touch' DNA. Someone with long fingernails penetrated and abraded the skin on Lyric's neck. As such, both Dr. Terzian and Investigator Zandy agreed that the abraded skin would probably be under the assailant's fingernails. Yet, Stebbins just claimed that any skin or DNA under the nails could have come from anybody in that household. Wow! Lyric must have been given one hell of a hug.

Throughout her remaining testimony, the shameful nature of her answers continued and then worsened. It's been said that

"Truth fears no questions." Stebbins' bizarre answers were a clear demonstration of her fear of the truth. Otherwise, her answers would have made a lot more sense. As it was, listening to her testimony was painful and made my head hurt. I watched and listened to a so-called professional crime scene investigator make a public fool of herself under oath.

For the most part, the testimony of Jemel Fields, Chucky's brother, was consistent with what he'd been saying all along. In other words, no surprises. However, there were times when he appeared to be incoherent and started babbling. At one point, it got so bad that his testimony was halted, and the judge asked if he was okay. After a few minutes, he claimed to be fine, and his testimony continued. Later, it was learned that he had diabetes, and his blood sugar may have been out of whack. Next up was his brother, Chucky.

Like his brother, the vast majority of Chucky's testimony was consistent with what we've already learned. However, there were a few interesting new comments made. The first one that jumped out at me was a direct contradiction to what he'd told his interviewers back in early February 2011. When asked who would change diapers, he said, "Me once in a while, but usually Haveen and Veronica." However, when asked that same question at trial, his answer left little doubt when he said, "No. I don't. I refuse to change any diaper." He was asked, "You refuse?" He answered, "Refuse. I don't do those." Then added that if they did need changing, he would have Haveen do it. Considering what he'd said earlier, we were pretty surprised by his answer. We wondered what prompted the change and why he was so adamant. Oddly, having Haveen change her siblings' diapers during the day was one thing but waking her in the middle of the night? Considering everything that had gone wrong so far, the thought did cross our minds that perhaps Chucky was told about the blood on the diaper. Either that or during his trial prep, a 'suggestion' was made about how to answer.

Another interesting comment he made, which he'd never said before, was that usually, as soon as Veronica got home from work, he would leave. But as we've already learned, that didn't happen on December 30th. Furthermore, when answering questions about what the kids did if they needed anything while he was babysitting, he said, "If they need anything, they come to me." Okay. So, what happens if one wakes up in the middle of the night with a messy diaper? Apparently, rather than change it himself, he wakes Haveen out of a sound sleep because he refuses to change any diapers. This was coming from a man who says, "I love kids" and "I want to run a daycare center."

Continuing, after admitting to fixing dinner for the kids and fixing four plates, he was asked if he had to call them out for dinner and said, "I did call their names." Then he also admitted going into the kids' bedroom to get Zoey out of her crib to eat. In so doing, he walked right past Lyric but never bothered checking to see if he wanted to eat? Then he admitted further to seeing all four plates empty and assumed Lyric had eaten. When asked about the dog peeing on the bed, he said the dog didn't pee there. It had peed on the bed at his house.

He explained once again about the kids' room being cold. With blankets on the windows to help keep the cold out. Later, he was asked why he had gone back to Veronica's apartment. He claimed he was allowed in to watch the place. He claimed further to have gone back with Veronica to get some things. However, as we've already learned, Veronica didn't go back to her apartment after. Chucky went alone.

I mentioned previously that we probably hadn't heard the last of Jesse Noel. As expected, he was called to testify right after Chucky. Once again, he repeated his lie, claiming that Veronica had confessed to murdering her son. Then admitted that he had first told the police that it was Chucky who confessed on three or more occasions. Telling him that he killed the boy because "Veronica was screwing around on him." For the most part, other than a few exceptions, his direct testimony was just a repeat of what we already know.

During his early cross-examination, he admitted that his relationship with Veronica had ended in October 2010. Yet, he claimed she had called him in the early morning hours of January 10, 2011, and confessed to killing her son. We knew that Noel had already told many lies and that liars can rarely keep their stories straight. As such, we were confident it would be no different now. Sure enough, in his testimony that followed, he often contradicted his prior statements or said things he'd never said before. Early in his cross, Dave asked, "Do you know Chucky?" He answered, "I know Chucky." Dave followed up with, "Well, you know Chucky from down in the city, New York City?" He answered, "No, no." Yet, he'd told the police during his post-arrest interview in June that he was familiar with Chucky from the Bronx where they grew up.

When asked whether he had contact with Veronica *after* Lyric's death before she called him on January 10th to confess, he said no. However, he claimed that he had gone over to her apartment on January 3rd or 4th, but no one was there.

Not surprisingly, Noel offered another new revelation when Dave asked, "Did she ever ask you to lie for her?" He answered, "That was the alibi. Chucky did it. Charles did it. That was the whole thing to help her out." Dave followed up, "No. Did she ever tell you to lie for her?" He answered, "Yes. Well, not ask me to lie, but can I help her out, help her." Dave asked, "All right. You never told anybody that until today, right?" He answered, "No." Dave asked, "This is the first time ever that you've mentioned that?" He answered, "Yes, it is." Under further cross, he admitted never telling the police that, even when they'd asked explicitly. Then he also admitted to never telling that to the grand jury. Later, he also testified for the first time that Veronica, during that same January 10th phone call, asked him to tell the police that Chucky confessed.

Turning to the hole in the wall, Dave questioned him about how he knew it was a "child-sized" hole that he'd told Investigator Wagner about during his interview. To start, Dave asked, "Has anyone ever told you that there's a child-sized hole in that wall outside of her bedroom in the living room?" He answered, "No." Dave then refreshed his memory about what he had told Wagner, and he agreed to have told him that. Continuing, Dave said it was either: one, you saw it yourself, or two, someone told you. Then he asked, "Which one?" Noel answered, "I saw it when I was over there." Dave asked, "So, now you're in the apartment after the hole?" He answered, "After the fact, yes, I saw it." Dave continued, "Okay. When was that?" He replied, "One of the times that I came over, I saw it." He asked, "After Lyric died?" He answered, "Yes. I can't recall when, but I did see it." Dave questioned, "Did she point it out to you and say that's the hole that I slammed him into right there – that's the wall or look at the hole that I left? Did she tell you that?" He nodded his head then said, "Yes."

We knew he was lying because he'd already testified earlier that other than January 3rd or 4th when no one was home, he'd never been back. Accordingly, Dave challenged him asking, "You said I've never been in that apartment, right, after his death?" He answered, "No, I never said that. I don't remember saying that." Dave said, "You've already testified to it here today." He replied, "No, I said I was there afterward. I said I went there." Then added, "That's where I saw the hole."

After that, Noel was turned over to DeLucia for some redirect. DeLucia couldn't resist trying to get some clarification as to whether or not Noel had gone back to Veronica's apartment after Lyric's death. He asked, "And you said that you did go over to her house after Lyric's death?" he answered, "Yes, I did." DeLucia asked, "Okay. Do you recall when you went over after that end of December period?" He answered, "Well, several times. Like, several times I went over." In his attempt to bolster his claim, he went on to say, "She would say she had no food. I would buy her some food, or she would say the kids were hungry. I would buy Chinese food, or she would say, "Jesse, can you come over." So, I don't remember exact days, but I know I was there several times after this happened."

Later, DeLucia asked, "The hole that you saw, when did you first see that? Can you give us a date or a day?" He answered, "Let me see. Well, it would have to be after the 10th, after I spoken with her and, as a matter of fact, it was the day that I had – I came home from work straight over to her home and brought Chinese food, and I remember the hole being there." He asked, "Were her children with her at that point?" He replied, "Yes. Yes, Haveen and the other sisters were there, yes."

What a bunch of nonsense. Nothing Noel just said was true. He was just making stuff up as he went along, just like he'd been doing from the very beginning. He was a big liar but not a very good one. He'd dug himself into a hole he couldn't get out of, so he just kept on digging. It was rather pathetic.

More troubling was the fact that DeLucia knew he was lying. He was desperately trying to salvage some of Noel's rapidly failing credibility. In doing so, he just knowingly elicited false testimony from his witness, knowing full well that Jesse Noel had never been back to Veronica's apartment after Lyric's death. Which meant he'd never seen Veronica, her children, or the hole in the wall. DeLucia knew it wasn't true for a couple of reasons: First, because after Lyric's death, Veronica didn't go back to her apartment, and second, he knew Veronica's children were in the custody of her mother. Busted.

Before wrapping up, Dave had a little more recross. Noel claimed once again having gone over to Veronica's apartment several times after the January 10th phone call. Later, when challenging him about his latest claim of Veronica asking him to alibi her, Dave referred to his earlier interview with Wagner. Then asked, "You told Wagner that Veronica never told me to do anything, never asked me to do anything, right?" He answered, "Yes." Then he was asked, "But now you're telling us today she did?" He answered, "Yes." Dave asked, "So, you weren't truthful back then? Even when you had the epiphany, you weren't truthful when you told them that? You were still lying to them, weren't you, according to you?" He replied, "No, I just said – no."

As a final line of questioning, Dave asked, "And you stated that you had been there several times and you saw her up in March at a bowling alley?" He answered, "Yes." Then Dave asked, "You told Wagner after the phone call I didn't speak to her until my birthday, March 21st?" He replied, "Sort of. No, I said that. I said that."

38

CPS LEGAL MATTER

Halfway through the trial, testimony was halted, and the jury was temporarily excused from the courtroom. Thereafter, Judge Cawley, opposing counsel, and a CPS attorney went into Cawley's chambers to discuss a pending legal matter. Earlier, the CPS attorney had filed a legal motion under section 422 of the Social Services Law, asking the Court to preclude the introduction or use of any CPS reports. Specifically, those that were unfounded. Then, asking further to prevent the testimony of the CPS caseworkers who authored the reports. They argued that the records were confidential and sealed by law and could only be released by a court order.

During the ensuing arguments in chambers, the issue as to how the police obtained access to the "unfounded" reports without a court order became a sticking point during their discussion. The Defense pointed out that DSS had simply given them to the police. Initially, DSS counsel denied it but later admitted they had. It was also noted that those same records had been turned over to the Defense during pre-trial discovery. DSS counsel reminded the court that the "unfounded" portion of the reports was confidential according to the legal statute outlined in section 422. After that, DeLucia argued that any "unfounded" reports should be kept out. However, Judge Cawley quickly pointed out that the reports, whatever their confidentiality, had already been released. In other words, the cat was already out of the bag.

The arguments in chambers lasted quite some time, and both sides made plausible arguments. Unfortunately, part of the problem was in the way the law was written. Section 422 of the Social Services Law was somewhat vague and poorly written, which was not only confusing but difficult to understand how it should be interpreted or applied. To make matters worse, all parties agreed they were unfamiliar and somewhat ignorant of the law, having never dealt with this issue before.

After oral arguments, Judge Cawley asked that all respective arguments be put in writing, which he would later review before deciding whether to allow or preclude the CPS reports. In the meantime, the trial resumed.

A few days later, Cawley reached his decision and summoned counsel back into chambers. During his review, he noted that the Court hadn't found any case which would allow the subjective determination of "unfounded" vs. "founded" to be presented to a jury. Then added, "I haven't been able to find anything that suggests that they can be given to this jury," thereby agreeing with the prosecution to bar the use of any "unfounded" report or testimony from its author from the jury.

Using those "unfounded" reports to impeach the cry-ladies' credibility had been a significant part of our defense strategy. Needless to say, we were very disappointed with the decision. It was a devastating blow to the Defense, which for the most part, would leave the damaging testimony from the cry-ladies unchallenged. It left the jury to believe their evil portrayal of Veronica was accurate.

39

TRIAL RESUMES

Lead investigator Jeff Wagner was up next. Senior ADA Josh Shapiro lead him through his direct testimony. At the time, Wagner had about 22-years of experience as a police officer and the last 12-years as an investigator with BPD.

During his direct, Wagner explained his response and subsequent observations upon his arrival at the crime scene. During the brief period that he was at the scene, he recalled seeing a small female child inside the apartment, dressed in pajamas. Shortly after that, he helped transport Charles Pratt from the scene to the BPD station with Investigator Cornell. Then from there, over to the hospital to speak with Veronica.

Later, during his cross-examination, he admitted Veronica had told him she was having a hard time remembering things. Then added, "I didn't know whether to believe her or not." During his direct testimony, he described the inconsistencies he'd noted when interviewing Veronica. Under cross, however, after Dave pointed out the differences between major and minor inconsistencies, he admitted that her only inconsistencies were about little things.

After acknowledging that Veronica was at work between 11:00 p.m. and 7:00 a.m., Dave asked, "So, the death occurred in that time. Is there anything she could add about what happened in that room based on personal knowledge?" He answered, "She wouldn't be able to add anything after she left for work."

Continuing, he was asked if he'd had any further involvement with Charles Pratt after December 30th? He only recalled a single interview at the DA's Office, possibly in February. He'd taken no notes and couldn't recall if anyone else had. Following up on Pratt, Dave asked, "Within a week after December 30th, did you have an opportunity to review Charles Pratt's video?" Knowing he was the lead investigator, I was blown away when he answered, "I still have not watched that video to this day." Later, he said he relied on what other officers told him.

When questioned about the autopsy, he said he did not attend. However, he did acknowledge knowing that the autopsy was performed on December 31st. Dave asked, "When was the first time after the autopsy was completed that you were made aware of any estimation of time of death?" Once again, I was blown away when he answered, "I don't think anybody ever gave me an estimation of the time of death that I recall." Later, he denied ever using an estimated time of death to help move along any investigation he'd ever worked. Having said that, Dave asked, "So, this is the first case?" He answered, "Yes." Dave asked, "And would you agree with me that the timing of this death is critical in this case?" He replied, "Yes. It was critical from the time we arrived at the scene." Dave followed up with, "Okay. Did you ever make inquiry as to what the estimated time of death would have been?" He answered, "With Dr. Terzian, we talked about it, and he said it was very broad. He couldn't pinpoint it. I believe his words were 9:00 p.m. the night before."

Wasn't that convenient? Notably, he just contradicted himself twice in the same answer. He just said a moment earlier, "I don't think anybody ever gave me an estimation of the time of death that I recall." And now he admitted they did talk with Dr. Terzian about the time of death. Then, he contradicted himself further by saying he'd heard Dr. Terzian say it was 9:00 p.m. Yet, just before that, he testified Dr. Terzian said it was very broad and couldn't be pinpointed. Like our President might say, "C'mon, man."

Questioning then turned to his January 31st assignment to confirm Veronica's work alibi at the Binghamton High School. Dave asked, "And did you confirm that she was at work?" He answered, "Yes." Dave continued, "Did you relay that information to anyone back at BPD?" He answered, "Oh, we let everybody know something like that, yes." Then Dave asked, "Well, isn't it true that you were aware of the time of death at that point, and you were being asked to go there to confirm she was at work during that time frame?" He replied, "No." Later, he admitted that their investigation confirmed that Veronica had been at work the entire time she said she was. Dave asked, "So, that…did that knowledge refocus you onto Charles Pratt?" He answered, "Sure, yes. I wasn't unfocused from Charles Pratt at that point."

Surprisingly, when questioned about any communication there may have been about Lyric's clothing and whether any evidence was found on them, he believed there might have been but couldn't recall. Then added that he hadn't inquired because he trusted his investigators to let him know if they'd found anything.

Investigator Anthony Diles was up next, and shortly into his direct testimony, he was asked about being at the autopsy. He said he was in attendance for about an hour. Then, just like his colleagues before him, he claimed that Dr. Terzian never told him or anyone else during the autopsy that the time of death was between 3:00 and 4:00 a.m. During his cross-examination, the questioning regarding the time of death was posed a little differently. Instead, he was asked whether anyone had calculated the time of death or mentioned an estimated time. Like the others, he said no. Later, Diles described how the autopsy findings were relayed to him later by other investigators. Dave then asked, "Was the time of death ever relayed to you, estimated time of death?" He answered, "No."

During Diles' testimony, Veronica's January 1st videotaped interview was played for the jury. After that, Dave pointed out and touched on the part where Veronica was asked about her fingernails. Diles admitted they had taken a brief look at her hands. Following up, Dave asked, "How did you know – why would you have looked at her hands?" He replied, "I'm not sure why that came up." Yet later, when questioned further, he admitted having seen fingernail marks in the photographs of Lyric's neck. In other words, he knew damn well why they'd asked to look at her fingernails.

Near the end of his cross, Dave asked, "Now, she's being accused of doing crack cocaine. You said to her, "We have information that you do crack cocaine," right?" He answered, "Yes." So, Dave asked, "And she said, I'll take a piss test right now?" He replied, "Yes, she did." Dave continued, "Did you take her up on that?" He answered, "At that point, we didn't have the means to do so." Dave asked, "Okay. But she was being accused of doing drugs, and she said, "I can prove it right now that I'm not." That's not important? That's not something that can be thrown into her face if she's lying?" He replied, "Well, it certainly could have been, but again, there was not an opportunity to do it right then."

The prosecution rested, and the defense was up next.

At the time of the trial, Sergeant Tom Eggleston had retired after 25-years of service. His last 2-3 years were served as the supervising Sergeant in charge of detectives. Dave wasted little time getting right to the main issue regarding his knowledge of the time of death. After acknowledging he was not present during the autopsy, Dave asked, "Okay. Now, after the autopsy, let's say, and going into January 1st, were there meetings between detectives down at the Binghamton Police Department?" He answered, "Yes." So, Dave asked, "How often would you have these meetings in this investigation?" He replied, "Correspondence with the investigators is ongoing but sit-down meetings, at least a daily basis." He then identified Wagner and Cornell as the lead investigators, as well as the other investigators involved. Continuing, Dave asked, "And at the time this boy was discovered on December 30th, was the time of death an important issue for you at that time?" He answered, "It was discussed, yes." Dave continued, "Okay. Well, was it important to you?" He replied, "Yes." Dave asked, "And you've been involved in numerous murder investigations, correct?" He answered, "That's correct." So, Dave asked, "And isn't it one of the first things you try to find out information about?" He replied, "Yes." So, Dave continued, "And did you, in fact, find out information about the time of death in this case on January 1st?" He replied, "It was talked about, yes, sir." Dave asked, "Okay. In those meetings with the other investigators?" He replied, "Yes."

From there, he admitted that he had provided CPS with information about the time of death, Lyric's body temperature, and the formula used to make the calculation. He admitted further to telling CPS that the body temperature loses two degrees per hour and that it could be quicker with a child. In answer to a question about what he'd told CPS, he added, "The rule of thumb would be the term that I would use...." So, Dave asked, "Okay. Did you tell her the rule of thumb?" He replied, "Yeah, I believe so." Again, referring to the information he shared with CPS, Dave asked, "In fact, you told her that Lyric died sometime around 3:00 a.m. to 4:00 a.m. timeframe, correct." He replied, "I believe that was an estimate."

Dave wanted to lock him in about what he knew of the time of death, as well as what was shared with CPS and his investigators. So, once again, referring to the CPS caseworker, he asked, "And she was at – you invited her over to a meeting at Binghamton Police Department, correct?" He answered, "Yeah." Dave continued, "And detectives were present?" To which he responded, "Yes." He asked, "And this time of death issue was discussed?" He replied, "Yes." He later explained how there had been numerous meetings after that, and the time of death was discussed frequently. As a final question, he went back to what he had told CPS and asked, "Were you deceiving her at that point in time?" He answered, "I was not deceiving her. I was providing information that was discussed." Shortly thereafter, the defense rested.

40

CLOSING ARGUMENTS & DELIBERATIONS

After two weeks of testimony, both sides rested their case. Before closing arguments, Dave filed a standard defense trial order of dismissal motion, claiming that the People had not met their burden of proof and that all charges should be dismissed. As expected, the Court denied the motion. After that, the jury heard closing arguments. Unlike opening arguments, the defense would go first, followed by the People who would have the final word. Each closing was about an hour long.

Dave went right to work. He started by referring to the cry-ladies as the "yahoos" whose only purpose was to make you angry and hate Veronica. Turning to the 9-1-1 call, he reminded them how horrible it was and said, "It was the most guttural crying sound that I've ever heard." He then turned to Pratt's injuries and bloody knuckles seen by the detectives and said, "We've got a child beaten to death. We've got fingernail marks. What do we do? Nothing. Oh, neat, you hit that wall, huh? Okay. And they drop it never to come up again."

Continuing, he mentioned Veronica's interest in CSI and how the officers were not ashamed to say it was ninety-five percent bullshit. Then added, "Apparently, even their own identification unit believes that also." That line made me smile. He moved on to the clothing Lyric had been wearing and how no one had paid any attention to what he was wearing when he was found. Then, he pointed out how the other children were all seen wearing their night clothing. He added, "Not one question in this entire case focused on why Lyric was wearing those clothes. They didn't even ask the mother what he sleeps in."

He hammered away at the testimony of Sergeant Stebbins regarding her bizarre claims that the blood on the diaper was of no value and that Charles bleeding on that diaper doesn't make him any more of a suspect. Dave couldn't help but add, "I almost fell over when I heard that." I thought to myself, "No kidding. Ditto that."

Moving on, he spent quite a bit of time on the time of death issue and pointed out, "Not a single officer on that stand brought by the prosecution acknowledged that the time of death was an issue. That it was a concern. That it was part of a discussion. Or, they had any knowledge of it whatsoever." He quickly pointed out that the testimony of Tom Eggleston, called by the defense, was just the opposite.

Following up, he said, "I like the police, okay. I deal with them all the time. I'm not here to trash them, but don't be disingenuous to try and put someone away for murder. Tell the truth." I was a bit surprised to hear him say that but glad he did because we'd discussed that exact thing during our many sessions together.

From there, he engaged in a comprehensive attack on Jesse Noel's credibility. Telling the jury, he was "a desperate man up there willing to do anything to get the hell out of jail."

Later, he moved on to DeLucia's bizarre assumptions about the so-called "extremely warm" environment where Lyric was found. He pointed out the testimony of his witness, Charles Pratt, who'd said, "It's cold in that room. It is. I couldn't even notice that Lyric was cold when I touched him because it's cold in that room. We put up things on the windows because it's cold in that room." Dave then added, "So, again, the assumption fails, everything fails."

Dave's closing was powerful, emotionally driven, and a heartfelt demonstration of the cause for which he was fighting. The life and freedom of his factually innocent client – Veronica Taft.

In fairness, DeLucia, too, delivered a powerful closing, albeit a very bizarre and warped interpretation of the evidence and Veronica's character. He even touted the thoroughness of the police investigation. From there, he downplayed the early time of death estimate, attempting to cast doubt on its validity, at first calling it a misnomer. Then, he described it as being "much broader" or more "fluent" than that. An inexact science. Later still, calling it a "bit of a wash."

Continuing, he told the jury, "Throughout the trial, many officers testified that there was discussion as to the time of death." There was? Not that I had heard.

Later, in his attempt to salvage the warm environment issue, he said, "He's [Lyric] in an insulated cocoon in there." Then added, "Diapers can be insulative in nature."

He spoke about the four plates of food Chucky had fixed for the kids and how he'd returned later to find them all empty. Once again, his explanation to the jury was built on his frequent use of assumptions and possibilities. He told the jury, "We know there was a puppy roaming about." Then said it was possible, "Haveen not only ate her food but Lyric's as well." Then added, "Or the dog gets it." Wow!! I just shook my head and rolled my eyes. An insulated cocoon? An insulative diaper? Haveen or the puppy ate Lyric's dinner? Astonishingly, he really did say those things.

Finally, DeLucia submits to the jury that the hole in the wall and the blood on Pratt's hands was nothing more than a red herring. If that's true, I suppose the bloodstains on the diaper were a red herring as well.

By the time DeLucia completed his final remarks, it was around 3:30 p.m. Since Court normally closed around 4:00, recess was called early and scheduled to resume in the morning. At which time the case would be turned over to the jury for their deliberations.

41

VERDICT

On Tuesday, August 28, 2012, deliberations began right on schedule around 9:00 a.m. Surprisingly, by mid-afternoon, there was a knock on the door – there was a verdict. Wow! Less than six hours. That was quick. Dave and I had been waiting in a small conference room just outside the courtroom when a court officer popped his head in and announced there was a verdict.

Having reached a verdict that quickly, knowing how much they had to talk about, we didn't know what to think. From our perspective, a not guilty verdict seemed more likely. We also believed that a guilty verdict could never have been reached so quickly. Regardless, we were about to find out.

All involved parties and spectators reassembled in the courtroom and took their seats. The judge called for Veronica, who joined us at the defense table. Once everyone was in place, after being summoned, the jury filed back into the courtroom and took their seats in the jury box. While walking in, their faces appeared somber, without expression, staring straight ahead, making eye contact with no one. Admittedly, I'm no jury expert, but my thought was, "This is not good."

Speaking to the jury, the judge said, "I understand you've reached a verdict." After answering in the affirmative, the jury foreman was asked to stand. After that, he was asked for their verdict on each of the charges announced one by one. Their verdict was the same on all charges – Guilty.

42

AFTERMATH

Even though we were optimistic for a favorable verdict, we were also well aware that there are no guarantees with a jury, as was Veronica. Sadly, what just happened here was a good example. Despite the lack of tangible evidence of guilt, an innocent woman was just found guilty of a crime she didn't commit. A cruel and tragic miscarriage of justice radically changed her status from an innocent grieving mother to murderess baby-killer.

Upon hearing the verdict, I was stunned briefly, but my thoughts quickly turned to Veronica as I placed my hand on her shoulder in a comforting gesture. Surprisingly, there was no trembling, no outburst, no tears, no hanging off her head. Remarkably, instead, she held her head high with a stern look on her face, showing no emotion. Later, after the jury was excused, we all stood for a moment behind the defense table as we waited for the court officers to come for Veronica. I was likely still shaken from the verdict and didn't remember all that was said.

Meanwhile, the court officers had arrived and were waiting to take Veronica. They were patient and allowed us to continue speaking for another few minutes. I remember Dave saying he would be filing her notice of appeal within the next couple of days. Shortly after that, Veronica turned and spoke softly, thanking us for everything we had done for her. Then gave us each a big hug. She'd likely seen the somber look on our faces and said, "Don't worry. I'll be okay." We wished her well and said goodbye as she stepped aside between the two court officers, still holding her head high as they walked away.

As hard as it was, once Veronica was gone, Dave did the honorable thing by going over to congratulate DeLucia and Shapiro. Initially, I had no intention of doing anything like that. However, following Dave's lead, as difficult as it was, I just sucked it up and also offered a half-hearted congratulations but didn't offer my hand.

Meanwhile, Veronica was hauled back to the jail to await sentencing. In disbelief, we slowly started gathering up all of our case file binders we'd used during the trial, taking our time to allow spectators to clear the courtroom. For a while, neither one of us said much of anything. Slowly, we began sharing some of our thoughts as we tried coming to grips with what just happened – at times, second-guessing ourselves as to whether we could have done anything differently. We both agreed it was one of the most disheartening verdicts we'd ever heard in our careers. With a bit of angst in his voice, Dave said, "That's Broome County justice for you. She was convicted before she even went to trial." I nodded and said, "Yep. I know what you mean. Once the jury saw those pictures of Lyric, she was toast."

At the time, I had been working in the private sector for about sixteen years. During which time, I'd experienced a few other injustices. However, what I just experienced here topped the list as one of the most egregious miscarriages of justice ever in my career – a wrongful conviction of a factually innocent woman. In other words, an orchestrated charade and insult to our system of justice.

Strangely, throughout the trial, there had been little or no media coverage. Even after being found guilty, the only notice of her conviction was a small brief from a staff report in Binghamton's *Press and Sun-Bulletin* Newspaper.

BRIEFS

Woman found guilty in son's death

BINGHAMTON — Veronica Taft was found guilty Tuesday of second-degree murder in the death of her 2-year old son Lyric on Dec. 30, 2010.

A jury in Broome County Court returned the verdict and also found Taft guilty of several other charges.

Veronica Taft

Lyric was found dead in Taft's apartment on Fayette Street.

— *Staff report*

43

SENTENCING

By law, in New York State, after a conviction and before sentencing, the court orders the Probation Department to conduct a standard pre-sentence investigation or PSI. Which normally takes two or three months. As such, Veronica's sentencing was originally scheduled for Thursday, November 29, 2012. However, shortly before sentencing, Sr. ADA DeLucia passed along some new information he'd received after the trial. As a result, Dave Butler requested and was granted an adjournment to explore the new information. After a brief assessment of the new information, sentencing was rescheduled and took place on Tuesday, February 26, 2013.

44

25 TO LIFE

It wasn't as if I didn't know what her sentence would be. Due to the brutal nature of Lyric's murder, I knew DeLucia would be seeking the maximum, and the Court would most likely agree. As such, it was showtime for DeLucia, and I had no interest or the stomach to listen to anything further. Therefore, I decided not to attend. After reading the article the next day in the *Press and Sun-Bulletin*, I was glad I didn't.

The headline read, "Taft gets 25 to life for son's murder," with the subheadline, "Continues to plead innocent in beating death." Staff crime reporter Anthony Borrelli penned the article. Writing that prosecutors portrayed Veronica Taft as a demeaning mother who answered her 2½-year-old son's natural expressions of curiosity and affection with escalating abuse – finally beating him to death. Then, before being sentenced to the maximum of 25 years to life in state prison, Taft sobbed and maintained her innocence. Later, Borrelli quoted ADA DeLucia saying, "That suffering was caused by the one person in the world who was there to keep him safe. No one, least of all a 2½-year-old, deserves that." Then added, "Even now, she is unwilling to accept responsibility."

Later, when Veronica was allowed to address the Court, he reported how she first wiped away her tears and struggled to keep her composure before saying she could never do something so horrible to her child. She then added, "I can't believe this is happening. To my beautiful boy – I will never give up on giving you the justice I was robbed of."

Borrelli also quoted DeLucia's response to some of Veronica's claims. That response was precisely the reason I didn't want to be there. Even when reading it in the news article, I found it upsetting when he said, *"This case is proof that those involved in the criminal justice system will try their best to make sure cases involving victims of child abuse, especially very young victims, are investigated thoroughly and prosecuted to the best of our ability."*

That comment almost made me sick. "Trying their best?" "Investigating thoroughly?" No, Mr. DeLucia, that's not what was done. There was no trying their best or thorough investigation. Instead, they were at their worst and anything but thorough. The evidence that Chucky was the real killer was lined up right under their noses. Veronica was right by saying she would never give up on the justice for her son, of which she was robbed.

Borrelli also reported that just before announcing her sentence, Judge Cawley described this as one of the worst child abuse cases he'd seen while on the bench. Then added, "How anyone could beat a child simply defies description."

VI

THE APPEAL

45

APPEAL

More often than not, the chances of a successful appeal are slim to none. Obviously, Veronica's conviction was a devastating blow to our pre-trial optimism that she would be exonerated. However, being overwhelmingly convinced of her innocence, believing that the weight of the evidence presented at trial didn't support a conviction, we were both confident that a strong appeal argument could be made. To start the process, Dave formally filed with the Court Veronica Taft's intent to appeal. Unfortunately, the process involved often takes several months or even years.

After sentencing, Veronica was returned briefly to the Broome County Jail before being shipped off to state prison the very next day. She was committed to the Bedford Hills Correctional Facility for women, a maximum-security prison in Westchester County, just north of New York City, with a housing capacity of more than 900 inmates. Now labeled "Baby-killer," she began serving her lengthy prison sentence while trying to adjust to a frightening new way of life.

| Bedford Hills Correctional Facility

In the days, weeks, and months that followed, I continued having troubling thoughts about the miscarriage of justice – at times, making it difficult to concentrate on other matters. Unfortunately, as much as I wanted to, there wasn't a damn thing I could do. I was anxious to learn who would be assigned to write Veronica's appeal. Whoever that was, considering my knowledge of the case, I was willing to offer any assistance I could.

Ordinarily, knowing there are times when the wheels of justice turn very slowly, I can have a great deal of patience. However, in this matter, I began losing patience because things were moving way too slow. I started checking in with Dave Butler every couple of weeks without a word. Sadly, more than three months had passed, and still no word on an appeal attorney.

Finally, on July 16, 2013, the first step began when we finally received word that Binghamton attorney Norbert A. Higgins had accepted the assignment. I'd been working in Broome County, NY, for years and never even heard of Higgins. Later, after speaking with Dave Butler, I wasn't overly thrilled to learn that the bulk of Higgins' experience was in family law, not criminal.

I waited a couple of weeks before calling and introducing myself to Higgins. He explained that he had just recently spoken with Dave Butler and already had my name. We discussed the case briefly, and I offered my assistance, telling him I would make myself available for anything he might need, even if it was just to answer a few questions. He mentioned he had just ordered the trial transcripts and added, "But it may take a while before I get them. They'll send them when they get around to it, but they usually take their sweet old time." "I figured as much," I said. I then put in a big plug for Veronica, briefly explaining how the system had failed her – miserably. I added, "It's all in the transcripts. You'll see." Veronica's life was now in his hands, and even though the appeal process had begun, the wheels of justice had slowed to a crawl. Without even a glimmer of light at the end of the tunnel.

Meanwhile, Veronica remained locked away in prison, where her fellow inmates often called her "Baby-killer" or "BK" for short. Others called her Casey Anthony for the famous mother who'd been accused of killing her young daughter Caylee. Fortunately for Veronica, she'd spent most of her life standing up to ridicule, bullying, and nasty trash-talking. Just as she'd been doing all her life, she wasn't about to start taking any crap now. That built-in trait of her character helped her manage to survive in such a hostile environment.

More months passed without nary a word. I didn't want to be a pest, but I decided to check in with Mr. Higgins for a progress report. He welcomed my call and said he had finally received the more than two thousand pages of trial transcripts and was still working his way through. Along the way, he was identifying and making notes of all potential appeal issues. He still had a long way to go but was making good progress. I was glad I called because that was the first encouraging news I'd heard in quite some time.

Months were slipping by as the clock kept ticking but still no word. Then finally, on May 20, 2015, after more than twenty-two months, Veronica's appeal brief was filed with the State of New York Supreme Court, Appellate Division, Third Judicial Department. I was anxious to read it myself, so I called Higgins and asked if he could send me a copy. Moments later, the fifty-page appeal brief was in my email.

I must have read through it at least five times. Higgins had a good grasp of the key issues, specifically the lack of evidence needed to uphold a conviction. He was aggressively arguing that the guilty verdict was against the weight of the evidence. Although I didn't agree with everything he wrote, for the most part, when it came to the more critical issues, he nailed it rather well. Our only hope now was that the Appellate Court would agree.

Throughout his appeal brief, Jesse Noel was repeatedly referred to as the "dishonest snitch." As for the cry-ladies, he referred to their "trash allegations" where caseworkers had found no credible evidence against Veronica Taft but nonetheless were introduced at trial.

For now, that significant first step was complete and would move the appeal process forward. But this was just the next step because Veronica's life had just been transferred into the hands of the Appellate Division of the Supreme Court. The wait continued.

Periodically, throughout this long waiting period, I corresponded back and forth with Veronica while she was in prison. Often, it was just a Christmas card, a brief note of encouragement, or to give her an update on the appeal process without making any promises or offering any false hope.

She would always write back right away. Usually, in a lengthy letter, first thanking me but then spilling her heart out about how much she missed her kids. She told me, "I talk to my kids. I get to once a month now. They miss me crazy like I do them. I lose my rights next summer if no family steps up to get them, so I'm stressed out to the max." Other times, she wrote about those who betrayed her and testified falsely against her – offering to forgive them if they would come forward and tell the truth. Near the end of one of her letters, she asked me to pray for her and her children and if I belonged to a church to have them pray also. That was already being done.

In another letter, she asked if I could locate and send some of the pictures of her children that we had in the case file. I found several of all the children. Included were several photos of Lyric, some of which had been taken during his second birthday party – sharing a moment with his mom, opening his gifts, and riding his new three-wheeler. Yet, DeLucia claimed she hated her son. Altogether, there were more than fifty photos from which to choose. From those, I selected about twenty to send to her. Later, as I was placing them in the mailing envelope, I thought to myself, "I'm sure she'll be glad to have these, but they'll probably make her cry." About a week later, I received her responding letter. Where she started out saying, "Thank you so much for the pictures. That means the world to me. They made me cry because I miss Lyric so much and pissed because I'm in here and don't see my other babies. It's like I lost all of them. In reality, I pretty much did."

Time continued to drag on as more months passed. Christmas 2015 had come and gone. It was now early September, the fifth anniversary of Veronica's arrest and incarceration, and more than a year since the appeal brief was filed. Yet, still, no decision. What was taking so long? Talk about stress. This was worse than waiting for a verdict.

Also anxious for the decision, Dave Butler's office monitored the Appellate Court decisions posted almost daily. Knowing there were some substantial appeal issues, we were both hopefully optimistic that sufficient cause would be found to reverse the conviction and grant Veronica a new trial.

46

APPELLATE COURT DECISION

Ordinarily, whenever Butler's office called, it came in from the office Secretary or Paralegal. However, on December 1, 2016, I received a direct personal call from Dave informing me that the decision had just come in. Anxiously, I asked, "Well, are we going back to trial?" He said, "No. No trial. It's better than that. You're not going to believe this. Their decision was unanimous. It's almost unheard of. They tossed out both the murder and manslaughter convictions." I said, "Yeah, but doesn't that mean she has to be retried?" He said, "No. I'm reading it right here. It says the verdict was against the weight of the evidence. It's over. By the way, the press is all over this, and they want to hold a news conference. Can you meet me at the office?" "I'm on my way," I said.

During my drive over to his office, my thoughts went immediately to Veronica. First, wondering whether she had received the good news yet. Then, realizing that after five-and-half years in prison, she would soon be coming home, which would at least bring closure to her physical nightmare of imprisonment. Sadly, however, the scarring left from her emotional nightmare would remain permanent – never to heal.

In my view, this decision was unprecedented. Like Dave said, almost unheard of. In fact, I couldn't think of a single case that I was familiar with where an Appellate Court had thrown out a murder conviction. It was overwhelming, but I took comfort in knowing that the Court's unanimous decision helped reaffirm everything we fought for in defense of Veronica.

When I arrived at Dave's office, several local media reporters were already gathered in the conference room, setting up their equipment. I remember Dave offering a few comments and then answering some questions. I may have provided a comment as well, but I don't know exactly. Whatever it was, I'm sure it included being pleased knowing that Veronica would be released soon and, hopefully, reunited with her children.

Later that same evening, a lengthy *Press & Sun-Bulletin* news article was posted online through *pressconnects.com*. Authored by crime reporter Anthony Borrelli, under the headline, "MURDER CHARGE DROPPED: Mom's conviction tossed on appeal."

The next day, the same article appeared in the print version of the *Press & Sun-Bulletin*, under the headline, "Judge tosses conviction of mother in murder of toddler." As well, a caption read, "Veronica Taft had been sentenced to 25 years to life in prison for what prosecutors called a 'depraved indifference' killing of her son." In the article, Borrelli described the decision as a bombshell ruling that tossed out second-degree murder and first-degree manslaughter convictions against Taft. Reporting further that the jury's verdict that proof established beyond a reasonable doubt she killed her son was *"against the weight of the evidence."*

Borrelli had also interviewed Taft's appeal attorney, Norbert Higgins. When asked for his thoughts about the decision, he was quoted saying, *"Unless something terribly wrong happened, they are generally reluctant to reverse a jury's verdict. It's certainly a tragic case, but there is life, and there is the law. And under the law, the decision was correct."*

The following is a brief synopsis of the Appellate Court decision:

The seven-page decision was written by Justice William E. McCarthy, with four other judges concurring. It basically tore apart the theory as well as the methods and evidence used by the prosecution, agreeing with the defendant that *"as to the convictions for murder in the second degree and manslaughter in the first degree, the verdict was against the weight of the evidence.* Further stating, *"In our weight of the evidence analysis, this Court "sits, in effect, as a thirteenth juror."*

From there, the decision moved into some of the specific issues, starting with, *"the sole scientific evidence that was introduced at trial indicated that the victim most likely suffered his injuries more than three hours after defendant had left the victim with the boyfriend and gone to work."* It explained further how the pathologist had relied on the victim's body temperature in determining the victim's time of death and wrote, *"the victim "most likely" died at approximately 3:00 a.m."*

Interesting to note that the decision also stated, *"Based on questions related to the pathologist's degree of certainty as to his conclusion, the pathologist testified that it was "technically possible" that the victim's time of death was 11:00 p.m. and that it was "within the realm of possibility," that the injuries could have been inflicted at 9:00 p.m. This scenario, however, would assume a 50% error rate in the time of death calculation and would have also doubled the amount of time that it took the victim to die from his injuries."* Exactly. I couldn't have said it better.

When addressing Pratt's acknowledgment to feeding all the kids after Veronica left for work and later finding all four plates empty, it was written, *"According to the People's theory of the case, the victim would have had to have been either mortally wounded or already dead at this point in time."* Right again.

The decision also referred to statements made by Pratt while making a phone call during his police interview and another while speaking with CPS. Specifically, his comment saying, *"I don't know my nigger, this little nigger be running around doing mad shit."* Then, later, telling a CPS worker, *"I'm not getting the death penalty for no accident."* In continuing, it was also written, *"Moreover, the boyfriend acknowledged at trial that he had been offered immunity if he testified against the defendant at the grand jury proceeding."*

The final part of the decision focused on the testimony of Jesse Noel, often pointing out and tearing apart what they noted as *"contradictory and inconsistent testimony."* Starting with, *"He acknowledged that he had reached out to law enforcement after his arrest because he had information about this case and other cases and because he had hoped to get the best deal that he could."* Then it added, *"On at least four different occasions, he told law enforcement and/or prosecution officials that the boyfriend had confessed to killing the victim."*

After that, the decision continued to point out several more specific contradictions and inconsistencies in Noel's testimony. Leaving no doubt that he was not credible and nothing but a liar, whose only interest was in *"trying to get the best deal he could."*

It was remarkable, as well as reassuring, to learn that the Appellate Court recognized the same nonsense by reaffirming nearly every vital issue argued during the trial. Then it added some of their own, which was not only welcoming but very impressive – judicial integrity at its finest.

Veronica had been hanging out in the prison gymnasium talking with a friend when she was approached by a counselor who had just learned of the decision and said, "You won." Initially, even upon hearing the good news, she felt uneasy, believing there would need to be another trial. Moments later, however, her feelings quickly turned to relief and elation after learning it was a dismissal that would set her free. There would be no retrial.

As mentioned, the decision of the Appellate Court was dated December 1, 2016. Accordingly, Veronica should have been released that same day, or perhaps the following day at the latest. Instead, she was detained for several more days without any word as to when she would be released. Thankfully, upon learning of the decision, Ms. Joan Mencel, a local Family Court attorney, stepped up to demand her immediate release. Otherwise, she may have been held even longer. On December 7, 2016, she was finally released.

Veronica's release came just shy of six years after Lyric's murder. With five-and-a-half of those years spent behind bars. Finally, the day she hoped and prayed for had arrived. During her escort to the front gate, she realized her prison nightmare had come to an end. As she stepped through the gate, she tried wiping away a mixture of tears that filled her eyes, joyful tears for herself, along with tears of sadness for Lyric. For both his death and the justice, he was denied. After clearing the gate, she stopped for a moment as the gate closed behind her. She then stepped ahead but glanced back one last time. The prison walls, topped with razor-wire, stood behind her now. The horrific prison she'd been forced to call home for nearly four years would soon be a bad memory. Moments later, the heavy weight she'd been carrying on her shoulders all that time suddenly lifted and was gone.

Soon after that, with a one-way bus ticket and a small backpack over her shoulder, she climbed aboard the bus and was heading home. However, even with her renewed freedom, the road ahead would not be easy.

APPELLATE COURT DECISION | 333

Veronica Arriving Home

VII

THE AFTERMATH

47

STARTING OVER

Veronica was no longer a convicted felon with the Appellate Court's dismissal of her murder and manslaughter convictions. However, due to the length of time that she'd spent in prison, the challenges she faced transitioning back into society and restarting her life would not be easy. Almost as if she was still a convicted felon.

After her release from prison, I had no clue where she had gone to live or whether or not she had ever been reunited with her children. Although, I was pretty sure she'd have no interest in returning to Broome County considering all that happened. After speaking with Dave Butler, I learned that Veronica had been in contact with him. He didn't have many details, but it was his understanding that there was a good chance she would be getting her children back. She'd also given Dave her current phone number, along with permission to share it with me. I was anxious to speak with her, but I decided to give her plenty of time to adjust to her new life. Besides, I was right in the middle of another murder case that was gearing up for trial.

I finally reached out to Veronica in May of 2017. She was

glad to hear from me, and we chatted for the better part of an hour. We hadn't spoken since her trial, nearly five years ago. She was still trying to put her life back together and still fighting to get her children back. She'd finally met and started a new relationship with a man who treated her well. They were living together in central New York. We spoke briefly about the Appellate Court decision and how they had reaffirmed all the key arguments we made during the trial. Later, she said, "I thank God. I'm so glad the Appellate Court saw through all that shit." "Me too," I said. Shortly after that, I wished her well and told her I would call again sometime. Then added, "But feel free to call me anytime."

A month later, on June 17, 2017, the story of Veronica's wrongful conviction made headlines once again. It was reported by *WICZ FOX-40 News* in Binghamton under the headline, "Binghamton Woman Wrongfully Convicted of Her Sons Death."

Veronica had agreed to a personal interview, where she answered questions and offered comments about her experience. When asked for her reaction after learning about the appeals court decision, she said, "*I was stunned. I was happy, and I was stunned. I was like I can get home to my kids.*" Later, she was quoted saying, "*Void of evidence and only the 67th case to happen in the world. It's the best declaration of innocence you could ever have.*"

Continuing, she also explained that the only thing that kept her going was that she would see her other children again one day. In a final statement, she added, "*I did everything at that place just to be able to send them stuff because you're working for less than five cents an hour. But I managed to do it. I sent them big packages, you know, handmade stuff that took a lot of time.*"

Even though I often thought about her, time just slipped away, and I didn't speak with her again for nearly three years. In the meantime, I wrote and published my first book, *Reign of Injustice*, which became my inspiration to write Veronica's story. It was another story that needed to be told.

Then finally, in June 2020, amid the coronavirus pandemic, we first spoke on the phone, then later met and talked for several hours. Before the meeting, we both agreed that no masks were necessary. Social distancing? Well. Maybe a little. Anyway, after introducing me to her family, she gave me a quick tour of her lovely new home – of which she was very proud. It was a significant step up from Fayette Street. Before getting into the specific details of her case, I briefly took her back to her childhood and early school years. When the topic of her youthful diagnosis of ADD/ADHD came up, I said, "I understand you were a bit hyper back then." She just smiled and said, "Yep. I still am, still am." "Okay. Well. I guess that explains a lot then," I said, smiling back.

| Veronica

We then started discussing some of the more critical details of her case. I offered a few comments and asked a few questions, but I let her do most of the talking for the most part. For Veronica, even after ten years, it was like it all happened yesterday. Remarkably, she recalled every detail, then added a few new things.

After reviewing her story, she fixed me a cup of coffee, and we started talking about her life in prison. She struggled with inmates urinating and smoking in the showers, being called "baby-killer," lots of drugs, and cockroaches everywhere. But the hardest thing she said was, "Not having any information about my kids." To help cope, she worked all day, every day. Either in the mess hall or as Equipment Manager in the gymnasium. Continuing, she added, "There was a lot of sexual harassment: COs having sex with inmates, women raping women. It was awful.

On the other hand, I worked with some pretty cool COs, but

the female COs? They treated me like crap." Later she added, "It was really hard when I found out my grandmother died, and I couldn't go to her funeral. I was depressed for a long time. We were very close. I'd even stayed with her for a few days right after Lyric was killed. It still makes me sad when I think about it. I never got to say the last goodbye."

Later, we turned to the struggles she had to get her children back after she was released. It took more than a year before Amira and Zoey were finally returned. Haveen, she said, "was a different story." She'd been placed in a pre-adoptive home and was on the verge of being adopted. "I could have lost her forever," she said. In as much, it took another two years before Haveen was finally returned in February 2020.

Continuing, she added, "The kids hated me at first. They'd heard a lot of bad things about me from their foster parents. They were really damaged. At times they'd have temper tantrums, and the cops got called. Then CPS would come and accuse me of all kinds of crap, and the same shit would start all over again. I'd end up back in Family Court again. One of the caseworkers from Syracuse actually said, "We're here about the old fatality." Can you believe that? It never stops. It's been horrible. Just one constant battle." Knowing how CPS works, I wasn't shocked to hear her say that. And her case was just one example. Later, I asked, "How are the girls doing now? Any counseling?" "Oh yeah, we all go, but they don't like it," she said.

Remembering that she'd had a child in prison before her trial, I asked if there was any chance of getting Omari back? "Well, I'm still working on that, too, but his foster parent moved out of state and took him with her. She wasn't supposed to do that, which makes things more complicated," she said.

On a more positive note, during one of her battles fighting for her children, she returned to Family Court in Broome County. She was surprised to learn that the CPS attorney in

Binghamton had actually written a supportive letter to Family Court on her behalf. Then later, he told her in person that he never believed she'd killed her son. She was surprised further by another Senior CPS supervisor who apologized to her, saying, "I'm so sorry." It would seem as though CPS knew all along, she hadn't killed her son, but at the time, their hands were tied.

One of the more surprising things she told me was about the cry-ladies. During the trial, Dave Butler often referred to them as the "yahoos." She chuckled when I reminded her of that. Later, when their names came up during our conversation, I was thrown for a loop when she said, "You know, they came up here to see me and apologized. They told me how sorry they were and how they got into drugs really bad because they couldn't live with what they'd done. It was a lot of guilt." I said, "You're kidding? Which ones? What did they say?" The three she named had given the most damaging testimony during her trial. She said, "What they told me was, the police had them believing I killed Lyric and needed their help. After that, they were pressured to say certain things, and it just snowballed from there." I said, "Well, that sounds about right." Continuing, she said, "But you know, I'm a big forgiver. They'd tracked me down and drove all the way up here to apologize face-to-face. That took some guts. But once they apologized and explained what happened, it all made sense, and I forgave them." I said, "Wow! That is pretty amazing, but we knew all along it was bullshit. I guess they couldn't live with the guilt. I have to give them some credit for that."

Continuing, I said, "By the way, speaking of pressure, I think that's exactly what happened with Jesse Noel as well." She smiled again and said, "Well, you probably won't believe this either, but Jesse called to apologize too. He told me how sorry he was and how guilty he felt. He told me that it was his third felony, and they were going to put the murder on him. And they'd threatened to arrest him." I said, "Well, they very well may have told him that. Or perhaps they'd just threatened to cancel his deal. Either way, he would have been fearful of going back to prison. So, he threw you under the bus to save himself. By the way, he did get his deal. He was released after just four months of time served."

Surprisingly, Veronica had also tried reaching out to Chucky to see if he would talk. She said, "He killed my baby. I want to know what happened. I need to know what happened. I want to hear it from him, but he never called." "And probably never will," I said. She added, "I wanted to try Jemel too but found out he'd died two or three years ago. Probably from his diabetes."

Our conversation then turned to her friend Deanna and the suspicious circumstances surrounding her death. She said, "You know. I think they killed her. In fact, I'm almost sure of it." I said, "That certainly is possible. Even with what little we know, that can't be ruled out."

The entire time I was there, Veronica's girls ran around, both indoors and out, doing their own thing. All very well behaved. One or the other would briefly pop in looking for a snack or to ask their mother something from time to time. Then take off again. Before leaving, I had a brief opportunity to speak with Haveen, who was now a pretty young teenager. Then again, all of her girls were pretty. With Haveen, however, I could see how much she was like her mother even during that brief period. Intelligent, strong-willed, and a bit feisty. Even after ten years, she claimed she could still remember having heard Chucky hitting Lyric that night and giving him a bath shortly after. At the time, however, she was way too frightened to say anything or tell anybody.

| Veronica's family today

Later, I made two separate attempts to contact both Noel and Pratt for comment. There was no response.

Undoubtedly, moving on and rebuilding her life after five-and-a-half years in prison was an ongoing challenge and an uphill battle. For Veronica, however, that was nothing new. She'd been doing that her entire life as one who would never back down – a scarred and battle-tested veteran. But it was that same strong will, persistent determination, and tenacity that maintained her drive to continue to fight.

Unfortunately, strong women are often perceived as having an 'attitude' of being mean or cold-hearted. Mainly because they refuse to be mistreated or taken for granted, they have no fear of standing up for themselves when no one else will. For some, that would describe Veronica perfectly. A cold-hearted woman with a mean attitude. Whereas others, especially those who knew her best, viewed it differently. That it wasn't attitude but rather a standard she used when standing up for herself.

Broken, betrayed, and mistreated by so many, she'd fought a thousand battles and cried thousands of more tears. Yet here she stands, with her head held high – strong, smiling, and walking with a proud strut in her step, with enough humility to forgive.

It had been nearly ten years since I'd last seen or spoken with Hope Taft. But in the aftermath of Veronica's release from prison, I wanted to speak with her again. When I called, she agreed to come to my office. As soon as she walked in, I recognized her right away. I said, "I can't get over how much you remind me of your daughter." I also realized it was more than just a physical likeness. There was a character likeness as well. As we stood in the doorway for a moment, I said, "Maybe not everyone would agree, but I've always seen Veronica as a very strong woman." Hope replied, "She is strong." I added, "Not only that but smart too. I've always been amazed by her ability to stand up for herself and not take any crap from anyone. Not even the police. There aren't too many women who can do that." She said, "She's always been that way. She just tells it like it is. But that didn't always go over too well with some of her friends." "Yeah. I know about that all too well," I said.

As she walked into my office, she hadn't even sat down before she said, "I've been anxious to speak with you. I'm glad you're writing Ron's story because someone needs to. I can't wait to read it. I actually thought about writing it myself." Then added, "I don't know how this whole mess ever happened. I probably never will. I'll never understand how it possibly could have happened. Because they knew damn well from the beginning who did this, but they let him go, with immunity no less. He'll never be held responsible. Even CPS knew Chucky did it. It was all written up in their reports. This whole thing is bull crap." Hmm! Where have we heard that before?

After mentioning CPS, she said, "Even before she was

arrested, they treated her horribly, forcing her to go to DSS for visitation. Have you ever seen that place? It's disgusting." I said, "Oh yeah. Veronica told me all about that." She added, "It was awful. I'll never understand why they wouldn't let her have visits at my house." I said, "I agree. That never made any sense to me either. But then again, there were a lot of things in this case that never made much sense." "Ain't that the truth," she said.

After that, we jumped around a bit as we rehashed some of the various details of the case. Even after ten years, some of the details that surfaced stirred up some emotion, which at times brought a few tears to her eyes.

Later, we started discussing the blood-stained diaper, Lyric's stomach contents, and the time of death. Like Veronica, she'd been following those issues closely. Then admitted how she was hooked on crime shows like CSI or others involving forensic science. Then added, "So, yeah, I knew how important those things were. So did Veronica."

I just had to ask her again about Lyric's SpongeBob pajamas. With a tear in her eye, she said, "He really loved them. Wore them every day. In fact, most of the time, he'd put up a fuss if he had to take them off." I asked, "And you said you never found them when you were in there that morning, right?" She said, "No. I was tossing things all around, looking for clothes for all the kids, but I never found his pajamas. I never found Haveen's comforter either. Ron had asked me about that."

As we were wrapping up, she mentioned how she and Veronica talked quite often now and that she'd been up to her new home to visit her and the kids. Earlier, we had discussed how difficult it was when Veronica first got her kids back. She agreed that it was a real battle, not only with the kids but also with Family Court. As a final comment, she added, "Yeah. It was a real struggle there for a long time, but things are a little smoother now." "I certainly hope so, but that's good to hear," I said.

48

POWER OF AUTHORITY

The very core of our justice system is built upon law enforcement institutions, comprised of highly qualified and trained individuals who are entrusted with the full-time responsibility of using their power and authority to serve and protect the interests of those they represent. Therefore, whether on duty or off, they are rightfully held to a higher standard. However, that does not mean they are deserving of our blind trust or allegiance. Should we cave in to that temptation, we surrender our obligation to ensure that justice is done each and every time.

Prosecutors, in particular, have more power and control over life, liberty, reputation, and freedom than any other person in society. When at their very best, they can be a valuable asset to our system of justice. However, when they engage in acts of malice and misconduct, they can be one of the worst. In doing so, they abuse their authority by bending, breaking, or creating their own rules. At times, they even justify committing criminal acts, all in the name of justice. Thereby undermining the integrity and jeopardizing the entire system they swore to uphold.

To make matters worse, they may actually believe they're doing the right thing. Yet, they engage in their misconduct surreptitiously while hiding behind the shield of their authority, knowing it's unlikely they'll ever be held accountable.

Understandably, police and prosecutors have challenging and demanding jobs. While most of these men and women work effectively within the constraints of the law, per their oath of office, others do not. Therefore, society's trust and allegiance must be earned. Especially now, when law enforcement tactics have fallen under heavy scrutiny, with protests springing up across the country, appeals for justice, and cries against injustice. Together, making their demands for much-needed change.

It's been said that "Trust, once lost, is like a stone that's been cast, a word that's been said or a time after it's gone." In other words, it can't be restored. Unfortunately, when errors or wrongful acts are discovered during the pursuit of justice, they're often viewed as a failure or sign of weakness. Sadly, they are sometimes remedied by turning a blind eye, avoiding, rejecting, denying, or even hiding their existence. When this happens, the integral foundation of our justice system is threatened – likely resulting in a miscarriage of justice.

Fortunately, there is an alternative. The discovery of any error or wrongful act can be viewed not as a failure or sign of weakness but rather, an opportunity to fix the problem. When you know something is 'not right' or 'not just,' there's a moral obligation to do something about it. In other words, if something is wrong, make it right.

49

A RUTHLESS KILLER

What really happened to little Lyric? Unfortunately, the only one who knows what happened is the killer. But we do know it wasn't Veronica. Seeing right through the nonsense, the Appellate Court destroyed the bizarre theory that Veronica was the killer, dismissed her convictions of murder and manslaughter, and left Chucky as the only possible killer. But the mystery as to what truly happened remains.

As bizarre as it was, the police theory that Veronica was Lyric's killer was made clear throughout this case. Unfortunately, the theory was built on nothing more than speculation, supported by broad assumptions, far-reaching possibilities, and untrustworthy witnesses, along with a bit of guesswork and wishful thinking. In other words, no proof of anything.

In fairness, when considering my professional training, experience, and knowledge gleaned from assessing the evidence, I should be allowed to speculate as well. Unlike law enforcement, my speculation carries no risks. By using an alternative assessment, I'll propose a more plausible theory as to what happened. I assert that during the early morning hours of

December 30, 2010, Lyric fell victim to the angry wrath of Charles Pratt. At which point, he was savagely beaten, placed back in bed, and left to die.

Author's note: I'm about to reveal a reasonable hypothesis drawn from the evidence, including a good-faith assessment of the known facts and information developed during my investigation and that of law enforcement. At times, it will require some speculation. Therefore, it should not be construed as being factually accurate in its entirety as some variations are possible.

By mid-morning on December 29th, 2010, Ray Ramos, Veronica's daytime babysitter, arrived to babysit so Veronica could run some errands and then later meet up with Chucky to pick up a few groceries. During her absence, Ramos fed the kids their lunch. Then later, around 5:00 p.m., just before Veronica and Chucky returned, he fed the kids peanut butter and jelly sandwiches. After that, Ramos left and headed home. Chucky took off to Max's house to smoke weed and play video games. Before leaving, Veronica reminded him not to be late because she had to work, and he was on call to babysit.

Veronica spent some time playing with the kids before sitting down, trying to relax a bit before the long night ahead, briefly nodding off at times. Later, shortly before Chucky arrived, she had all the kids in their PJs and ready for bed. After that, it was quiet time. Following their routine, the kids went into their shared bedroom and started watching their favorite movies – usually, *Mean Girls*, *Winnie the Pooh*, or *Mrs. Doubtfire*. The TV and VHS player sat on top of the dresser near the window, making it easy to watch from the bunk bed. Haveen, being the oldest, was charged with starting and stopping the movies. Each of the four kids climbed onto the bunk bed, choosing a spot from which to watch. Even baby Zoey, who slept in a nearby pack-and-play, had a place on the bunk bed at movie time.

With the kids settled in watching their movies, Veronica took advantage of the quiet time and decided to lay down for a few minutes before going to work. She fell into a deep sleep, then woke up in a panic, thinking she may have overslept. Checking the time, it wasn't as late as she thought, and Chucky hadn't arrived yet. As she readied for work, Lyric wandered in, needing a diaper change. After changing his diaper, she watched as he wandered back to the bedroom. Shortly after that, Chucky walked in, followed by his brother Jemel and Lynette Pica, the girl from downstairs, a few minutes later. Lynette joined Veronica in her bedroom, where they sat on the bed discussing plans for New Year's as Veronica finished dressing for work.

A car horn sounded, alerting Veronica that her ride to work had arrived. She quickly popped her head into the kids' room, threw each a kiss, and said a quick goodbye. Then, as she was hustling out the door, she reminded Chucky to be sure and feed the kids.

Before leaving, she'd already set the oven to pre-heat for some Mac & Cheese, French-fries, and Tater-tots. Shortly after she left, Chucky put the food in the oven. Including enough for each of the four kids as well as himself and Jemel. He then walked into the kids' room to say hello and tell them dinner would be ready soon.

Once dinner was ready, Chucky fixed plates for each of the four children, one for Jemel and another for himself. The four kids' plates were set on a small table in the living room corner where they always ate. He then stuck his head in their room, telling them it was ready, and to come and eat. Haveen stopped the movie as the others climbed off the bunk bed, and they all came out to eat. Chucky and Jemel took their plates into the game room, where they ate and played video games.

| Chucky

The kids were all hungry because they hadn't eaten since 5:00 p.m. with those peanut butter and jelly sandwiches. As such, they scarfed it all down quickly, leaving nothing behind on their plates. Once finished, well ahead of Chucky and Jemel, they left their empty plates on the table and headed back to the bedroom to continue watching their movie. Later, when Chucky came out of the game room, he added the four empty plates to his own and went into the kitchen to clean up, followed shortly after by Jemel with his empty plate.

Just before 11:30 p.m., Chucky's phone rang. It was Veronica. A routine call, just like every night she worked, checking on the kids and making sure they'd been fed. Chucky assured her the kids were all fine and that they'd all been fed. He assured her further that they were now back in their room.

After cleaning up in the kitchen, Chucky joined Jemel in the game room, where they began drinking and playing more video games. By now, he'd already changed into his sleep clothes after telling Jemel he was tired and thinking about going to bed soon. They played a little longer when, around 12:30 a.m., Jemel said he was getting tired as well and decided it was time to leave. He'd been staying at Chucky's place, so he headed back there for the rest of the night, leaving Chucky alone with the kids.

Somewhere around 1:00 a.m., Chucky received another phone call. It was Veronica again. This time, she asked him to locate a movie and the 3D glasses needed to watch it. She told him that she might come home and pick it up for her and her coworkers to watch if there was enough spare time. During the call, Chucky told her all the kids were in their room sleeping, and he was cleaning up in the kitchen. Before the call ended, Veronica said she'd call back later to let him know whether she was coming home for the movie.

It was now somewhere between 2:00 and 3:00 a.m. Presumably, all the kids had been fast asleep for the past two or three hours. As for Chucky, it's uncertain whether he was asleep or still awake doing whatever. Regardless, what happened next was an unexpected interruption of whatever it was he was doing.

Something had caused Lyric to wake up. Perhaps a nightmare, messy diaper, or tummy ache from his late-night meal. Or maybe, he was just thirsty. Whatever it was, he was awake and in need of something. Knowing his mother was at work, he turned to Chucky.

During the trial, Ray Ramos spoke of one occasion when he'd spent the night babysitting. He explained how Lyric had woken during the night, frightened from a nightmare, and came to him. To comfort him, he had Lyric curl up next to him in the game room, watching a movie. Within a matter of minutes, he fell back asleep.

Whatever Chucky was doing, he'd been interrupted by Lyric's sudden appearance and was not happy. He never thought to ask why he was up or what he needed. Instead, he became angry and scolded him, yelling and demanding he go back to bed. Whatever Lyric tried to say fell on deaf ears because Chucky wasn't listening or didn't want to hear it.

Instead, he grew even angrier, and Lyric was cut off immediately, demanding and yelling again to get back in bed. Lyric just stood there helpless and confused but still in need of something, so he started to cry. Chucky's anger grew more intense. Fearful that his crying would wake the others, Chucky reached out, trying to grab Lyric, hoping to silence him. By now, Lyric was not only confused but one terrified little boy. Chucky was furious, yelling at him and now trying to grab onto him. Even at two-and-half years of age, his survival instinct was telling him to run. Trying to escape Chucky's grasp, he quickly backed away, turned, and started to run. Notably, this was precisely what Chucky later told his brother over the phone, "This little nigger be running around doing mad shit. And that ain't right."

In that tiny apartment, there was really no place to run. Lyric was defenseless and no match for Chucky. As such, it didn't take long for Chucky to catch up with him. Unbeknownst to Lyric, his attempted escape from Chucky's wrath had only bolstered his anger. By now, Chucky's anger had grown totally out of control.

Lyric was still trying to run when Chucky caught up from behind, wrapping his long fingers around his little neck and yanking him up off the floor. Lyric's arms and legs began flailing wildly as he let out a frightful squeal. Again, fearful that Lyric would wake the other children, he needed to silence him – quickly. With Lyric still suspended in the air, Chucky tightened his grip around his neck, causing his fingernails to penetrate deep into his skin. Still holding him by the neck, he started whipping him back and forth like a rag doll as he made his way across the room, where he slammed his forehead into the wall – twice. While doing so, the back of Chucky's hands raked across the wall, painfully tearing the skin off his knuckles, and they began to bleed. Instantly, his anger turned into a full-blown rage of fury, and he forcibly threw Lyric onto the hard wooden floor. So forceful that the back of his head bounced off the floor after it hit.

Lyric's arms and legs went limp, and his flailing stopped. His whole body laid motionless and silent on the floor. Unfortunately, Chucky's rage-filled assault wasn't over. His adrenaline level was near its peak but still pumping.

Immediately after throwing Lyric to the floor, he reached down and punched him in the head with a closed fist, leaving knuckle marks on his face. Then he stood up and stomped on his chest, followed by a powerful kick to the abdomen, injuring his foot in the process. Then he continued booting him across the room like a soccer ball into the kitchen, where he was left bleeding internally from his injuries. Two of which would be fatal: one, a bleeding head injury, which caused his brain to swell, and two, a lacerated liver, detached from his spine, with half his blood volume oozing into his abdomen. He was dying from exsanguination. In other words, he was bleeding to death.

Chucky's ruthless assault was finally over. From start to finish, it was likely over within a matter of several seconds. And whatever Lyric's need was, had cost him his life.

As Chucky stood there in the kitchen surveying what he'd just done, seeing Lyric's body still lying there motionless, he knew he had to do something. Otherwise, he'd be in big trouble. So, he decided the best thing was to get Lyric back in bed and pretend nothing happened. Unfortunately, he was about to learn that his plan wasn't quite that simple and was about to become a bit more complicated.

He decided it best to wrap Lyric in a blanket before moving him back into his bed to start. So, he snuck quietly into the kids' room, grabbing Haveen's pink Barbie comforter that Lyric had been using earlier. Returning to the kitchen, he started covering him with the comforter. Then, as he was rolling him over to pick him up, he suddenly noticed, much to his chagrin, that Lyric's

SpongeBob pajamas were covered in excrement. Poop, if you will. While looking around, he saw even more spread across the floor, with some even on the front of his pajamas.

There were only two ways this could have happened. Either Lyric had already messed his diaper, which might explain his reason for seeking Chucky's help. Or, considering what just happened, he may have soiled himself during the assault.

Author's note: I learned from both Veronica and her mom that Lyric, ever since he was an infant, had difficulty with bowel movements, usually from constipation, which caused stomach pain, crankiness, and occasional misbehavior.

For his plan to work, Chucky needed to clean up his mess, including Lyric. A thorough cleaning that would leave no incriminating evidence of what happened. He started by carrying Lyric's limp body into the bathroom, where he stripped off his soiled SpongeBob pajamas and diaper, filled the tub with water, and washed him clean. This left a large wet white towel with brown staining on the floor, alongside a wet blue washcloth. After that, he set Lyric on Veronica's bed, grabbed a new clean diaper, and fastened it on. As it was, Chucky's skinned knuckles were still open and bleeding, with a small amount of blood running across his hands and down along his fingers. As he put on the new diaper, specks of blood from his fingers transferred onto the diaper, including his bloody thumbprint on one of the fastening tabs.

| Wet & Stained Towel

Rummaging through the laundry, Chucky couldn't find another pair of Lyric's pajamas. Pressed for time, he chose instead to dress Lyric in blue jeans, T-shirt, and a hoodie he'd found. By now, it was unknown whether Lyric was dead or alive. Regardless, Chucky picked him up and carried him back to his room. Carefully placing him on the bottom bunk next to his sister, Amira, and covered him up. Then cowardly walked away, leaving Lyric in his bed, either dead or dying, while his sisters slept nearby.

Chucky returned to the kitchen to finish cleaning up his mess, using the clean portions that remained on Lyric's PJs and the pink comforter to clean up the floor. Once that was done, he stripped out of his soiled pajamas and wadded everything together. Then he searched around for a place to hide it all. Without leaving the apartment, his options were limited. But his most immediate concern was to get everything out of sight before Veronica got home. So, he stuffed everything into a large black plastic bag, tied it shut, and set it in the small closet in the kids' bedroom.

Well before Veronica arrived home, Chucky had everything cleaned up. The kitchen was spotless, looking better than it ever had. He'd also changed into his regular clothes and stashed away all the soiled items. There was no sign that anything ever happened. Yet, he still feared what would happen once Veronica arrived home, knowing that typically, the first thing she would do was check on the kids. According to his plan, he stood at the door and greeted her as soon as she walked in, assuring her the kids were okay. Then he reminded her how tired she was, insisting she just lay down and get some sleep.

At the time, Veronica was still weak from her miscarriage a few days earlier and exhausted from working all night. So, she hadn't noticed anything out of the ordinary or otherwise suspicious as she walked in the door. When Chucky greeted her at the door, Veronica readily accepted his assurance that the kids were fine, as well as his offer to just climb in bed and get some sleep. She was without a single clue that her son was seriously injured and was either dead or dying in his bed.

I'm reminded of the late Paul Harvey, who always concluded his radio commentary by saying, "And now you know the rest of the story."

50

SUMMING UP

Due to the severity of Lyric's murder, authorities were under a great deal of pressure, along with a sense of urgency to solve his brutal murder and make an arrest as quickly as possible. Ironically, once the decision was made to abandon Chucky and pursue Veronica, the investigation that followed was drawn out for months. The irony is that had they continued their pursuit of Chucky, with the evidence found shortly after, he could have been arrested within days. Instead, the absence of any evidence against Veronica dragged the investigation on for eight months. Even then, they were forced to rely on the 'trash allegations' of the cry-ladies and the desperate lies of their 'dishonest snitch,' Jesse Noel. In so doing, they brushed aside, rejected, or completely ignored the more compelling evidence lined up right under their noses. All of which pointed right at Chucky.

As a brief reminder, the following is an itemized review of what that evidence was:

- Lyric's diaper – blood stains on the exterior + a bloody thumbprint.
- Stomach contents – Lyric's last meal. Consistent w/potatoes.
- Estimated time of death – 3:00-4:00 a.m.
- Early onset of rigor mortis.
- Veronica's work alibi – 11:00 p.m. to 7:00 a.m.
- Chucky's bleeding knuckles.
- Chucky's injured foot.
- Chucky's words: *"It was on my watch."*
- Chucky's words: *"I knew his plate was empty."*
- Chucky's words: *"I heard Lyric's voice."*
- Chucky's words: *"This little nigger be running around doing mad shit."*
- Chucky's words: *"This is life or death if you know what I mean."*
- Chucky's words: *"I ain't getting the death penalty for no accident."*
- Missing – Lyric's SpongeBob PJs.
- Missing – Haveen's pink Barbie comforter.
- Missing – Chucky's sleep clothes.
- Lyric's ear – burn mark.
- Lyric's neck – penetrating gouge marks (abraded skin) from long fingernails.
- Wet towel w/stain on the bathroom floor.
- Plastic bag w/stained pink material.

I could likely add a few more, but it's not complicated. What more do we really need?

In contrast, the following was the "compelling" evidence they used against Veronica:

- Cry-ladies

- Jesse Noel
- "Extremely warm" temperature – 74 degrees.
- Black plastic spoon.
- Assumptions
- Possibilities

There was nothing complicated about this case. In fact, if anything, it was relatively straightforward. In as much, it could have easily stayed that way. Unfortunately, after dumping Chucky to pursue Veronica, the investigation that followed was anything but straightforward. Whether by action or inaction, everything after that became much more complicated.

Without question, the tragic miscarriage of justice experienced by Veronica Taft never should have happened. Initially, the early stage of the investigation was clearly on target for a successful and just conclusion, believing that Chucky was Lyric's killer. Unfortunately, less than two days later, a very premature decision turned the tides against Veronica, which led to an early rush to judgment. The investigation that followed traveled down a dangerous path, leading to one calamity after another – at times, perpetuated by ignoring their best evidence, casting doubt on irrefutable proof, or rejecting it entirely. Then shamelessly, replacing it with innuendo, far-reaching assumptions, broad possibilities, and untrustworthy witnesses.

During the first 48-hours of the investigation, Charles Pratt was the prime suspect for good reason. Unfortunately, soon after the tides turned, an ugly picture started developing rather quickly, which turned into a total train wreck. Frankly, this train wasn't even up to speed before it fell off the tracks.

One doesn't need to like Veronica Taft to understand what happened to her was wrong – seriously wrong. And no one was doing anything to make it right. Instead, they pushed forward in a united team effort, setting aside well-tested forensic procedures, including the basic investigative protocol, such as their haphazard crime scene searches. Then, they tried to explain it away, saying, "Well, we didn't know it was a homicide," or, "It may have been a SIDS death." Both of which completely contradicted the lead investigator, who said, "I think it would be remiss if we didn't handle it as a murder right from the beginning."

The botched crime scene work was bad enough, but there was more – much more. When referring to the evidence, how often did we hear the words "insignificant" or "no evidentiary value?" Apparently, the only physical evidence they felt was significant was that "extremely warm" temperature in the kitchen three weeks later or that black spoon three months later. Where in contrast, when considering the more compelling evidence, such as the blood-stained diaper or Lyric's skin under fingernails, there was "no evidentiary value." Or, "It could have been anyone in that household." Similarly, according to Investigator Zandy, the fingernail marks he saw and photographed on Lyric's neck were of no significance. Even though his other injuries made it clear he'd been severely beaten. Evidently, that wasn't significant enough to alert investigators to recommend getting DNA and fingernail scrapings. All of this, coming from two forensic crime scene investigators with several years of experience.

Additionally, according to the trial testimony of Zandy, Wagner, and Diles, the early morning time of death was never discussed. Diles must have forgotten what he told Jemel Fields during his interview and later wrote in his own report: *"The results of the investigation and the autopsy clearly put the time of death in the early morning hours."*

According to Wagner, regarding the blood-stained diaper, he was never informed or consulted about any evidence found on Lyric's clothing. In other words, he did not know about the transfer bloodstains found on the exterior of the diaper, the bloody thumbprint on a fastening tab, or the vomit-stained mattress cover. Yet Stebbins said, "It's my practice to keep the investigators working the case abreast of what I find and what I don't find." For someone calling himself the lead investigator, I found it rather remarkable how little he claimed to know.

For the most part, when looking at what Wagner knew or didn't know as lead investigator, according to his testimony, he didn't seem to be very knowledgeable of his own case. Strangely, even though he admitted Charles Pratt was an early suspect, he'd never watched his videotaped interview. He never had any discussions about the time of death, didn't know when the autopsy happened, and was never informed about the blood or thumbprint on Lyric's diaper.

Although, in fairness, I'm not convinced some of this may have been caused by a breakdown in communications. But, as lead investigator, his failure to review Pratt's videotaped interview was inexcusable and irresponsible. He completely ignored a nearly four-hour videotaped interview of a major suspect overflowing with valuable information that could further aid the investigation. Maybe he readily embraced DA Mollen's early decision to flip from Chucky to Veronica and decided it was unnecessary.

As mentioned repeatedly, the time of death in this case was crucial. During her interview, Veronica had expressed her interest in the time of death and made inquiries several times. She knew that once it was established, it would prove her innocence and point to the real killer. The crucial aspect was created by the 12-hour plus window, between the time Lyric was last seen alive until his discovery. It was crucial because Veronica was proven to have been at work for eight-and-a-half of those hours. In comparison, Chucky was alone with the kids the entire time. No need to check with Captain Obvious there. Yet Wagner, as lead investigator, even after admitting the time of death was critical, contradicted himself, insisting there was no discussion about that with other investigators. Recall what he said? "I don't think anybody ever gave me an estimation of the time of death that I recall."

To accept that answer, you'd have to believe that Sergeant Eggleston and Investigator Diles, who both shared that same information outside their agency, never shared it with members of their detail. Does that make any sense? Of course not. Furthermore, Eggleston wasn't even at the autopsy. So, if it was never discussed, how would he know? Someone had to tell him. What's one of the most elementary questions asked of a pathologist? "Hey Doc, what are we looking at for a time of death?"

Recall what happened right after the autopsy on December 31st? Wagner and Cornell drove straight over to Binghamton High School and verified Veronica's work alibi. She was at work on the night in question from 11:00 p.m. to 7:00 a.m., just like she'd told them. Later, when asked whether he'd relayed that information back to the other investigators, he said, "Oh, we let everybody know something like that, yes." Then turned right around to deny that his knowledge of the time of death was his reason for doing that.

More importantly, the defense testimony of retired Sergeant Tom Eggleston, whether he realized it or not, totally undermined the testimony of his former colleagues. He admitted knowing of the estimated time of death and sharing it with other investigators and CPS and admitted that it was discussed frequently during daily case briefings. Now that makes a lot more sense.

Throughout the story, several references were made to what I described as "lost opportunities" during the police investigation. Conceivably, any one or more of those, had they been done, may have helped steer the investigation in the right direction. There were several, but I'll mention a few of the more significant lost opportunities briefly. Many of which could have been done easily, with minimal effort.

On day one, during Veronica's interview, she'd offered to take a polygraph to help clear up any doubt they might have regarding her involvement. What was she told? "Well, we'll keep that in the back of our mind. Do you think we should give you one?" Yet, they never did. They forfeited the perfect opportunity to learn whether she was truthful or deceptive. Moreover, *they* should have been the ones asking *her* to take a polygraph.

That same day, after learning about the fingernail marks on Lyric's neck, they never obtained any fingernail scrapings, DNA, or photographs. They failed to do the same with Chucky, who was also there the first day, which was even more critical because his knuckles were bleeding. Strangely, there was not even a photograph.

Stranger still was the so-called crime scene searches and processing during the execution of three separate search warrants. Where other than the photographs and diagram, it was a total debacle. For crime scene investigators with years of experience, there was no excuse for their rushed, ignored, or incomplete work at the crime scene. They routinely overlooked or completely ignored even the most elementary crime scene protocol, never bothering to look through drawers, cabinets, closets, garbage bags, laundry baskets, or even under the beds. Even when returning to the crime scene with two additional search warrants, they still never recovered those tiny blue-jean pants Lyric had been wearing. They were still lying there on the floor, where EMTs left them, in plain view right next to Veronica's bed.

Previously, when asked, Veronica denied using any illicit drugs. However, during her second interview, she was confronted with the cry-ladies 'trash allegations' of being a crack cocaine user. Of course, she wanted to clear up that issue once and for all and said, "I'll take a piss test right now." Yet at trial, when Diles was asked why they never did that, he answered, "At that point, we didn't have the means to do so." Then he tried pointing the finger at someone else, saying, "It wasn't necessarily my decision." Regardless, they'd forfeited yet another opportunity to learn whether she was lying or truthful about her drug use. In light of the accusations, *they* should have been the ones asking *her* for a urine sample. "We didn't have the means?" That's absurd. Besides, how hard is it to take a urine sample from a volunteer no less?

During her interview with the DA and BPD before her arrest, Veronica mentioned having messages on her phone between her and Chucky that might help eliminate her as a suspect. Even though she didn't have her phone with her at the time, she had offered to make it available if they were interested in looking at it. There was no interest. However, when she was arrested six months later, her cell phone was seized and placed into evidence. Presumably, they would be conducting a forensic autopsy of her phone to review everything that was there. In search of anything that might aid their investigation. A very routine function that, more often than not, provides valuable information. It's irresponsible not to. Yet, it never happened.

For the most part, at least initially, examining the physical evidence had started fine. Lyric's diaper, T-shirt, hoodie, and vomit-stained mattress cover from his bed had all been properly secured and placed in separate evidence bags, and tagged accordingly. Thereafter, Sergeant Stebbins retrieved the items of clothing from the evidence locker and commenced her examination. During her preliminary naked-eye examination of the T-shirt and hoodie, she found nothing remarkable. Yet, they were never submitted to the crime lab for any further testing.

However, as we've already learned, what she found during her visual examination of the diaper was a different story. After discovering those five transfer bloodstains on the exterior of the diaper, including one that looked like a thumbprint on the fastening tab, she didn't stop there. Instead, she spent a significant amount of time describing the bloodstains then preserved them with numerous photographs. At times, she used little red sticky arrows to pinpoint their locations. Once that was done, the only thing left was to have it tested for DNA. But first, she'd have to brief her superiors of her findings.

Strangely, however, Stebbins' lengthy examination of the diaper was in direct contrast to her trial testimony when she said, "There was no evidentiary value to it in our opinion." Then added, "It could have been anyone in the household." The point being, if they truly believed the diaper had no evidentiary value, why examine it at all? Why go through all that effort just to abandon it and pretend there was no value?

Equally important, the actions of DeLucia himself created another contradiction to Stebbins' current opinion that there was no value to this evidence. Recalling, four months after her initial examination of the diaper, DeLucia examined it personally. However, he had no interest whatsoever in Lyric's shirt, hoodie, or vomit-stained mattress cover. Just that blood-stained diaper. But now, it has no value? That's insulting.

The bottom line is that blood-stained diaper was extremely valuable, and they knew it. As such, if they were truly confident in their theory and looking for supporting proof, it would have been tested. But confirming its true value would ruin everything. So instead, fearing the risk of learning its true value, they chose to eliminate that risk by not testing it, even knowing that a young woman's life was at stake. It was a shameful and cruel act of misconduct that was immoral, unprofessional, and unethical.

During her second interview, Veronica had made inquiries not only about the time of death but Lyric's stomach contents. She knew, once analyzed, it would prove that Lyric had, in fact, eaten potatoes *after* she left for work. Furthermore, she'd already been told his stomach contents were consistent with potatoes. Then, just days later, it was reported that the stomach contents had been sent out for analysis to the Onondaga County Crime Lab. Suspiciously, for reasons unknown, the results of that analysis remain a mystery because they were never disclosed.

Later, however, during a recent call to that office, I learned that evidence was submitted for analysis in January 2011 with a case number assigned. I learned further that the submitting agency was the Broome County DA's Office. According to their records, the analysis had been completed, and the results returned to the Broome DA's Office. Unfortunately, they were not authorized to provide me with a copy of those results. Later, I even tried a FOIL request, but their denial was like a typical Catch-22 when advised I would need approval from the DA's Office.

Ironically, imagine, if you will, what would happen if the analysis of the stomach contents turned out instead to be the remains of a peanut butter & jelly sandwich? Most assuredly, they wouldn't be trying to hide it. Instead, they would have been shoving it right under Veronica's nose, arguing that it was proof of her killing her son *before* she went to work.

On a related note, remember the suspected vomit stain on the mattress cover from Lyrics' bed? It was never sent to the crime lab for any testing other than photographs and a quick visual exam. Again, if you're not going to do anything with it, why bother taking it in the first place? Briefly, let's say it had been sent to the lab. What would they be able to do with a suspected vomit stain? It would involve a three-part examination. First, to confirm that it was vomit. Second, an attempt to identify any unknown substance present in the vomit. In other words, another way to identify Lyric's last meal. The final step would require an affirmative DNA match to Lyric. Complicated? No. Valuable? Yes.

Unfortunately, when it came to the more valuable evidence that pointed to the real killer, they turned a blind eye, brushed it aside, ignored it, or rejected it entirely. They called it insignificant or having no value, replacing it with worthless evidence that proved nothing whatsoever. In essence, they were trying to hide the truth but doing a lousy job, like trying to hold a beach ball under the water.

When that wasn't enough, to make matters worse, they turned to the loathsome cry-ladies, who offered their 'trash allegations' against Veronica – calling her an unfit mother and a crack-dealing 'street walker' who was physically abusive to her children. From there, they leaped and called it a motive for murder. Afterward, portraying Veronica as a physically abusive mother, filled with so much hate for her son that she killed him.

The bottom line was other than the 'trash allegations' of the cry-ladies, none of whom were credible, there wasn't a single shred of physical evidence linking Veronica Taft to her son's murder. No eyewitnesses were claiming to have seen her beat her son. While entertaining the cry-ladies' complaints, CPS conducted numerous unannounced visits to Veronica's home, checking her children for injuries or any evidence of physical abuse and performing on-the-spot drug testing on Veronica. Never once did they find any evidence of her children being injured or abused. As for Veronica's drug tests, she was clean every time. As a result, they were never able to substantiate any of the allegations. Instead, they were found malicious, vindictive, or deemed not credible and, thereafter, reported as unfounded.

The final nail in her coffin was Jesse Noel. Notably, without his testimony, there was no case against Veronica. But we've already learned everything we need to know about Jesse Noel. A perpetual liar whose non-stop lies never ended. Recalling early in the game, he claimed it was Chucky who confessed to Lyric's murder and told authorities that on four separate occasions. Then late in the game, he tried making himself look like some righteous saint, claiming he didn't want to see the wrong person go to prison. Or how hard his decision was because he still had feelings for Veronica. Bull-sh.., I mean, Baloney. It was never about his feelings for Veronica or about sending the wrong person to prison. His only interest was Jesse. He knew there was no murder confession by Chucky or Veronica. The moment he was told that Veronica was about to be arrested was his cue to throw her under the bus to save himself. A cowardly and selfish way out just as he'd been saying all along, "I was hoping to get the best deal I could."

As a medical professional, there were several things related to Dr. Terzian's very disturbing involvement. One of the most crucial issues in this case was the time of death. Yet, in Terzian's approach, it was treated more like amateur hour. This case certainly wasn't his first time dealing with a time of death issue. In his years of experience, he was well aware of other available means that could be used in addition to the standard 'rule of thumb' formula he shared with the police. Including the stomach contents already mentioned could narrow down the time by identifying Lyric's last meal. But remember what he said when asked about that? "Oh, I tried to do that, but I couldn't find anybody."

He never mentioned or ever tried using the more advanced Henssge's Nonogram[1] formula. Unlike the single temperature Glaister formula, it uses ambient air temperature and body mass parameters. Then further allows for additional corrective factors that may be available, such as the thickness of clothing. Instead, he stood steadfast with his standard rule of thumb formula based on an average size adult, knowing darn well, for a two-year-old child, the formula would need to be adjusted for a more accurate calculation.

Even more troubling was his testimony and offering an expert medical opinion based on far-reaching possibilities and fact-less assumptions. Briefly, let's jump back to his grand jury testimony where DeLucia was questioning him about the possibility of Lyric being killed between 12-14 hours earlier and asked if it was 'within the bounds' of possibility? Of course, Terzian agreed and later said it could be as much as 18 hours. Then, a year later, he testified that it was 'within the realm' of possibility during the trial. That being said, I think it's safe to say that any number of things are possible that may fall within the 'bounds' or 'realm' of possibility. By definition, the word itself encompasses an extensive range. But eventually, when using our logic and common sense, we draw a line between that which is realistically possible vs. that which is unlikely. Unfortunately, that broad spectrum of far-reaching possibilities offered by Terzian clearly defined which side of the line he was on.

As bizarre as that was, that's precisely what he did. Although it's well known that Dr. Terzian has always been very pro-police, which isn't necessarily a bad thing, I'm certain he was just trying to be helpful. Here, however, he was really pushing the envelope and going above and beyond his professional expertise to try and help the cause. Firstly, by shirking his professional responsibility to try and narrow down the time of death. Then, by pulling a 50 percent error rate out of the blue to use in his calculation. By the way, that wasn't just a wild guess. Otherwise, why 50 percent? Why not ten or even 25? Because he'd obviously been doing his homework, searching for the error percentage needed to make it fit. Then suddenly, voila! Fifty percent will do it. Just throw in the assumptions, and there you have it. With that, the time of death could be pushed back to the desired time. How convenient.

Fortunately, and thankfully, the Appellate Court saw right through this nonsense as well. Recalling what was written,

> *"Based on questions related to the pathologist's degree of certainty as to his conclusion, the pathologist testified that it was "technically possible" that the victim's time of death was 11:00 p.m. and that it was "within the realm of possibility," that the injuries could have been inflicted at 9:00 p.m. This scenario, however, would assume a 50% error rate in the time of death calculation and would have also doubled the amount of time that it took the victim to die from his injuries."*

As previously noted, other than the inconsistent and often contradictory testimony of Jesse Noel, the 'dishonest snitch,' there was absolutely no evidence that Veronica was Lyric's killer. In fact, the evidence they did have, supported her innocence. Where in contrast, the more compelling evidence was lined up and waiting right under their noses. With everything pointing directly at Chucky. Piecing it all together was simple. The only requirement was honesty, professionalism, and some basic due diligence – otherwise known as integrity or doing the right thing. With integrity, however, there's no allowance to pick and choose when to use it.

Earlier, I described a large black plastic bag that appeared in a police photograph sitting on the floor of a small closet in the kids' bedroom. The photo had been taken during the second search warrant. If you recall, the top of the bag had been opened slightly, revealing a pink-colored fabric with a large brown stain on it. The bag was full and bulging from the other items or material underneath. Interestingly, once Veronica saw the photograph, she said, "I have no clue what that is or what else might be in there. I've never seen it before. All I do know is, I didn't put it there." However, when taking a closer look, she thought perhaps it was Haveen's missing comforter. Unfortunately, since they never bothered to look, we'll never know. If they had, they would likely have discovered all those missing items, which could help answer those elusive questions as to what happened with regards to a motive or means.

| Bag with pink stained material

---

1. *Henssge's nomogram*: An elaborate system developed to establish the time of death from body cooling, using the main influencing factors of body temperature, ambient temperature and body mass.

RETURN TO FAYETTE STREET

The rare dismissal of the murder and manslaughter charges against Veronica Taft had caught the eye of *New York Times* Bureau Chief Jesse McKinley. As an investigative reporter, he was intrigued after reading the decision and reached out to Dave Butler's office to learn more. A few days later, we all met at Butler's office to discuss the details. From there, he set out to pursue his own investigation.

As part of his investigation, McKinley had returned to the old block in Binghamton, where he reported that the memory of Lyric's murder had largely faded, saying further that he had spoken to Jennifer Clay, the current occupant of Veronica's former apartment. Ms. Clay had never heard of the case until approached by McKinley.

Interestingly, while speaking with Ms. Clay, he learned of a strange coincidence involving her six-year-old daughter Alyssa. She'd long had an imaginary friend she played with in the same back bedroom where the murder occurred. "She'd sit on the bed and talk and giggle," said Ms. Clay, who then added, "There were even times when she would buy toys as gifts for her imaginary friend." Things such as cars or trucks and the like.

McKinley then asked Ms. Clay, "What does she call him?" She turned to Alyssa and asked. The name wasn't familiar to her mother, so she said to Alyssa, "Spell it out on the blackboard for me." Mr. Clay then spelled it out for McKinley. The little boy's name, she said, is Elrick.

52

THEY CALLED IT JUSTICE

Even though it took more than five years, justice for Veronica finally prevailed. But at what cost? The emotional scars and painful memories from those years of living hell will never fully heal. Neither can they be erased. They will remain forever permanent.

The Appellate Court's decision came as a rather sharp slap in the face for those who advocated for Veronica's arrest and conviction. And rightfully so. But they were calling it a sham. A mockery of justice. An insulting violation of the rule of law. What they did was a scheming charade that used innuendo, deception, and bogus emotional testimony in a combined effort to portray a poor young mother struggling to support her children as a baby-killing monster. Sadly, I'll never understand how authorities here, who typically conduct themselves with integrity at the highest standards of professionalism, failed so miserably. It seemed surreal only because it was so unlike them.

It reminded me of what Jesse Noel was told just before his sudden epiphany at the jail when his attorney, Mark Rappaport, said, *"All I can say, Jesse is I'm not one of them. I'm over here with you, but*

I'm also saying to you, they don't want the wrong person to go upstate. They're not just trying to get a conviction to say yeah, we got somebody. They want to get the right person. If they don't get the right person, then they haven't done their job, you know? I'm often on the other side, but I do know that most of them, and these guys, in particular, try to do the right thing and not just the easy thing, especially in a serious case like this."

Therein lies the conflict. The authorities created the battle of what to believe. It was somewhat like the dissonance experienced by Veronica early on. Still, in this case, the confusion involved two opposing questions: did authorities genuinely believe they were doing the right thing, or did they frame an innocent woman? Frankly, I have trouble believing either one – a frame job or doing the right thing? Which was it? Unfortunately, a conclusive answer is unlikely. Authorities would never admit to intentionally framing an innocent person. But with all things considered, whether intended or not, that's what they did.

The brutal and devastating consequences for Veronica Taft were at least three-fold: a factually innocent victim, interrogated, arrested, convicted, and imprisoned for a murder she didn't commit, a young family torn apart with the surviving children yanked away and placed in foster care, and two-year-old Lyric was denied and robbed of justice by offering his killer Immunity for Murder. A ruthless killer just walked away, never to be held accountable. And they called it justice.

*Those who sow injustice reap calamity
And the rod they wield in fury will be broken*

— PROVERBS: 22:8

VIII

ADDENDUM

NOTICE OF CLAIM

On September 24, 2018, on behalf of Veronica Taft, the Syracuse, NY law firm of DeFrancisco & Falgiatano, filed a Notice of Claim with the Court of Claims and New York State Attorney General. Filed under Section 8-b of the Court of Claims Act, otherwise known as the Unjust Conviction and Imprisonment Act of 1984, the claim detailed a myriad of damages incurred during years of confinement in prison as the result of her wrongful conviction. She is seeking monetary compensation for reasonable and fair damages from the State of New York. The claim is still pending.

54

CAREER CHANGES

The Appellate Court's powerful decision debunked the ill-fated investigation and prosecution of Veronica Taft. It also dismissed her wrongful murder and manslaughter convictions and set her free. However, it did nothing to disrupt the careers of any of the foremost advocates of the case.

Instead, even though longtime DA Gerald Mollen was voted out of office in 2015, he accepted an appointment as Deputy Commissioner of Prosecution Services at NYS Division of Criminal Justice Services. Similarly, Peter DeLucia took a new position with the NYS Attorney General's Office. Likewise, Joshua Shapiro was appointed Special Counsel to New York Court's Administrative Judge for Town & Village Courts. At the same time, Investigator Jeff Wagner moved into a new position as Broome County's first Overdose Investigator. Sergeant Michelle Stebbins transferred to the Broome County Sheriff's Department, then later to Johnson City PD, continuing her work as an ID tech. Back at BPD, Investigators Corey Minor and Anthony Diles received promotions. More recently, Diles was hired as an Investigator with the Broome DA's Office.

NOTE FROM THE AUTHOR

Although harsh at times, any criticism of the Binghamton PD, Broome County DA's Office, Broome County CPS, or any of its members was offered strictly from a professional perspective as it relates to this story alone and should not be construed otherwise.

ACKNOWLEDGMENTS

To Anna, my wife of nearly 50 years. A strong supporter who was always there for me. Often encouraging me to keep writing the stories that need to be told – most of which, she lived and breathed with me. I always value her perspective as a woman as well as offering a second opinion, especially in this story, with so many female characters. They were characters, alright. Anyway, thanks again for all you've done and continue to do. Love you always.

A special thanks to Veronica's defense attorney, David Butler, and his legal staff at Butler & Butler Law. For your dedication and heartfelt commitment to the pursuit of justice. All were driven by believing in Veronica's factual innocence and defending her accordingly. It was a pleasure working with you.

To Jesse McKinley, as Bureau Chief of the *New York Times*, who once told me, "We need to breathe life into this story:" It was a pleasure meeting and working with you. Thank you for your investigative interest, time, input, and most notably, your independent affirmation of a tragic miscarriage of justice. It seemed rather clear from the very beginning that we were both on the same page. Thank you.

To all my early beta readers for their interest, valued suggestions, and honest opinions. Including my wife Anna, son Damon and later my friend Jim Corbin. I'm sorry I kept you waiting and didn't let you read the whole story until now. Hopefully, I didn't disappoint too much. Besides, I just decided to buy you all dinner. Anyway, thanks again – much appreciated.

A special thanks again to Katherine "Kat" McCarthy at Evening Sky Publishing Services, who helped me with my first book as well. For her continued editorial, formatting, and cover design skills, as well as my fine-looking website. Just tell her what you need, and the magic begins. A real professional, who I look forward to working with in the future. And I already have another story in mind.

To the State of New York Supreme Court, Appellate Division, Third Judicial Department. For their sharpened ability to see this case for what it really was. Doing so without bias and with the professional integrity that helped reach their correct and unanimous decision. Well done.

I've always had a strong faith and spiritual component in my life. Although some might disagree, I strongly believe our Almighty God is not only mysterious and loving but also a God who loves justice. My prayers weren't always answered on my timeline or in the way I thought they should have been. Yet I was always amazed after realizing He finally did answer. And for that, I give Him thanks.

ABOUT THE AUTHOR

David M. Beers holds a Bachelor of Professional Studies Degree from Empire State College. Previously, he served six years in the United States Marine Corps. Thereafter, received an honorable discharge at the rank of Staff-Sergeant. Thereafter, Beers became a sworn member of the New York State Police. As a trooper, he excelled in his regular  duties and became a police instructor. Later, helping to develop, implement and teach a state-wide highway drug-interdiction program. After being promoted to the rank of Investigator, Beers received additional training and experience and served in several specialized venues, including narcotics, major crimes, violent felony warrants, and forensics. Where he attained experience and proficiency in several forensic disciplines including, evidence collection and preservation, crime scene investigation, fingerprints, arson awareness, fire cause and origin and blood stain/pattern analysis. Over several years receiving numerous commendations, while routinely maintaining excellent and/or outstanding performance evaluations.

Beers' career in law enforcement ended prematurely as the result of what later became known as the, New York State Police, Troop 'C' evidence tampering scandal. Beers, who was initially cleared of any wrong doing was later falsely accused of a host of crimes related to his work as a police officer. After a two-year legal battle, including two trials, he was exonerated of all criminal charges. But despite his complete exoneration, Beers was fired from his position as a police officer. Even though his law enforcement career had been ripped away, his training and experience had not.

Over the next two years, Beers transitioned his training and experience into the private sector and became a licensed private investigator. With his combined experience as a Marine, police officer, defendant, and now as a private investigator, Beers developed a unique perspective of the criminal justice system. Thereafter, starting his own investigation and consulting business he justly named: *New Perspective Investigations*. Where he continues working today.

Contact David
Email at davidmbeers.author@gmail.com
Visit his website at davidmbeers.com

ALSO BY DAVID M. BEERS

REIGN OF INJUSTICE: The Cal Harris Story

On September 12, 2001, Michele Harris went missing from a small town in upstate New York. She has never been found, and the mystery surrounding her disappearance remains. Four years after she went missing, her wealthy husband Cal Harris was arrested and charged with her murder.

With neither a body nor a murder weapon, Cal was shockingly tried and convicted of her murder. Then, new evidence surfaced. His conviction was overturned, and a new trial granted. But once again, he was convicted and sentenced to 25 years to life in prison. That conviction, too, was overturned on appeal. The saga continued as Cal went on trial for the third time. This one ended in a mistrial. By the time Cal went on trial the fourth time, Michele had been missing for nearly 15 years.

Defense investigator David M. Beers worked on the Cal Harris case from start to finish. His account *Reign of Injustice* walks you through the details and events of the case never before revealed. It provides an inside view of the scandalous case facts you will not find elsewhere, including why he considers Cal's story a reign of injustice.